FROM HUMANISM TO SCIENCE

FROM HUMANISM
TO SCIENCE

1480-1700

ROBERT MANDROU

Professor of Modern History,
University of Paris X

TRANSLATED BY BRIAN PEARCE

HUMANITIES PRESS

This edition first published in 1979 by
HUMANITIES PRESS INC.
Atlantic Highlands, New Jersey 07716

First published by Editions du Seuil 1973
First published in Great Britain by Penguin Books Ltd. 1978

Library of Congress Cataloging in Publication Data
Mandrou, Robert
From humanism to science 1480-1700.
Translation of Des humanistes aux hommes de
science (XVIe et XVIIe siècles.)
Bibliography: p.
1. Civilization, Modern. 2. Renaissance.
3. Humanism. I. Title.
CB401.M3613   909'.08   78-10510
ISBN 0-391-00541-3

Printed and bound in Great Britain by
Redwood Burn Limited, Trowbridge and Esher

CONTENTS

AUTHOR'S NOTE

I am particularly grateful to Mr Brian Pearce for the meticulous care with which he has set about rendering all the nuances of the French text.

INTRODUCTION

A HISTORY of European thought? The general title of this series matters less, it seems to me, than the title given to this volume of the series: *From Humanism to Science*. For we are not here concerned with the history of ideas as it has been pursued for so long by the university philosophers and their imitators, and as it is still secretly cherished by those who are fond of sustained filiations and patiently rediscovered continuities. Thought and the works of thought are not – indeed, people accept this nowadays as a commonplace – ethereal things that float above the clouds and come down into the midst of human societies in response to chance flashes of genius and unforeseeable changes of wind. Intellectual and spiritual inheritances do exist, of course, and weigh the more heavily insofar as institutions of education and communication take care staunchly to transmit them. There is no pioneer, however great a genius he may be, who can flatter himself that he has completely broken with the heritage inculcated in him since childhood through the environment of his family, his school and the community in which he works. The sixteenth century provides a thousand and one examples of this truth. It is therefore not at all unjustified to link firmly the innovations of the Renaissance with earlier strivings in Italy, as, for a century now, all the historians of humanism have shown themselves able to do. But the diffusion of new ideas is not to be understood, any more than the maintenance of traditions, without reference to a general climate which involves the main social relations, the institutions concerned with promoting or disciplining intellectual life, the intervention of political

or religious authorities, and the technical means available both
to those who had something to say and to those who listened
to them. Here, too, the beginning of the modern period
illustrates very well those connexions which always bring the
historian back to men living in their own particular time, just
as much as, if not more than, to any 'systems'.

The temptation is great, of course. What better title than
one in which we symmetrically counterpose two 'isms',
referring to closed and coherent philosophies which can be
broken down into elements that are logically interconnected,
and formed into entities that can be identified in a process of
the development of ideas that is wholly governed by a long
tradition in the history of philsophy? From humanism to
mechanism, say . . . True, in the worthy histories of that order
which have been written, humanism has not enjoyed a good
press, owing to its extreme diversity, which refuses to lend
itself to rigorous classifications. But, at the other end of the
chain of development, what satisfactions are in prospect, with
Newton and Leibniz! However, the most serious problem
obviously lies elsewhere. Intellectual life is not confined –
especially not in the period being studied – to the elaboration
and diffusion of one or other of those great systems which
impress us even today with their logical rigour. It is made up
of gropings, rough sketches and confrontations which often
prove futile (in the eyes, that is, of those whose converse is
solely with geniuses) but which were certainly needed in
order that a great philosophy might be perfected, and which
contributed in no small degree to winning recognition for this
philosophy. Without indulging in any paradox, one may
suggest that, contrary to the notions generally accepted in this
field, those perfected systems have most often served to
sterilize the life of the mind, especially when they have enjoyed
the support of a powerful institution ready to impose and to
protect them. It seems clear to me, moreover, that all intellectual life must signify thinking in that broad sense, still

recognized by the men of the seventeenth century (Descartes, among them), which includes imagination and emotion: doubting, conceiving, affirming and denying, wanting and not wanting, imagining and feeling. Whoever has immersed himself in the battles of ideas in which men faced each other in the entourage of Francis I, or in the Royal Society, cannot but acknowledge the great part played in these debates by sentiments and passions: there was more cantankerousness than charity, without any doubt, whether the antagonists were named Leibniz and Newton or Budé and Erasmus. Thereby was affirmed in a particularly lively way the direct relationship between these matters and the general conditions of their time. On more than one occasion the witness of the arts and of artists will be brought forward to evoke precisely those correlations which are essential to a true understanding of what changed and what stayed unchanged. Similarly, we shall refer to the technical, economic and social conditions which determined to a large extent the expression and the diffusion of 'new forms of thought', and also the resistance they met with. A history of men voicing their thoughts, their dreams, their likes and dislikes, in their own historical setting, in so far as we are able to reconstitute this today – that is the task.

This does not mean, though, that the object of this brief essay on a huge subject cannot be defined more closely. Whoever has thought about the place occupied by intellectuals in societies whether ancient or modern has seen that they fulfil a specific function – broadly, that of developing ideology. As Gramsci emphasized so strongly, although the intellectuals, discoursing and discussing, play a role which is doubtless not so fundamental as that of the producers of goods and services (in our present-day societies, at least), yet what they have to say matters a very great deal in relation to that social regulation the need for which is appreciated by every society. The intellectuals, whether what they provide is authority, persuasion or escape, occupy an important place in society, which gives them a livelihood, encourages and watches over them, and either supports them or forces them to hold their tongues. Social hegemony, which is to a certain extent unavowed, is unable to exist without a corresponding ideological hegemony. Brute force alone cannot regulate relations between men and between antagonistic groups, especially in modern societies. Periods of crisis, when accepted value-systems are called in question, reveal clearly this role performed by the intellectuals. But what difficulties and mishaps are encountered in defining this function: the submissive, disciplined intellectual, carrying out with devotion the task thus assigned to him, is not easy to train, to mould and to keep in hand. The well-known division of medieval society into the Three Alls can give us a falsely idealized picture, with the definitions reduced to the formula of that society's signboard: 'I pray for all, I fight for all, I work for all'. Even within a firmly hierarchical and strictly disciplined institution like the Roman Church of the Middle Ages conflicts were always breaking out which showed what tricky handling this ideological control required. There were heretics breaking with the Church and having to be brutally silenced; rulers who sought to encroach on the prerogatives of the clergy and even to impose their own conceptions in those spheres; obscurer resistances, often hard to identify nowadays, on the part of the laity, directed against the prescriptions regarding worship and morality laid down by the clergy . . . With this background, the heritage at men's disposal at the end of the fifteenth century was certainly rich in traditions that were contrasting and even contradictory. The upheavals which profoundly transformed intellectual life in the second half of the fifteenth century may well have created quite new conditions and given a new dimension to all these problems, if only by multiplying the numbers of intellectuals, both within and without the institutional frameworks; it was nevertheless the case that, long before Gutenberg and Columbus, the Church had been subjected to the test of those difficulties that were inherent in the functions it took upon itself in Western and Central Europe.

The task I have chosen is, therefore, to reconstruct the role played by the intellectuals both within the institutions consecrated to them and also without these institutions, so as to estimate, as far as possible, what impact they had in their own time: a risky undertaking, to be sure, since it aims at evoking the speakers, what they said, and the impression made by this upon their contemporaries. There are many other ways of tackling the subject, even for an historian – starting with the study of the subsequent history which a particular movement or a particular work enjoyed. That is not the purpose of this series, however, which aims to reveal the stages (which were not linear) and the mutations through which thinking Europe passed, without claiming to add to our knowledge of filiations and revivals. Consequently, the main thing I have to do is to analyse and reconstruct the complex relations which linked the intellectuals with different social milieux, those to which they belonged and those to which they were opposed; the frameworks which were offered to them, or imposed upon them, those which they rejected and those which they themselves established, in accordance with their own preferences and ambitions. There is indeed no other way if one wants to give back to these battles of men and ideas their human density and their true significance in the development of modern societies.

But the path chosen is not without its uncertainties. Intellectuals, hard to categorize in present-day societies, as the works of sociologists show well enough, do not lend themselves to easy classification in the Early Modern period, either. When the institution of the Church broke up they ceased all to belong to an 'order', in the juridical sense of the word, and so eluded a relatively simple social definition. Yet their activity, the demands of the occupation they undertook to follow, gave them a place apart in a world which traditionally accorded men and groups a position determined by their distinctive activity or by their birth, and by the honours associated with these circumstances. When we follow them in their new careers, and hear them often speaking in an authoritative manner, they give the impression of possessing a certain aristocratic status. Already in the sixteenth century they lay claim to a nobility which is not linked with name or lineage but is determined by the honourable trade that they practise. Furthermore, the conditions under which they practise it – the cost of the books they need, the absence for a long time of any system of authors' royalties (for the less famous authors at any rate), and the lack of those priestly livings which ensured daily bread to the traditional clerisy – all this presupposed a good social position to start with. Without it, the intellectuals were needy fellows reduced to seeking employment as occasional tutors, proof-readers, public letter-writers, or even mercenary soldiers, like one famous seventeenth-century philosopher. Aristocratic in their turn of mind, they might also, indeed, be aristocrats by birth, or by ambition, and there are plenty of examples of this, from the humanists to the sophisticates of the early seventeenth century. But it was sociological conditioning that was doubtless the most important factor here: the new intellectuals, like the former clerics, were not drawn from the lower strata of society but from strata possessing a measure of material security which allowed them to engage in intellectual speculation and adventure – bourgeois from good merchant families, magistrates enjoying both leisure and substantial incomes, noblemen with pretensions to learning, these were the most usual categories, until the time arrived when those new professions became established in which intellectuals could find employment for their knowledge and talent: counsellors or stewards in the service of princes, historiographers or diplomatic secretaries, court astrologers, astronomers in seaports. Taken as a whole, these intellectuals thus belonged among the dominant groups of the societies of the Ancien Régime, and it was no accident that they concerned themselves so rarely with the traditions and lore of the common people.

To reconstruct the changes in intellectual life by following the guiding threads thus defined, across two centuries and all of Europe, is clearly not an easy task. It has been necessary to jettison a good deal, in all directions, for the abundant life of these innovating centuries does not let itself be embraced with ease in the frame of so rapid a sketch. Why not say something about the scientific concerns of Leonardo da Vinci, the utopian visions that flourish in *Simplicius Simplicissimus*, or the *De republica ecclesiastica* of Marco Antonio de Dominis? It is certainly a question of perspective, of the need to concentrate on major explanations, that compels such omissions; they are made not without regrets, into which it would not be useful to enter here. Similarly, I have chosen to take as epicentre the Christian West, which was torn asunder in the middle of the sixteenth century and in which innovations came to be amassed in wave after wave during the first half of the sixteenth century and throughout the seventeenth. To limit my territorial scope like this would have seemed legitimate to the men of that time, if we are to believe Commines when he says in his memoirs, already in the fifteenth century, that he has 'seen and known the better part of Europe'. The Eastern and Mediterranean borderlands cannot offer us much subject-matter in a period when the crusading spirit was dying, and degenerating into commerical 'capitulations', and in which the Eastern Mediterranean was becoming an object of curiosity for travellers who were almost tourists already – a time when Eastern Europe, almost unknown so far as its northern part was concerned, was known in the south-east only in the form of the Turkish invader whose advance by sea was held in check after Lepanto (1571), but remained a threat by land until the raising of the siege of Vienna in 1683. Even when thus curtailed, Europe, from Poland and Hungary to

Spain, and from Sweden to Italy, remains a vast area. The correspondence of learned travellers assures us of that fact, by steadily accumulating the most curious observations on the manners and customs of those countries, near and far, whose strangeness they discover. Within this spatial framework I have had to select and rearrange in great masses, sometimes overturning chronology, so as to find as accurately as possible – repressing the digressions that, at every step, a theme like this incites one to – the essential elements of explanation, those that best account for a transformation as profound as it was polyphonic, and from which our Europe of today, however much she may sometimes try to deny it, has in fact emerged.

Chapter 1

NEW WORLDS AND
NEW INTELLECTUALS
(1480–1520)*

THE terms of the change that took place have long since been
well established, as is shown by the fact that the expression
'the Renaissance' has continually become enriched as historians
have striven to identify the circumstances and details of a
mutation which did not occur in a day. Some include in the
Renaissance the transformations experienced by medieval Italy
from the thirteenth century onward, while others use the
word and the concept to describe the Carolingian revival in
the ninth century. But this means diluting the specific
character of the change which was experienced during the
century between 1450 and 1550 and which gave the clergy,
and part of Europe's high society, a new vision of the world.
It was not only a matter of the great discoveries and the
invention of printing, since the rediscovery, on a grander scale
than before, of Antiquity both pagan and Christian was something more than merely that turning back to the distant past
of which the early Middle Ages had provided several examples.
The new worlds that fascinated the intellectuals of the
sixteenth century were not so much the Indies – West or even
East – but those ancient worlds which the study and comparison of long-forgotten texts kept revealing as having been
richer and more complex than had been supposed. Italy, the
initiatrix, played her part to the full during that long period
when the clergy were taking step after step in new directions,
their activity enabling them to become aware of the manifold
knowledge that was preserved in the libraries of bishoprics,

* The dates given at the head of each chapter are only approximate.

monasteries and universities – a period when, throughout Europe, new intellectuals who were not churchmen, either having never entered the Church or else having left it, were making their appearance and devoting their lives to the study of these little-known worlds of Antiquity. Here we can see exactly what the break with the medieval heritage amounted to, and the degree of boldness shown by these discoverers who happily mastered knowledge of such great variety, lying outside the well-trodden and well-delimited paths enclosed by the traditional institutions.

I. THE INHERITANCES

In the forefront rises the ecclesiastical organization which dominated the whole of Europe's intellectual life in the last centuries of the Middle Ages. Even when the growth of cities and the rise of the bourgeoisie put forward new requirements in this field, the Church maintained its grip, creating new religious orders – the mendicants, better adapted to the needs of city-dwelling believers – and multiplying universities and colleges to provide teaching for an increased population of students. The functional monopoly which had been established in a long-past period was not yet challenged, except from within, by those who questioned doctrine or discipline.

In this sense, Gramsci was right when he wrote: 'The most typical intellectual group is that of the clergy, who for a long time monopolized a number of important services – religious ideology (that is, the philosophy and science of the age), together with schools, education, morality, justice, charity and good works.' Even if the two last-mentioned items matter less in our present context (though, in everyday life, the exercise of those functions made no small contribution to strengthening the social prestige of the clergy) it is easy to see that the list, as a whole, gives a good analysis of the different aspects of this institutionalized domination. From the diocesan schools up to the universities, the Church laid down the educational framework by which young men were trained – for the priestly life, in the first place, but also for 'good works' (medicine) and for the administering of justice (canon and civil law). By its sustained and solemn preaching, by the sacrament of penitence, and by the sanctions it could bring to bear to threaten the laity (excommunication, interdict), the Church kept control both of the definition of morality and of the respect to be shown to it. Together with the training of jurists, the presence of clergy in the civil courts (not to mention the ecclesiastical jurisdictions themselves, the *officialité* courts) ensured for the Church control, either direct or indirect, over that regulation of social life which it was the role of the judicial apparatus to maintain.

This ideological grip possessed by the Church is certainly not to be measured in the same way in all these different spheres. It is comparatively easy to follow the development of the universities in the period immediately before this age, the increase in the numbers of teaching staff and of students, the expanding influence ensured for the doctrine of St Thomas Aquinas from the time when his *Summa* became the universities' official doctrine. It is equally easy to observe the progress made in methods, down to the age of the Schoolmen, when the teachers, by their lectures, the university copyists, who reproduced notable lecture-courses and good texts, and the ushers in charge of preparation in the colleges combined their efforts to instruct ever more numerous students in the four Faculties. But it is a more delicate and subtle task to measure the degree of control ensured by the training of jurists and by the priests' repressive role in all the miscellaneous occasions of everyday life at parish level. We know about the system of justice, its codes and its sentences are available to researchers; but religious practice at parish level is not at all easy to reconstitute, and the studies carried out in the field, such as those of Toussaert and Adam, reveal a disparity in behaviour that doubtless conforms to the Catholic tradition which allows a variety of channels through which the Church's monopoly can be exercised. The revival of preaching, and at the same time that of the surveillance of heretics, both effected by the mendicant orders during the last centuries of the Middle Ages, expressed clearly the capacity possessed by the Church to adapt itself to social changes and transform its structures so as to deal with new situations. Taken as a whole, then, the formulation offered by Gramsci is undoubtedly valid for defining the reality of the Church's function in European society in the middle of the fifteenth century.

It is certainly harder to follow him when he says that 'the category of clergy can be regarded as that category of intellectuals which is organically linked with the landed aristocracy' – not that the role of the clergy in medieval society, integrated in the feudal and seignorial system, contradicts this statement, but because, on the eve of the sixteenth century, in more than one European country, the clergy can be seen to be linked no less organically with that political apparatus which was then steadily increasing its power over individuals and groups, namely, the monarchy. In the Empire as in the kingdoms of the West, the clergy put themselves at the service of the sovereign not only by participating in the counsels of government and in the administration, but to an even greater extent by reinforcing the monarchs' authority through an entire doctrine grounded in theology and law, to which might be added a belief in the miraculous powers of royal persons (as in France and England), a doctrine that consolidated dynastic sovereignties on firmer foundations. Witness to this is borne both by the major debates on the Two Swords, in the times of Gregory VII and Boniface VIII, and by the simple Sunday prayer: *Domine, Salvum fac regem* . . . Apart from this qualification, however, it remains well established that the clergy in medieval society, taking upon themselves all those functions which distinguish between good and evil and show the path to salvation for individuals and communities, constituted a category of intellectuals in possession of a monopoly, at the summit of the social hierarchies, firmly implanted and long engaged in defending its function and its teaching.

In that field the ecclesiastical institution had been remarkably well safeguarded, since much earlier times. This protection was ensured, first, by a separation, expressed even in the Sunday ritual of Communion, between clergy and laity, between those who know and can obtain men's salvation, and those who know little, cannot accede to greater knowledge, and must be content with the provender given them, to be taken in through their ears when they listen to the sermon or through their eyes when they gaze at the capitals of columns or at stained-glass windows. The pastor who spends his life at the head of his flock and who cannot fail in the exercise of his essential function, the distribution of the sacraments, belongs to a different order from other men, above the common level: his ordination, his celibacy, the ceremonial precedence given to him, all express this distance between him and the laity, a distance which was steadily stressed all through the last centuries of the Middle Ages. How many took it upon themselves to recall this distance, when the laity demanded a bigger share in the everyday life of the Church! A correspondent of Pierre Viret's gives his view without beating about the bush, in 1565, nearly fifty years after the explosion of the Reformation, concerning the learned works written by the Fathers of the Church: 'Simple folk can get no profit from reading these curious books, but must be satisfied with the simplicity of faith, without pressing on too far and tormenting themselves to reach wisdom and knowledge of high matters. It has always been the Church's custom by pastoral authority to convene councils to take cognizance of doctrine, and not to assemble craftsmen and merchants to judge of this.' A fine nostalgic declamation, in a time-honoured tradition, wherein exclusiveness finds expression, and even the social significance of this exclusiveness, with its reference to craftsmen and merchants, those 'mechanicals' who spoke up, loud and strong, all through the sixteenth century.

Secondly, the Church set in motion a whole system of judicial machinery which enabled it unfailingly to cast out of its bosom – and to doom to physical disappearance – those of the clergy who, though trained in its schools and its orders, chose to challenge its dogmas or its discipline. The inquisitorial procedure which performed wonders in Southern France, in Spain and in Italy succeeded in disposing of the most serious temptations to heresy, which were sometimes backed by whole communities in which the laity were allowed to express themselves more freely, such as the Cathari and, especially, the Vaudois, who suffered at the hands of the Dominican inquisitors. But the advocates of a renovation in religion, Wycliffe in England and Jan Hus in Bohemia, enjoyed no better luck. The amazing adventure of Hus and his comrades, backed by a large part of their country's population, took a tragic turn after winning remarkable successes, the greatest achieved in the tormented Europe of the first half of the fifteenth century. After having stirred the masses of the Czech people to their depths, having swarmed over all the near-by countries, to east, west and south, the Hussites were crushed by armies summoned from every part of Christendom to fight them. The repression that descended upon the kingdom of Bohemia illustrates well the power possessed by the Church, helped by the secular powers, when dealing with those who for a moment had managed to upset the established order. At a time when unauthorized preachers were becoming more and more numerous throughout Europe – hardy men, orators who addressed their words to anxious crowds – the Church's discipline seemed all the more necessary. And all the rougher, too, if it be true that the persecution of rural witches, male and female, entrusted to the civil magistrates, was inspired by the same will to maintain with severity the good order of orthodox beliefs, in a situation where Satan was playing the tempter in the villages. These were all so many clear indications of the struggle that the institution was capable of waging in order to uphold its hegemony.

However, the heritage into which the innovations of the Renaissance came to set themselves included also Italy, Europe's teacher in the Flamboyant period, that Italy which, as everyone knows, was the first to relearn the lessons of Antiquity, present so abundantly in her monasteries and on her soil – alive, so to speak, as an everyday evocation in the landscape, both rural and urban, of Rome, Liguria and Tuscany. That centuries-old striving of the northern peoples towards Italy which did not cease until the end of the sixteenth century is not to be explained solely by the importance of the survivals of ancient civilization to be found there. In the domain of letters and of thought the boldest initiatives came from the world of the clergy, and in a period when all spiritual life was controlled by ecclesiastical institutions it is clearly platitudinous to emphasize this source – to note, after many others who have done this, the vitality of the universities of Italy, Padua and Bologna especially. But it is not paradoxical at all to make the point that the Italian cities, richer in Churchmen than any others in Europe, and closer to the papal authority, constituted the setting that was most apt to stimulate the study of ancient texts and pre-Christian thought. Doubtless, the Italian clergy in the universities were obliged, as elsewhere, to cope with a new demand, coming from the bourgeoisie (or, better, from the citizenry, the 'bourgeois' in the original sense of the word) for knowledge of the profane sciences of law and medicine. Doubtless, too, the maintenance and even the increase of relations with the East, Moslem-dominated since the eleventh and twelfth centuries, facilitated the 'provisioning' of the libraries of Italy with manuscripts which made available to the Italian clergy a

large part of that highly esteemed Oriental learning that gave
new life to medicine, in particular, in the last centuries of the
Middle Ages on the shores of the Mediterranean. But another
factor of importance was the presence in great numbers of a
body of clergy who were all the less inhibited in conduct and
language by virtue of their closeness, through ties of neighbourhood or kinship, to the highest authorities ruling over the
universal Church. The Roman administration of the Church
protected the audacities of those clergy who were hardest to
please, such as Lorenzo Valla, with his sneers at 'Gothic
ignorance', or Leonardo Bruni, the 'restorer' of Aristotle.
Lorenzo Valla, honoured at the beginning of the sixteenth
century as the master-humanist, conducted for thirty years in
the universities of Italy (along with Francesco Filelfo, Guarino
Veronese, Gasparino da Barzizza and Vittorino da Feltre) the
debate about the true Aristotle, his physics and his morality.

In the first half of the fifteenth century all the Italian
universities, from Naples to Rome and Milan, were alive with
these disputations in which the first modern humanism was
forged: revivals of the famous quarrels between the Lyceum
and the Academy; apologias for Cicero's rhetoric, which was
needed for the development of every branch of learning, even
dialectics and theology; restoration of the great works of
Antiquity discovered in monasteries as far away as the Alps
and even France – all these features became well established in
the universities of Italy, especially in Florence, long before
1450. While the universities and colleges elsewhere in Europe
were bogged down in routine-ridden discussions about
realism and nominalism (the example offered by the Sorbonne
at the beginning of the reign of Louis XI is the most typical),
Italy's universities were going forward, in the direction
wished for by Petrarch, ignoring scholastic quarrels and undertaking instead a fresh restoration of the pre-Christian Cicero
and, especially, of Plato, whose *Phaedo*, *Phaedrus* and *Gorgias*
had been translated before 1420 by Leonardo Bruni in

Florence. This Italian humanism which challenged the Aristotle of the Schoolmen, as petrified in orthodox doctrine, in the thirteenth century, thus came to flower in a long debate which developed in favour of Plato, of the Academy against the Lyceum, its course passing through many petty quarrels in which attacks *ad hominem* also played a big part. But, on the whole, nothing checked the advance of these innovating polemics, and they were restricted by no prohibition from the Roman Curia. It was in the heart of Christendom, in Rome itself, that the renewal of learning by the study of ancient texts was undertaken, by clerics who compared the new readings of restored manuscripts with the doctrine that had been taught officially for more than a century. The universities of Italy absorbed the impact, in this early period, of the most dangerous audacities, while, far from Rome, condemnations and rejections in the name of orthodoxy were still the rule.

Most certainly this effervescence of Italian humanist thought is not to be separated from the artistic movement which quickened the life of the cities of Italy throughout the fifteenth century. The coming of a portrayal of space based upon perspective, which has been so remarkably analysed by Pierre Francastel, belongs to this same context, in which artists multiplied their creations at the request of urban patriciates. The first generation of the Quattrocento, whose work culminated around 1450 (Fra Angelico, Uccello, Brunelleschi and Donatello) and who were exact contemporaries of the great university humanists, showed a boldness comparable to theirs in the representation of space. The new Italian masters, whose ranks were renewed in the next generation, after 1450, in the age of Alberti, presented to the northerners a scene of artistic life marked by innovation, just as the intellectual life of the Italian cities enthralled the scholars and students, satiated with disputes about nominalism, who came to pursue their studies south of the Alps. Italy was teacher to all Europe. This function of hers as 'initiatrix' extended amazingly all along the roads of commercial and ecclesiastical communication, as plentiful evidence shows us to this day. The cities of Southern Germany which were in constant relations with Venice and Rome bear the marks of Italian influence from before 1500. Southern France, and Lyon in particular, with its fairs and its merchants, felt the attraction of Italian examples (the Thomassin house in Lyon, among many other monuments in that city, bears witness to this) long before the soldiers of Louis XII and Francis I crossed the Alps, to bring back from their unlucky expeditions on the other side of the mountains so many trophies and mementoes, like the barbarians discovering the civilized world – which does not mean that their passion for Italy remained unproductive, for all through the first half of the sixteenth century the building of châteaux and houses in the Italian (and even the Tuscan) style provides most striking proof to the contrary, still visible in the landscape of France. In other directions too, farther away and later in time, the Italian school re-surfaced in Prague and in Cracow – so deeply did the southern patterns, both artistic and intellectual, set their lasting mark upon Europe's cultural life.

In what was inherited from the Middle Ages this primacy of Italy matters no less than the institutional solidity of the ecclesiastical world, both because it contains the leaven of renewal which was to take effect in the sixteenth century and also because it shows the contradictions that are inherent in any institutionalizing of intellectual life. When Lefèvre d'Etaples went to Italy in 1494 he stayed in Florence, and there both followed the teaching of Marsilio Ficino and Pico della Mirandola and listened to the terrifying sermons of Savonarola. These encounters of his tell us all too well how weighty were the examples to be found in the capital of the Medicis. This 'priority' of Italy, which has so often been extolled since Burckhardt, points to the presence of a pole of cultural development which was unique in its time. No country escaped the attraction of Italy. Distance, together with the resistance inspired by parochial patriotism, accounts for the variations and hesitations in the response given to this attraction, which were particularly explicit on the intellectual plane. The case of Paris is very clear in this connexion. The great masters of the Sorbonne at the beginning of the fifteenth century, like Gerson and Clémanges, borrowed nothing from the life of the Italian universities, nor did their immediate successors. Only in the second half of the fifteenth century was a chair of Greek assigned to an Italian, who taught for a few months in the Faculty of Arts. But this first step, taken in 1457, was not followed up for over ten years. It was in 1470 that a young doctor of divinity, Guillaume Fichet, on his return from a mission to Milan which had introduced him to the debates going on in the Italian universities and the humanistic orientations being taken up everywhere in that milieu, decided to bring these new notions into the Sorbonne's teaching. His position as librarian enabled him to take the essential initiative. He installed a printing workshop in the college itself, so as to have printed without delay the works of Gasparino da Barzizza and Lorenzo Valla, and of Sallust and Cicero. In this way, Europe became Italy's pupil, thanks to the new techniques of communication which developed over several decades. The examples set by Italy remained dominant for a long time, but Italy's leading role was eventually lost as these new techniques spread wider. The example of Flanders, where an advanced degree of urbanization had long favoured the growth of active centres of intellectual and artistic life, provides the best illustration of this relationship. The greatest humanists of the new generation – which was European, and no longer merely Italian – were editors of ancient texts.

2. THE NEW PROFESSIONS

The most spectacular innovation was concerned with book-production. It is very difficult today, after four centuries of a print-based civilization, to appreciate all the changes that were implied in 'the coming of the book', the transition from the spoken word and the picture, engraved or painted, to printed writing, reproduced in hundreds of copies, which placed at the disposal of a wide public a *ne varietur* text, cleansed of the errors due to fatigue which had been committed by copyists and perpetuated through the years. Anecdotal history stresses the rivalries between different groups of workers, the hard feelings against the new machine entertained by those who copied out university lectures by hand, but what was most important certainly lay elsewhere, in the profound changes made in the way that the expression of thought was transmitted and preserved: in teaching itself, wherein recitation and techniques of memorization no longer needed to play a big part, and in the diffusion of knowledge of all kinds, from short stories bound up in little books to the heavy folios of the theologians.

Printing, with its rapidly accumulating technical improvements, engendered a new kind of intellectual: the bookseller-cum-printer-cum-publisher who united in his person functions which have today become distinct, a true entrepreneur who installed workshops and presses at great expense in order to produce books which he had often selected and edited himself, and the selling of which he subsequently undertook. In a period when editions were limited to a few hundred copies, when the skilled workers needed were scarce and expensive, and when the paper-mills which grew up around the cities or in a few specialized districts like the Livradois were not adequate to the demand, the book producer needed substantial capital and could not survive failure to sell his goods. He sought reliable orders, those that could be provided by the clergy or the princes, who very soon made use of the printers to serve their needs. In 1523 the Bishop of Nevers, Jacques d'Albret, gave an order for 600 breviaries to a printer in that town, and, the year after, the Bishop of Senlis had

400 missals printed. As his business succeeded, the bookseller-publisher hunted around perseveringly for unpublished manuscripts and documents which were routed out from the remotest monasteries. This master-craftsman was thus also a good connoisseur of ancient literature, and more than one such made a name for himself in that role in the 'republic of letters': the brothers Estienne in Paris, Sebastian Gryphius in Lyon, Aldus Manutius in Venice, and Plantin, from Touraine, who set up his business in Antwerp in 1549. But the managing of these new enterprises called for a long apprenticeship, which the young printers pursued all across Europe. The Amerbach brothers, of Basle, were sent to Paris in 1501 to gain experience of the methods of work that were in use in the workshops of that city, and their father, careful to guide the progress of his heirs, was not sparing of pertinent advice to them regarding this apprenticeship.

The point to be appreciated is that these printing establishments cannot be seen as ordinary craftsmen's workshops. From the printing to the binding and the gilding of the boards and spines, they were like a production line, in the modern sense of the expression, which employed detail workers at each stage of the manufacturing process. The compositor who assembled the letters and the corrector who read the first proofs to emerge from the hand-press belonged, too, to that new category of 'non-clerical clerks' who knew Latin and Greek as well as their own national language. It is not a matter for surprise that these printing workers, conscious of their key role, insisted on high rates of pay, and all the more vigorously in that, learning their trade on the job, as they did, they were not a plentiful commodity in the labour market. It was not unusual to see humanists of all ranks and every level of renown take service under the entrepreneurs of the book trade and work as correctors in a printing workshop for a few months, or a few years: neither Erasmus nor Budé scorned these chores. Jodocus Badius, who was a publisher in Lyon and later in Paris, employed in his business Lefèvre d'Etaples, Budé and Berquin: Sebastian Gryphius, in Lyon, used the services of Rabelais, Marot, Maurice Scève and Dolet. Alongside these highly skilled specialists there worked on the presses, and at cutting, binding and engraving, a number of workers, whose jobs were sharply defined and who were no less attached than the compositors and correctors to the privileges of their corporation – privileges which became established in the course of a few decades, as printing workshops were set up all across Europe.

For hundreds and thousands of these books, which were inevitably expensive – everything contributed to this: the raw material, paper, leather, ink, type, as well as labour – were being produced in Europe at the end of the fifteenth and the beginning of the sixteenth century. The maps which have been compiled to show the spread of printing establishments are eloquent, containing as they do considerably more data than those giving the distribution of the medieval universities: the northern and central parts of Italy are covered with these enterprises as early as 1480, as might be expected, but at the same date Brittany had printers' workshops in little towns like Tréguier, Loudéac and Lantenac, and in 1500 there were over fifty bookseller-publishers in Lyon alone. More remarkable still is the spreading of these enterprises across Germany, where the whole movement had begun in the middle of the fifteenth century. Before 1470 all the great cities of Germany – Cologne, Mainz, Nuremberg, Augsburg – possessed their own presses. But in 1500 small towns with a few thousand inhabitants, at most, also had one or more printing workshops: examples are Schleswig, Memmingen, Offenburg, and Lauingen (the birthplace of Albertus Magnus, on the Danube) – altogether, more than fifty towns in the Holy Roman Empire as a whole. Progress was no less marked in the southwest of Europe: before 1470, Seville alone had a press, but in 1500 about thirty towns were so equipped, including Gerona,

Burgos, Lérida and Tortosa, none of which was a major centre
of intellectual activity. This all-European development, which
spread so much further than the university framework,
covered the towns where fairs were held and large-scale trade
carried on, the centres of international traffic, both by land and
by sea, like Augsburg and Lyon, Rouen, Nantes and Antwerp,
and also the political centres, the capitals of principalities:
sometimes even of puny ones like Parma or Lüneburg. On the
scale of the entire continent it shows clearly how fast these
new means of reproduction, installed everywhere, succeeded
in ensuring a wider diffusion of ideas than Europeans had ever
been able to conceive as possible.

Under conditions of complete freedom the new technique
imposed itself everywhere, without much difficulty, despite
some outcries by the trades dependent upon hand-work in this
field. This invention, celebrated by contemporaries as God's
finest gift, did not fail to disquiet the authorities, political and
ecclesiastical, who were soon to assert a right to supervise the
large-scale production of printed books, just as, earlier, they
had supervised the slow output of the copyists But in the last
years of the fifteenth century the organization of censorship
was still only embryonic. Even later, when censorship
regulations had been laid down (in France already in 1521 for
all publications relating to Holy Scripture, and in 1539 for all
publications in general), the way they were operated was as
lax as the means of checking on the output of books remained
mediocre, and nobody was surprised to see republished in 1528
a humorous piece (*Les Heures de Nôtre-Dame*) which had been
condemned in 1525. Actually, the life of the book trade was
dominated at first by the infatuation of the public created by
the book itself: the installation of printing workshops, the
multiplication of editions, the production of spurious copies,
all this responded to the huge demand which was revealed
within a half-century by this new means of communication.

The fever of publication followed the graph of the discovery of ancient learning. For a century at least the two movements advanced together: reading, identifying, correcting, editing, writing commentaries, all that work done by scholars intent upon the rediscovery of the ancient worlds in their abundant richness passed through the hands of the master-printers, engravers and publishers, who were much more than mere auxiliaries – they were full participants in this intellectual adventure. Thousands of men were involved, throughout Europe, organized in new corporations, independent of the ecclesiastical authorities and in an ambiguous social situation: they were lay intellectuals, most certainly, by virtue of the activities they carried on, at once traders in and creators of goods – that is, they obeyed the rules common to business as it was practised in their time. But these master-printers and their workers put into circulation a durable commodity which was handed down from generation to generation like furniture or jewellery, and which, moreover, travelled easily across all countries, a product of high value in little bulk (apart from the folios): a commodity destined for a limited public, although reading aloud, a common practice in those days, might considerably enlarge its audience, and which was something more than just an object for consumption – it was a message and a 'leaven'. Very soon these craftsmen, who developed their specializations and their traditions within a few decades, became aware of their place in intellectual life: very soon, too, they became aware of the risks entailed in making themselves responsible for the diffusion of these books, both big and small, which so often gave cause for concern to the authorities.

Less spectacular and less commented on by contemporaries, the change brought about by the great geographical discoveries in the trades connected with the sea was no less remarkable. The sudden enlargement of the known world effected in some thirty years, between Columbus and Magellan, certainly did not disturb the outlook of the great

majority of Europe's inhabitants, who were countryfolk
for whom the sun continued to rise in the east and set in
the west every day and who were indifferent to a change in
the way things were represented which made no practical
difference in their own familiar horizon. But for the
sailor, the shipowner and the merchant whose lives were
bound up with the sea, and who wanted to make something
for themselves out of these new lands, the change was of vital
importance. Long before mathematicians and astronomers had
put forward their new world-system – that infinite universe
which was to replace the conception, inherited from Antiquity,
of a flat earth, the centre of the universe, around which moved
the sun and the stars – seamen had had, gropingly, to construct
for themselves, by multiplying improvised maps, a new
picture of a round earth on which they could locate the Indies,
West and East, and an empire on which the sun never set. The
sailors who took part in the first crossings of the Atlantic, and
who learnt from experience to mark out the safest routes –
from the Canaries to the Caribbean, using the trade-wind, and
from the Bahamas to the Azores, using the west wind – had
the hardest job to do, since the excessively crude instruments
they possessed for taking their bearings, and the lack of maps,
left them for a long time at the mercy of the regularities and
caprices of the winds. Subsequently, however, as the identification of the new lands progressed and as the measurement of
latitude was accomplished (though not that of longitude,
which was mastered only much later), these long-distance
voyages to the Americas and the Far East resulted in the
production of works that for a long time were more
practical than theoretical, being intended to provide sailors
with the means of safer navigation across these unknown
waters.

Astronomers, cartographers and geographers worked
together in this field. The first-named studied the fixed points
that were available to navigators for keeping to their path

and for determining their position when far from any land-mark. The second group applied themselves to constructing and drawing the maps that these navigators needed in order to determine the quickest and safest routes, and to identify the places where they would interrupt their voyages and engage in trade. The last-named made it their business to give to all in Europe who were interested in the new worlds descrip-tions of the countries concerned, their inhabitants and their resources. All of them had to work over the ancient knowledge which had been diffused by the printers, even though this was found to be, in part, useless. In 1469 the Elder Pliny was published in Venice, in 1475 and 1478 Ptolemy's *Cosmography* appeared in Vicenza and Rome, and in 1533 Ptolemy's *Geography* came out in Basle, with a preface by Erasmus.

This slow labour was accomplished amid the ardours of a world that was alive with initiative, in ports and in the courts of princes, everywhere that the demand for these instruments of cognition was a pressing one, and it went on all through the sixteenth century: in the last years of the century, the States-General of Holland and Philip II of Spain both offered a prize – of 6,000 ducats in the one case and 10,000 florins in the other – for the perfecting of a method of measuring longitude. The stages of this slow and difficult task, covering the whole world that had now become known, are marked by the most famous successes achieved, and those that have been best conserved down to our own time; but one needs to leaf through collections of old maps, arranged in chrono-logical order, before one can visualize what was meant by this long-continued labour, the sailors' demands and the tentative efforts of the draughtsmen and calculators who worked to meet them. In 1539 Kremer (Mercator) constructed his first map, showing the principal coasts identified since 1492–1520, and thirty years later he published the well-known planisphere established in accordance with the projection that bears his name, which enables all the lands known on the surface of the globe to be shown together. At the same time, Sebastian Münster, who had become known in 1535 through his publication of a Hebrew Bible, was devoting himself to the establishment and production of maps, dozens of them, a task that he continued to the end of his life, his chief work being the famous *Cosmography* published in 1544. Similarly, the geographers, using the first travellers' tales and describing men, animals and plants by reference to the species known in Europe, were furnishing the sailors with tools for everyday use. Schöner, who attempted in 1520 to construct a globe, published in 1533 his *Opusculum geographicum*, the best-known treatise of this kind written at the beginning of the sixteenth century. All these successes were the achievement of Flemings or Germans, who worked for the Hanseatic ports or for Antwerp (Münster spent a large part of his life at Duisburg) and found in that part of Europe, rather than in Lisbon or Seville (which nevertheless had their cartographers, who worked under the wing of a *cosmographo mayor*: Martín Cortés, Rodrigo Zamorano), the milieu rich in information and in technical means (for engraving and printing) that they needed in order to carry out their work. The direct relationship with the users of their work (who were at the same time their suppliers of data, more elaborate year by year and to a large extent replacing earlier information) is in this case absolutely obvious, and explains to a certain extent how it was that this work could develop pragmatically over a very long period without giving rise to anxieties and interdicts, although the essential assumptions involved in it constituted a challenge to an important part of the doctrine enshrined in Holy Writ.

For every graphic representation of a round earth, turning both upon itself and around a fixed sun, clearly contradicts by implication the Ptolemaic system to which the Old Testament alludes: a flat earth in the centre of the universe, with a firmament arranged in relation to this earth (indeed, to

Palestine) – that traditional conception of the cosmos no longer made sense to anyone who used the new maps and engaged in long-distance navigation. While the theologians continued to teach the old world-system in the universities, cartographers and astronomers, in their day-to-day practice, reasoned on the basis of facts acquired through the experience of sailors and gradually verified by their own calculations which established the new image of the earth. Doubtless, they did not all, when employing the new conceptions, appreciate the reversal of perspectives that these implied: the sailors embarked for very long voyages round the world who continued assiduously to pray to their patron saints, to the Virgin and to Jesus, hardly suspected the implicit contradiction between their cartographical practice and the 'astronomical' pronouncements found in the Scriptures. The sphericity of the earth and its movement upon itself entered into the current practice of seamen, without much difficulty. They obviously raised more questions for the printers and scholars who worked on these new ways of representing the world (often without giving up their old astrological and meteorological pre-occupations) but who nevertheless felt few scruples in getting on with their work. Mercator's planisphere, the best formulation of the new system, affords the clearest expression of this practical priority, of technical needs over articles of faith, and at the same time the uncomfortable coexistence that was established *de facto* (for a minority, at least) between the two. On the one hand, a recognition of the fact that the earth was spherical, accepted with all its consequences; on the other, an assertion contradicting this, and regarded as revealed truth, not subject to discussion – and both together under the same hat. We do not need to ponder upon what dramas of conscience this must have meant, since it does not appear that the boldest of the cosmographers and cartographers were embarrassed for very long by such scruples, or hesitated to take account – map after map, line upon line – of the data of new experience accumulated by navigators. It was otherwise with the astronomers, including the greatest of them in this generation, Copernicus.

The Copernican revolution is, in a way, a rather mysterious affair. This learned man, born in Northern Poland in 1473, who studied in Cracow and then in Italy in the last years of the fifteenth century, spent forty years of his life (while practising medicine) in building a new theory of the world, in conformity with the facts provided by the great discoveries and supported by a considerable mass of calculations concerning the position of the earth in relation to the sun and to the moon. Established at Frauenburg (Frombork), he carried on an extensive correspondence with an impressive number of mathematicians and astronomers, including some illustrious cardinals of the Roman Curia, such as Bernardus Clesius, Bishop of Brixen, to whom Copernicus was able to submit, little by little, the new calculations he had made to determine the curve of the earth's orbit round the sun, and the limits of the finite world which has the sun for its centre. The heliocentrism of Copernicus describes a new firmament, but one which is also defined as limited: much vaster, to be sure, than that of Ptolemy the Alexandrian, but not yet the 'infinite spaces' of Pascal. During all this time, however, in which he was repeating approximations which wholly assumed negation of the Ptolemaic system, he encountered, it seems, no blame or formal opposition on the part of the ecclesiastical authorities. His correspondents in Rome, just like the other scholars who were working along the same lines and who congratulated him on his successes, lavished upon him encouragement which one cannot, given their level of understanding of the phenomena involved, regard as being due to unawareness or ignorance. Yet Copernicus advanced, apparently, quite soon after his return from Italy in 1504, towards his construction of a total concept which situated all the elements of the solar system and defined them mathematically in relation to each other: but he published nothing, remaining satisfied to communicate to his usual correspondents hypotheses and propositions supported by calculations that were as exact and as full as the means of observation then available permitted – although a man more for calculation and deduction than for observation, Copernicus nevertheless made a fair number of recorded observations of stars (about sixty in all). He was in no hurry to publish, leaving it to his few disciples to proclaim his system. Doubtless he was mistrustful of the critics to whom he referred unkindly in his book: 'I hesitated long whether ... it were better to follow the example of the Pythagoreans and others who were wont to impart their philosophic mysteries only to intimates and friends, and then not in writing but by word of mouth ... as fearing lest these so noble and hard-won discoveries of great men should be despised by such as either care not to study aught save for gain or – if by the encouragement and example of others they are stimulated to philosophic liberal pursuits – yet by reason of the dulness of their wits are in the company of philosophers as drones among bees.'

Then, in 1543, he published at Nuremberg, a few months before his death, his famous treatise, *De revolutionibus orbium caelestium*, the first, and incomplete, exposition of a solar cosmology, which set forth in good Latin all the relationships between the different elements of the solar system. This was the capital work upon which all subsequent astronomers leaned: Tycho Brahe in Denmark at the end of the sixteenth century, Kepler in Prague and Galileo in Italy in the first decades of the seventeenth century. After 1543 there was certainly no more room for equivocation on this plane, for anyone who claimed any acquaintance with astronomy: Copernicus had set forth as clearly as possible all the co-ordinates of the new system which ruined the traditional geocentrism sanctioned by scriptural authority and by that of Aristotle and of St Thomas. All the more remarkable, therefore, was the silence that followed the publication of *De revolutionibus*. Condemned in 1539, even before publication, by Luther, the work made its impression in the small circle of initiates capable of following the calculations presented by the Polish master, but it led to no prosecutions of Copernicus's disciples when they arranged for reprintings, nor of any astronomer or cosmographer who based himself upon this new authority. The Copernican revolution remained, so to speak, a silent revolution until the appearance of the works of his great successors mentioned above. The dichotomy in their consciences which we must assume in the case of many of the technicians and scholars who emerged after the great discoveries was accompanied by an institutional duplicity: the Church, which concerned itself so quickly, in other instances, with heterodox propositions put forward in the first half of the century, did not worry too much about a work that was difficult to read, and reserved by its very nature to a small élite, numbering not more than a few hundred persons in all Europe. Unless, that is, the metaphysical and doctrinal implications of the Copernican theories were, in fact, not immediately grasped by the dignitaries of Rome ... A. Koyré, in his book on *The Astronomical Revolution*, does not rule out this possibility.

Altogether, at the beginning of the sixteenth century, intellectual life had thus been fundamentally made new, as a result of a great variety of processes. In the wake of the innovations of the cartographers and geographers, other disciplines were to establish themselves, drawing, in all sorts of ways, upon Europe's entry into the previously unknown worlds. The curiosities which became material for collections of rare objects, and the accounts of voyages which accumulated descriptions of the newly explored countries, served as preludes to the recasting of the sciences of man and of nature which Montaigne was soon to assess. Just as the necessity to evangelize populations which had not had the chance to learn the truth of Christianity raised many problems for Europeans who paid attention to the letter of the Scriptures and who were also conscious of the virtues of these native peoples, so the progress made in knowledge of these new worlds called in question some of the learning inherited from earlier centuries and codified in teaching. But this kind of innovation made its way rather slowly, as the relations between Europe and the transoceanic countries became regular and as information was accumulated: more slowly, that is, than the galleons of Spain brought back their cargoes of treasure. More slowly, especially, than the wealth of the cultures of Antiquity was being revealed by the persevering labour of the humanists, who were more numerous and more prolific than all of the innovators whom we have just been considering.

3. THE HUMANISTS AND THE KNOWLEDGE
THEY RECOVERED

In order to obtain a true idea of these men who stood outside of the traditional intellectual framework we need first of all briefly to refer to the degree of confusion and decrepitude to which the medieval universities had sunk in the second half of the fifteenth century. The best-known example, that of the University of Paris, described not so long ago by A. Renaudet, is not the best that could be given. Yet the Sorbonne, which had launched itself into political conflicts – it was pro-Burgundian under Charles VII, Gallican and Conciliarist in opposition to the popes, was ill-used both by the kings of France (Louis XI) and by the Roman Curia, and its sources of revenue were ruined by the effects of war – was indeed, perhaps, the university most seriously affected. With professors who no longer taught, students who gave themselves up to debauchery, monasteries deserted or else transformed into havens for the gay life, long periods when the university was on strike or closed down, Paris suffered a whole succession of the gravest disorders.

But the other universities of Western Europe were not in much better health. Shortage of theologians to carry on teaching; lack of staff for the attached colleges; sometimes no students, since these, at a loose end or disappointed by the teaching they received, either wandered from one university to another or else gave up all work in order to lead a merry, boisterous existence protected by the university's privileges, which began to be felt as a burden by the civil authorities. The religious orders which sent their novices and young monks to study in the universities were aware of the decline being suffered by the institution. The Chapter-General of the Dominicans observed at Ferrara in 1494: 'In nearly all our provinces, teaching has become weaker, and we can now foresee its collapse in the near future.' Everywhere the disturbances caused by rowdy students and teachers, the continually revived conflicts over the privileges granted when colleges and universities were founded, and which were now being challenged by promoters of reform, the endless disputes caused by the debates that started up regarding the primacy of the papal power and the authority of Councils, and even regarding scholasticism and mysticism, all came together to discredit both the institutions themselves and the regular clergy who made up the population of many of these universities. During the last years of the fifteenth century there were young clerks who dared, in the heart of the Sorbonne, to revive the theses of Wycliffe and Hus and proclaim that the Church had fallen prey to Caesar and Mammon. It was amid this troubled context that humanists and scholars chose deliberately to turn their backs on a community bogged down in its own contradictions, its futile attempts at reform, and its domestic quarrels.

These men were given the label of 'humanists' only quite late in the century. Montaigne contrasted 'theologians' and 'humanists' in a brief phrase, but the formula established itself only much later. Whatever may be the validity of the term 'humanist' (it now figures in the most up-to-date terminology of the humane sciences, and even in present-day political polemics), it would be better to speak of a 'learned man of letters', since this indicates more clearly what it was that such men did, and what their aims were. In order to restore the civilizations of Antiquity in their full complexity, all of these men needed to be able to read and interpret the works of ancient literature which had now been recovered. Erasmus had reached the age of thirty when, in 1500, he wrote: 'I have turned my entire attention to Greek' (*ad graecas litteras totum animum impuli*), realizing how important a mastery of this language and ability to read Greek works in the original would be for his understanding of the ancient world. Consequently, these men were all philologists in the usual sense of the word: all of them practised during their years of study that examination of a text which begins by identifying the terms it uses, eliminating the errors due to poor transcription, establishing the correct reading of the text, and providing it with a translation and an adequate commentary. All of them hastened to sit at the feet of good teachers, who became known through their sureness in these preliminary exercises and the reliability of their consequent interpretations: they followed the lectures of John Colet, at Oxford, and those of Lefèvre d'Etaples at the Collège du Cardinal Lemoine.

This necessary apprenticeship, which was pursued even into the printers' workshops, set its mark on these men who, through several generations, practised the same trade and used the same methods, with a rigour that became the more certain as working tools became available – in the first place, grammars and dictionaries, like Estienne's *Thesaurus*. Even the men who advanced further, abandoning those philological workplaces which remained well-frequented for such a long time, did not forget them or what they had learned there.

Calvin, when he had become the head of a Church, did not forget his early training as a philosopher and a jurist, at Orleans, and did not fail to recall his participation in the common task, when he attacked those timid ones, the Nicodemites, who had not followed him. It is enough to read a page annotated by Luther, as in his commentary on the Psalms, in 1503, to appreciate the extent to which this method had become a matter of everyday behaviour for them. Disparaged nowadays by those who have kept at a safe distance from severe disciplines, these 'philological' methods were an extraordinary school of critical thinking, which brought together into play both knowledge of the ancient tongues, with their linguistic formalism, and mastery of wider learning about all those matters which made up the civilization of Antiquity.

None of these scholars, moreover, who were in love with Latin or Greek, confined himself to publishing the text and translation of some work brought back to life from a medieval library and zealously dusted off. It is not detracting from the merit they acquired in this stage of their *cursus* (especially when the works in question included Aristotle's *Logic*, published by Lefèvre d'Etaples, and the plays of Euripides) to mention the logical progression whereby these scholars went on to study the armies and political institutions, and even straightforwardly the history, of the ancient world, as recounted by Polybius and Livy, Sallust and Herodotus. From commentaries they proceeded to paraphrases and then to narrowly specialized researches. Guillaume Budé (Budaeus) wrote a treatise on the Roman currency, *De asse et partibus ejus* (in which, besides, he talks at length about many other matters, remote from the monetary problems of Rome but relevant to his own time, and reveals the same preoccupations as those of all the other humanists); Lefèvre composed an introduction to the *Ethics* of Aristotle; Josse van Clichtove wrote a treatise on the division of the sciences and the arts.

After language primers, which made possible a rapid apprenticeship to the ancient tongues, it was guides and catalogues of various kinds that enjoyed most success (or so it would appear from their many reprintings). In Rome, Francesco Albertini published in 1510 his *Opusculum de mirabilibus novae et veteris urbis Romae*, a guide to the city which was reissued in 1515, 1519, 1520, etc. In Strasbourg the manual of ancient mythology published by Hermann van der Beeke, *Elucidarius carminum et historiarum*, enjoyed equal success under its other title: *Vocabularius poeticus*. It is enough to dip into the mass of new publications which every year enriched the collective patrimony of this republic of learning to find evidence of the scholars' devotion, to which their correspondence provides a generous echo, testifying to the interest with which they followed each other's work – one man is worried because he has not received a certain book, and begs his correspondent to get him a copy, or else he comments emphatically on the author's success in giving renewed life to some aspect of ancient civilization.

Within the limits of this book it is not possible to give a list that would properly represent all this scholarly activity. The humanist bibliographers, with their dry-as-dust inventories, alone fill entire volumes. The subject-classification normally employed to survey this activity (the politics, morality, etc., of the humanists) fails to take account of the variety of concerns which all these men displayed: even the least important letter to a friend tells us more, because in two or three pages it touches upon several subjects, quite different in kind according to our classifications, which all form part of the humanists' field of inquiry. It was not just the going over from 'historical' problems to questions of faith that was remarkable here: there were no limits at all to their curiosity, to their hunger for knowledge. And this could not fail to disquiet, in several ways, the holders and dispensers of classified learning who were then in control of the universities.

This happened in the first place, no doubt (even if this reason was not always made very explicit), because these men of more or less universal learning worked and made themselves known outside, to some extent, of the institutional framework. Not all of them, certainly, nor even all the time: but, on the whole, it does indeed appear that, from the first decades of the sixteenth century, the scholars who were rediscovering Antiquity were much more numerous outside the universities than inside them. Then, secondly, it soon became clear that this passion devoted to the rediscovery of pagan Antiquity could not but reveal, to researchers who burnt the midnight oil in company with the greatest writers of Greece and Rome, the richness and fecundity of pre-Christian civilizations, which the collective memory had not been helped to remember much about during the medieval period. That was so not only at the level of the instruction currently handed out to the mass of the faithful, for whom the history of the Chosen People and of the birth of Christianity, the Old and New Testaments condensed into a few dozen lectures in the course of a year, could not leave much room for the Greek, Roman and Hellenistic worlds, but also at the level of more elaborate learning, which was based upon a small selection of authors, as commented on by the Fathers of the Church and interpreted in accordance with the strict doctrine of the Schools. Long before Montaigne, his library stocked with the results of a century of diligent toil, expressed his enchantment with this rediscovery, many had wondered about the correct interpretation of Aristotle, about the merits of Plato and Socrates, about the evolution of the pre-Christian societies of the Mediterranean. In this field, as in that of astronomy, the letter of the Scriptures was not compatible with the historical accounts that were widely diffused already at the end of the fifteenth century.

The 'gap' established between the practice of navigators and cartographers and the Ptolemaic doctrine confirmed by

Holy Writ and by the Church could not be maintained here. This was so, first, because many of the documents put into circulation by the humanists' efforts referred directly to events belonging to Jewish and Christian history: the historians Tacitus and Flavius Josephus, along with the minor Greek writers of the Hellenistic period who dealt with the Jewish diaspora or the conflicts between Jews and early Christians, contributed evidence that seemed trustworthy. This was so, secondly, because the Apostles and the Fathers of the Church – St Paul and St Augustine especially – had given a series of impressions of ancient culture, both Roman and Hellenistic, which did not always accord with what could be found elsewhere, on the basis of other, non-Christian works, contemporary or subsequent in date. Therefore, where Christian Antiquity was concerned, at least, the mere circulation – that is, the mere making accessible to study – of pagan authors of the period presented problems that could not be solved without going against the teachings of the Church.

But there was something even more serious implied in the application of the critical method to those texts which were related to, or which actually constituted, the sacred books of the Church. That exacting philology which made it possible to restore the authentic form of an ancient work, getting behind all the glosses and faulty readings, could not be confined to the writings of pagan antiquity. Before the fifteenth century was out, the humanists had tackled St Paul and the Gospels, and found that corrections were needed which seemed to them similar to the many that they had made in the case of 'ordinary' writings. Lorenzo Valla was undoubtedly the one who went farthest, by attacking the text of the Vulgate, which he found rotten with copyists' mistakes and faulty translations. John Colet, at Oxford, gave commentaries on St Paul and the Gospels, in lecture form, which he waited a long time before publishing. When Erasmus found at Louvain in 1504 Lorenzo Valla's notes on the Latin version of the New

Testament, he had them published by Jodocus Badius, accompanying them with a preface which set out admirably the logic implicit in this critique of Scripture. The sacred text must be examined like any other, by the grammarian whose task it is to establish correctly the letter, without which the spirit cannot be grasped. If the letter is corrupt, it must be corrected with the care and respect that sacred texts demand. Theology is certainly the queen of all the sciences, but she cannot do without the services that her humble attendant the science of words (*pedissequa grammatica*) can render her. Erasmus knew well beforehand the objections that would be advanced by theologians defending Tradition, and the Vulgate in particular, and his plea aimed to ward them off. Nevertheless, he did not vacillate for one moment regarding the validity of the method, which had long since proved its worth: so many texts restored and even the implicit competition between the greatest scholars, those who knew all three languages – Latin, Greek and Hebrew – constitute arguments enough to prove that. Some time had already passed since a brilliant proof had been furnished by that same Lorenzo Valla's demonstration of the falsity of the Donation of Constantine, in categorical terms that were often quoted during the discussions about the Gallican Church and the power of Councils (notably by Jean Lemaire de Belges in 1511). In a letter to Dorpius (Martin Dorp), Erasmus explains very clearly his position, which must be that of every philologist: 'There is no danger that anyone will suddenly depart from Christ if he happens to hear that a passage has been found in the Scriptures which an unskilled or drowsy copyist has corrupted or some translator or other has rendered inexactly. That danger springs from other causes, which I prudently pass over here.' Thus, the humanist method called in question the Catholic Church's most fundamental traditions, by the very procedure that it followed: there was a direct relation between philological criticism and discussion of the

elements making up the Tradition of the Fathers, based upon
the sacred texts in the form and interpretation which had been
adopted during the Middle Ages. If one is justified in separating this work of criticism from the reform movements
strictly so called, then it is because some of the clerics who
preached an instauration of the Church found themselves
establishing new institutions, that is, new Churches, while
many humanists of the great period cared for science, in the
strict sense of the word, more than for anything else.

Certainly less numerous than the philologists, and less
honoured by posterity because their work was rapidly surpassed from the seventeenth century onward, these science-
orientated scholars nevertheless counted for much in the
intellectual evolution of the age. It is well known that
Leonardo da Vinci and Albrecht Dürer were concerned with
matters of this order for many years. Dürer offers an example
which, though less striking than that of Leonardo, is perhaps
more convincing, by virtue of his works devoted to theoretical
problems – his treatise on measures, published in 1525
(*Unterweisung der Messung*) and the amazing posthumous
work which came out in 1528, his four books on the propor-
tions of the human body (*Vier Bücher von menschlichen
Proportion*) and by the workmanship of his paintings and
engravings, in which symmetry, calculation and perfection of
detail are always present: in *Melancolia*, or *St Jerome in his Cell*,
for example, or in the well-known *Hare*, 'from which no hair
is missing'. It is certainly easy nowadays to carp at the talent
for compilation shown by many of these scholars, who were
carried away by the revelations that reading the Elder Pliny or
Avicenna brought them, or at the veneration with which a
whole school surrounded the memory of Albertus Magnus,
the Swabian who became a master of all sciences at Cologne
and who wrote such a lot on all sorts of subjects. But these
men were in the grip of the same fever as the humanists. What
they discovered was treatises and discourses of astrology and

astronomy, chemistry and alchemy, and they strove first to
identify the terms used and then to put them in some sort of
coherent order. The desire that can be discerned, however, in
the eagerness with which they sought to master this twofold
inheritance, medieval and ancient, is clear enough. Convinced
by the Schoolmen that the world of Nature and of Man is a
secret which men can master and gradually unlock only with
the greatest of difficulty, they intended to lay hold of everything that their predecessors offered, with a view to discovering some part of this unknown. Albertus Magnus wrote about
the secrets of women and about the secrets of the nature of
things, and they followed him, there as elsewhere, for their
approach was absolutely single-minded. For them there was
no distinction between permissible sciences and occult ones.
There was no difference between the quest for the philosopher's stone and research to find out how fever is contracted,
because their way of classifying the sciences was different
from ours; and because all relations were plausible to them
once they had been affirmed by some authority, no matter
whether this be a learned doctor in the Hippocratic tradition
or the possessor of some empiric knowledge. In this sense
they were indeed comrades-in-arms of the philologists, since
they too proposed to master learning that had been lost, or
else for a long time only poorly known. Once they had
recovered this knowledge they would be able to work more
confidently, sure of being able to relate it to whatever they
might themselves observe, and sure, too, that they would then
be able to make their own discoveries known. Brunfels
revised the Elder Pliny, publishing his *Flora* in Strasbourg in
1536. Agricola studied metals on the basis of the mines and the
classifications of the ancients. In the same year, 1543, that
Copernicus published his treatise, the surgeon and physician
Vesalius published his *De corporis humani fabrica*, in which he
used his observations from dissections to correct Hippocrates
and Galen, whose works had been published in Venice twenty

years before. But all the scholars of this type brought something different into the game: what they proclaimed was the coming acquisition of power over beings and objects, in so far as the knowledge they sought would enable them both to find the hidden springs and, of course, to work them. The reciting of an invocation that could at any moment free a patient from sickness, or protect an animal, opened up more utilitarian prospects than the writing of a treatise on Cicero's orations against Catiline. The presence of scholars of this kind alongside the humanists or even outside their circles, was not always so plainly perceived by contemporaries, but study of a few careers enables us to see it in full clarity.

As a first example let us take the Rhenish astrologer Johann Lichtenberger, who was born in the middle of the fifteenth century and died in 1503. A physician, doubtless, as well as an astrologer, this Johann Grumbach who became Lichtenberger carried out research on the influence of the stars and of precious stones upon human destinies. He was employed at the court of the Emperor Frederick III (*astrorum judex sacri imperii*) to inform his employer every day how the stars stood in the heavens, and on this basis to advise him how to spend his time. Lichtenberger's reputation was so great at the end of the fifteenth century that disciples came to live near him so as to learn this art of astrological prediction. The 'Master', as Peter Creutzer calls him, also published works in which he imparted some of his doctrine: a *sortilegium* (defining the days that were favourable for different activities), a *Wetterbuch*, various horoscopes, including that of Duke Ludwig of Bavaria-Landshut, and, above all, in 1488, a *Pronosticatio*, which can be considered his major work. This was a long dissertation on the astrological cases which he had succeeded in compiling from ancient writings, and which he interpreted in his own way, devoting his attention to remarkable conjunctions of the stars, such as the encounter of Jupiter with Saturn at the end of November 1484. This *Pronosticatio* had much to say about the

Church and the Holy Roman Empire, about the Turks, and about the proclaimed coming of a second Augustus. Obviously inspired by the prophecies of Joachim of Fiore, Lichtenberger announced a new age in which the Church would be made new, when the Emperor had purged Rome and an angelic pope had arrived, capable of suppressing luxurious indulgence and of preaching the Gospel. Frederick III's astrologer was accused of committing plagiarism in this book, by a rival, Paul of Middelburg, who brought out in 1492 an *Invectiva in supersticiosum quemdam astrologum*, denouncing 'borrowings' which are the harder to deny in that all these astrologers worked upon common sources, exploited the same astro-logical themes, and took responsibility for the same pre-dictions – alarming so far as the immediate future was concerned, but rich in long-term hope. Lichtenberger did not even reply to the accusations of his colleague: another characteristic of the time. Nevertheless, his book enjoyed a fine career: between 1488 and the end of the fifteenth century fourteen editions appeared (in German, Italian and Latin), another thirteen between 1526 and 1530, and, altogether, by the middle of the sixteenth century, about fifty, including the excerpts and summaries made after his death by faithful disciples keen to make their teacher's masterpiece more widely known. Quite certainly, at the end of the fifteenth century astronomical and astrological description and explana-tion constituted one of the most highly esteemed branches of science, and this not only in the political circles in which Lichtenberger pursued his career but also among a wider public who believed that the stars exerted a direct influence on human lives and who sought to know what the relevant coordinates were.

A more significant figure still, owing to the repercussions of his work, was Theophrastus Paracelsus, who in the first half of the sixteenth century (1493–1541) occupied a high place among the most learned. His career is not well known,

since all that is certain is that he studied medicine in Italy, at
Verona. His was a universal range of learning, according to
the university standards of the time – he was a doctor of
divinity, of law and of medicine – and also with respect to
the newest branches of knowledge, for he studied everything
and wrote about everything. He led a wandering life for a
long time, hidden in the silence of the mountains in the heart
of the Swiss cantons. Then, for the rest of the century, he
inspired a whole procession of disciples, such as Cornelius
Agrippa and Giovanni-Batista della Porta, who did much to
make Paracelsus's works known. This man, whom his contemporaries seem to have thought of chiefly as a physician,
who applied himself to relieving suffering close at hand, while
also preaching a reform of religion and morality (in which
there was nothing original for those days), wrote about all
scientific subjects with a really exceptional power of comprehension. In the first half of the sixteenth century he was
without doubt the man who most strikingly endeavoured to
gather together a huge body of learning drawn from all
sources. His great work, the *Philosophia sagax*, contains the
elements of universal knowledge, with reflexions upon Nature
and God. He also wrote about meteors, the origins of invisible
diseases, an explanation of the whole of astronomy, the 'Great
Mystery', the foundations of wisdom and the arts, and the
magical secrets of precious stones. One of his treatises is even
entitled *De generatione stultorum* ... His favourite fields were
certainly alchemy, in which he long figured as the master-
possessor of the rarest secrets, hidden in his writings, and
medicine, for which he employed the 'raw material of the
elements', to use the terms of his own philosophy. Amid his
bulky complete works the medical writings alone account for
thirteen volumes.

There is reason to believe Paracelsus when he declares that
he owed all his knowledge to his own efforts alone, to his
perpetual investigations, wherein he ascribed as much

importance to empiric knowledge (the elements of which he collected during his travels) as to the bookish learning dispensed from under their doctoral headgear by the university teachers – whom he regarded as ignorant louts. Paracelsus collected and integrated with his learning all sorts of popular practices, the prescriptions of barber-surgeons and old women, the methods used by smelters in the silver-mines, and also folk-tales. A contemporary of Dr Faustus, who had the reputation of being a magician at Würzburg and Heidelberg, Paracelsus differed from him by this constant recourse that he had to empiric lore collected in the course of his travels. Whereas Faustus was the scholar who had read all the books, Paracelsus was the professor at the University of Basle (for a short time only) who led his students out to botanize in the countryside and listen to the peasants whom they met on the way. Instead of scholastic learning, classified according to Aristotle, Paracelsus invoked the spirits of the dead, ghosts, amulets, and the magic formulas repeated by old women at the bedsides of the dying. He cured people by using a complex chemistry which included remedies made up of metallic elements and powders which could not but seem bizarre in an age when the pharmacy of the Schools was surrounded by mysteries beyond the understanding of the layman. Paracelsus banished medieval science from his medical practice, as from the teaching he gave to the disciples who accompanied him in his wanderings, in favour of a new science which showed confidence in Nature and in life – which were, by definition, magical powers.

A pugnacious and inexhaustible genius, Paracelsus made more enemies than friends in his zeal to polemize against the official science of his time, with his readiness to abuse bad teachers who were arrogant but incapable of helping their fellow-men. This determination of his that he was in the right in his disputes, together with the deliberate hostility shown by the constituted authorities, suffice to account for the

ings of Paracelsus. Movement from place to place was
acteristic common at this time to all these men of
learn.. ig, even the literary humanists, who were also great
travellers. These new-type intellectuals multiplied what today
we call personal contacts.

4. THE LINKS BETWEEN THE NEW INTELLECTUALS

Defining the bonds that were established between these men,
devoted to learning, who stood outside the universities and
traditional institutions (monasteries, episcopal schools) is not
too easy a task: first, because evidence regarding any new
organization is by no means plentiful, and, second, because the
ambiguity of the men's careers contributes a substantial extra
obstacle. All these humanists and scholars were themselves
clerics: they had received their education, in part at least, on
the benches of the Schools, and sometimes they remained
associated with them for many years. Some, like Jacques
Lefèvre d'Etaples, never even thought of leaving the particular
academic setting in which they had lived for so long; and,
while it is true that Erasmus asked his superiors at Steyn, after
many years, to release him from obligations that had never
weighed very heavily upon him, he nevertheless remained, in
the eyes of everyone, friend and foe alike, a churchman to the
end of his days. Yet all these men were also in conflict, whether
consciously or not, with these same institutions which had
shaped them, and all or part of whose teachings they now
rejected. Copernicus, Budé, Colet and Reuchlin were all
capable of appreciating the insecurity of their situation, in that
their work could not fail to arouse the frowning criticism of
the traditionalists, zealous defenders of established learning,
when the latter was called in question. Hence the practical
solidarity constantly expressed, in the first place, in the
hyperbolic eulogies exchanged, those formulas of esteem that
swarmed with superlatives. These certainly expressed mutual

recognition, and not only gratitude for work carried on in common and for the new contribution, celebrated with all the needful praise; also, and above all, they were the signs by which these men testified that they all belonged to the same community of discoverers, who were pushing forward together, against wind and weather, despite all threats and dangers, the frontiers of knowledge in a variety of fields. They signified readiness to come to each other's aid if need be.

This solidarity was shown at several different levels, with different implications. First, there was correspondence, in the widest sense of the word – exchanges of letters, books, information regarding work in progress in this place and that. Across all Europe information was passed in this way, on a basis of mutual trust – except where rivalry and competition arose in connexion with the interpreting of a text or the use to be made of a discovery. We know about this so far as Erasmus is concerned through the monumental Latin-and-English edition of his correspondence, and it is no less obvious in the case of the other scholars and humanists, who were unable to do without such exchanges. Doubtless the volume of each one's correspondence depended on the fame achieved by the different writers. Behind the greatest names, which literary and intellectual history has preserved, there were arrayed many hacks who participated less actively in such exchanges. Furthermore, the most thorough reconstitutions of their correspondence reveal – quite apart from losses due to the damage done by time – the occurrence of interruptions, quarrels, even ruptures of relations which bear witness plainly to the strain to which these relations were subjected, in the uneasy atmosphere of a kind of research which always implied the challenging of accepted notions and established teachings. The best example of this is provided, perhaps, by the breach between Budé and Erasmus, after many years of sustained and friendly exchanges, a breach accomplished without very lengthy explanations or perfectly clear discussions: just the ending of a relationship, like the breaking of a link, effected on the initiative of the French humanist, without his correspondent having been able to ascertain what really underlay their quarrel. But the exchanging of letters had become current practice in intellectual life. Erasmus published in 1522 a treatise on good usage in this form of writing (*De conscribendis epistolis*); and the authorities, political and religious, soon understood the advantage to be gained from keeping an eye on such exchanges. In 1514 Erasmus himself recommended prudence to one of his correspondents, Servatius: 'Do not put anything confidential into a letter, unless you are quite sure where I am staying and have secured a messenger who is to be trusted absolutely.' Others thought it more clever to publish the letters they received without informing those who had written them. Here too one had to look after one's interests, even if this could only be done by ensuring, oneself, the publication of letters that had really been written for a public wider than the nominal addressee.

Next in line came a more direct form of solidarity – hospitality and mutual aid, on a Europe-wide scale. Everywhere that printing and the initiative of adventurous clerics had brought a group of scholars into existence, informal associations were created for reading, commentary and discussion of new publications: these *sodalitates litterarum* were the basic cells of that famous Republic of Letters which was invoked so often in the first decades of the sixteenth century. Comrades in research among the manuscript treasures preserved in a monastery, co-disciples of a great humanist or scholar of reputation, assembled for readings or lectures, lovers of literature who were fascinated by the discoveries of Greco–Latin Antiquity – these promoters of the new associations were certainly not all capable of corresponding with Erasmus or Paracelsus, but they were all ready to contribute to the exchanges which made up the life, and the joy of life, of these men as the fruits of their work began to pile up. When they travelled across Europe from one town to another, the *sodalitates* constituted the setting that was spontaneously available to receive and welcome them. This hospitality was not at all disinterested, to be sure (as we see from the example of Erasmus), since the traveller would be asked to take part in some meetings, to give his views of a new book, or to outline to those interested the work that he was engaged in.

The republic of living literature thus provided itself with a framework which was in no way a heavily formalized and organized institution: it had no entrance fee, no initiation ceremony, and no obligations were imposed on members – except to take part in the common effort and to be able to put to each one's credit the publication of some previously unknown work of Cicero's, or a description of a Roman monument, or a discussion of a learned treatise of astronomy. Neither academies *avant la lettre*, nor schools in the established meaning of the word, these associations constituted the freest conceivable form of gathering open to all who were working in the same direction. Assembled in the homes of hospitable individuals, or even in monasteries which had been won over to the new learning, the *sodalitates* gave to their participants a very strong feeling that they belonged to a community united in solidarity against those who scorned and hated them. And this was so despite the rivalries and conflicts which soon set against each other, all across Europe, the boldest and the most senior, as with the 'Ciceroniani' of Italy, who claimed to be sole guardians and sole judges of the quality of Latin, and even to be more genuinely devoted than others to the literature and values of pagan Antiquity, in contrast to the new groups which had sprung into existence in the Rhineland and throughout North-western Europe.

Nevertheless, the limits to this solidarity soon made themselves felt. The spotlight of historical study has been focused on the greatest of the new scholars, those who have been the first beneficiaries of this study and who attracted the most

attention from princes. Remaining in the shadow are all those
who made up the rank-and-file of the movements, the minor
scholars whose work brought them only a poor living and
who might bask for many years in their pride at having
approached Erasmus during one of his journeys, or met Colet
or Fisher at Oxford, or received a letter from Budé or Gaguin.
Those who kept up the continuous activity of these associations without financial endowments or paying pupils
experienced anxiety and anguish that were all the harder to
bear because books were expensive and they could not carry
on their work without frequently purchasing them. If, in
order to live, they became printing workers, for years at a
time, they lost contact with the circles of the new learning.
More commonly, they preferred to teach, outside the
traditional framework, as needy tutors instructing little groups
of children in Greek and Latin: they were poorly paid, and
persecuted by the Church authorities when their illicit
activities became known. It was for them that Philip
Melanchthon wrote his *De miseriis paedagogorum*, in which he
described the woes of these penniless scholars vegetating in
petty teaching posts. The striking evidences we have of the
prestige won by the humanists ought not to create illusions:
Budé by the side of Francis I at the Field of Cloth of Gold, or
Erasmus as councillor to Charles V, were not really typical. It
is better to observe the care which all these writers, of whatever standing, take to fill the opening pages of their works
with flattering dedications, long, rambling discourses which
are so many appeals to the generosity of the great: a pension
for a few years, or even just a lump sum, a few hundred
Rhenish florins. True, the enthusiasm of the learned spread, at
the beginning of the sixteenth century, to the sovereigns and
their courts, from Rome to London and from Lisbon to
Prague. La Croix du Maine records this as still being the case
in 1579, when he evokes the 'rooms full of wonders', stocked
with 'rare books, medallions, portraits, statues or effigies,

precious stones and other pleasing curiosities which are to be seen in the homes of princes', when they 'hoard such magnificent objects as these'. Doubtless the practice of the paid-for dedication became established without difficulty, as may be judged from all those preambles to books that soon constituted a definite *genre*, with its own rules (enumeration of titles, mention of attachment to literature and learning, recalling of personal relations), with regard to which the historian would like to be able to study the financial return obtained – something a great deal more significant than the flattering missives addressed by princes to scholars, warm invitations in which the asker barely conceals the pleasure and reputation he expects to obtain by this means.

The important question in this field is that of the competition with the traditional universities and colleges represented by the bearers of the new learning. As the ranks of the latter increased and printed books became more numerous, testifying to the fecundity of their methods and the range of the studies that were being recast by them, the need for an organized system of transmission, a teaching organization, became more and more obvious, outside those scholarly circles into which beginners did not enter. It was for the religious and civil authorities to respond. The institutional weight possessed by the former could not but encourage them to resist, that is, to refuse to do more than tolerate, within the framework of the existing colleges and faculties, the presence of a few innovators whose boldness we can appreciate only if we realize the nature of the established tradition: men such as Lefèvre d'Etaples, teaching a conception of Aristotle that was new and close to the text at the Collège du Cardinal Lemoine in the 1490s. More decisive initiatives, however, could come only from the ruling princes, who might override the bans and warnings of the Church, taking a calculated risk for the sake of the political and cultural advantages they expected to gain.

Three creations are significant in this connexion. In the

second decade of the sixteenth century, the humanists were everywhere appealing for the establishment of new centres in which they would enjoy an assured position. But the welcome they received was not always very cordial. At Louvain, where the theological faculty was so cautious that Erasmus came to dread his visits to this town, even though he had many good friends there, the problem arose through a testamentary endowment. Hieronymus Busleiden, a canon of Malines and a front-rank personage in Flemish literary circles, donated to the university the funds needed in order to set up, within the framework of that institution, a Trilingual College (*Collegium Trilingue*) in which there should be taught the three biblical languages (Latin, Greek, Hebrew), taking account of the advances in philology that had been made in the preceding quarter-century. At the time when Busleiden's endowment was being accepted, a professor of theology named Jacobus Latomus, though he was not regarded as a conservative, took it upon himself to compose a dialogue in which doubt was cast on the usefulness of knowing these languages for purposes of theological study. Erasmus, personally affected by this argument, and very much concerned to see the new college established, was obliged to answer his adversary and to take many steps before he succeeded in his aim. The new teaching, for which no fees were charged, began in September 1518. At Louvain the new school was thus placed within the framework of the university, and so was indirectly under the supervision of the four old Faculties.

In the same period, a similar project was put forward to Francis I in Paris by Guillaume Budé (Budaeus). But the King of France, favourably disposed though he was towards 'good letters', was not deaf to the objections raised by the Paris Faculty of Arts to any proposal which would imply a profound change in teaching – and all the less so because of the troubles he had just experienced with the Parlement and the Sorbonne in getting registered in his kingdom the Concordat he had signed with the Pope at Bologna in 1516. Budé discussed with Erasmus the idea that the latter should settle in Paris, to take part in this new teaching, but that nomadic scholar, no more anxious to settle in Paris than in England, whither his mighty friends at the court of Henry VIII were calling him, several times declined the Frenchman's proposal, and Budé's scheme therefore remained unconsummated for a dozen years. After much discussion, the University of Paris decided to reject the establishment of a college *intra muros* on the Louvain model. In the end, Francis I, urged by those around him, who were concerned to restore his prestige, which had been compromised by his period as a prisoner in Madrid, resolved in 1530 to get over the difficulty by creating a royal college completely independent of the University of Paris. This 'Collège de France' functioned thanks to royal generosity – which soon proved to be capricious and inadequate. The teachers, Budé and his friends, who taught not only the three languages but also astronomy and mathematics, experienced some difficult times. Attacked by the university all the more harshly because the lecture-halls of the college were always well-filled, they had to cope with insults and affronts in order to keep their new school going: but its reputation became firmly established, despite these painful beginnings. A century later the jurist Cardin le Bret celebrated the boldness shown by Francis I, and the wretchedness of the medieval university: 'King Francis, who deserved his appellation of Father of Letters, surpassed all his predecessors in magnificence. Seeing that the University of Paris had become very slack and that the study of good letters was wholly neglected there, and as though sunk in barbarism, he set up this famous college of twelve royal professors of all manner of arts and sciences.'

A third remarkable instance is provided by England, where the young King Henry VIII was living, at the same period, surrounded by a pleiad of scholars to whose advice he gave ear. Fisher became Chancellor of the University of Cambridge in

1517 and saw to the teaching of Greek there, and Thomas More became Chancellor of the Exchequer in May 1521: later, between 1529 and 1532, he became Lord Chancellor. The foundations due to the English scholars were effected both within the framework of the universities, by the creation of new colleges, and also outside this framework. Thus, on the one hand, in 1516, at Cambridge, John Fisher officially opened St John's College (for which a charter had been granted in 1511), and in the same year Richard Fox was authorized to found the Erasmian college of Corpus Christi, at Oxford; while, on the other, in 1518 Tunstall persuaded Henry VIII to set up the College of Physicians, a sort of medical university, which functioned in the house of one of its first members, in the form of readings of learned papers. The establishment of new colleges went on for some years more, right down to 1527–30.

The immediate and, *a fortiori*, the long-term consequence of these innovations in the field of teaching was to accentuate the decline of the medieval university system throughout Europe. In 1519 a school for the teaching of Greek was established at Zwickau (a *sodalitas* transformed into an institution with the backing of the municipal authorities, who had been won over to the cause of 'good letters'), Bishop Lubranski's academy was set up in Poland, with similar aims, and in December 1520 an academy of the sciences was founded at Padua.

The last point which clearly emerges from all this is that the movement of learned men, humanists and scholars which brought about so profound a change in European thought in the sixteenth century did not take the form of a struggle to promote a particular doctrine. It was a process of seeking, carried on in a cheerful spirit (until about 1520), by men of many-sided learning, who did not want to create a doctrine, a philosophy, in the strict sense of the word. If their view of the world contrasted with that of their traditionalist contemporaries, still chained to the teaching of the Schools, that was in the first place owing to their aptitude to receive new knowledge and put it to the test: more than any construction of an ordered system of thought, it was their openness to the world that mattered. In other words, it is futile to try to discover a single humanist 'line', so great is the distance between the political morality of Erasmus, the practice of Thomas More, and the theory of Machiavelli when he wrote *The Prince*. Nor did they display any one morality, nor any 'humanist metaphysic', inasmuch as none of them wanted, or was able, to impose uniformity of thought where critical confrontation was the prime rule. True, all of them did, in different ways, evoke a world that differed from the one in which they lived. All of them dreamt of changes, as their very vocabulary shows: the *bonae litterae* they advocated were obviously counterposed to others that were not so good. All of them were innovators, more or less, and the most significant work produced by their movement was undoubtedly Thomas More's *Utopia*, that description of an imaginary island in a new world where everyone would be subject to the rules of the Republic of Letters, and would be free to investigate . . . There was, indeed, no humanism but only humanists and scholars, each labouring in accordance with the spirit that moved him, proud of his discoveries and his works, as the list thereof lengthened.

The best example is offered by the prince and pattern of humanists, Erasmus himself, a triumphant figure down to 1520–21. This little cleric from Holland, an Augustinian canon at the age of nineteen and ordained priest in 1492 at the age of twenty-three, gained all-European recognition within a dozen years. He studied in Italy and learnt the usual lessons from masters whom later he was to censure for their paganism. He travelled much, not hastily, but yet without taking rest, in England (where he stayed with Colet and More, who were always his friends), through Flanders, where at St-Omer he met Jean Vitrier, and in France. Until 1520–21 he kept up this ceaseless wandering, which was a protracted quest, in company with all those who sought, as he did, to find at the springs of ancient wisdom a truer knowledge of men and of the world. Like many others he edited works that soon became classics: the *De officiis* of Cicero. In a more original way, he then collated from his reading in Latin and Greek the sayings of ancient wisdom, the *Adages*, which he published for the first time in 1508, often thereafter adding to and reissuing it: eventually, a collection of more than 3,000 proverbs. Having mastered the Latin and Greek tongues, he did not shrink from attacking all who mangled these languages in their teaching of them in the universities, where nothing was as it should be: the *Praise of Folly*, published in 1511, was first and foremost a virulent critique of these institutions and of those who lived by them.

From that first decade of the sixteenth century onward, Erasmus was definitely the most famous of the humanist scholars. He was a European figure, as has often been said, or, more precisely, as he himself claimed, a citizen of the world (*civis mundi*), by virtue of his fame and also of his travels – since he never resided at Steyn, near Gouda, and was continually being welcomed in the Rhineland or in Italy, at Bologna and Venice – and of the correspondence which he kept up assiduously with the scholars of the entire Continent: an activity that devoured his time and for long prevented him from getting on with his own work. All the great names of triumphant humanism figure among the correspondents of Erasmus, and even lesser celebrities, too, like Konrad Peutinger, the Augsburg political personality, or the printers he worked with: his friend Froben in Basle, and Aldus Manutius in Venice. Already in that same period, his works were becoming sold out and having to be reprinted more rapidly than any others. The *Praise of Folly*, of which 1,800 copies were printed (in an epoch when printings normally never exceeded 1,000) was out of print in a month. Some people saw fit to publish letters they had received from him, without even asking his permission. After the years of misery he had known between 1493 and 1500, at the beginning of his travels, Erasmus had become, at the turn of the century, the first writer in the world's history who was able to live by the income from his own printed publications. Received everywhere as the greatest of men, flattered by the *sodalitates*, pensioned by Charles V, his 'natural' sovereign, and also by Henry VIII of England, he certainly established himself as a model for others, by his genius for the study of Antiquity, and also by the clarity of his Latin style – but above all, and more than anything else, by the logic of his thinking, which led him to preach reform of the Catholic Church. It is impossible, where Erasmus is concerned, any more than with many others, to separate the humanist student of Antiquity from the reforming Christian. The restoration of ancient letters was indissolubly bound up with that remaking of the Church for which he called from the beginning of the sixteenth century. In 1504 he published his *Enchiridion militis christiani*, and this 'Christian soldier' suddenly became as famous as his translations of Terence and Cicero. Together with his English and Flemish friends he challenged men and institutions, dreaming aloud of a return to the original purity of a primitive Church which had not drifted far from the pristine teaching and the fundamental precepts. The two attitudes can be separated for purposes of study, and can even be divided chronologically, in so far as in 1520–21 the knell was sounded for hopes of reform of the Catholic Church from within. But it was always a question of one and the same existential approach, made by the same set of men.

Chapter 2

FROM CHURCH TO CHURCHES
(1520–60)

WHILE pursuing their researches, the scholars of the sixteenth century were all preoccupied with their salvation in the Church. Born and bred in that constraining religious framework, to which they belonged 'from the cradle to the grave', they never failed to give thought to the life of the Church and the question of how it could be improved. More than one of them even convinced himself that the time he devoted to pagan letters, however necessary that work might be, could not be prolonged indefinitely. After toiling over the restoration of secular literature the humanist scholar ought, inescapably, to proceed to the study of the sacred texts and to discover, through immersing himself in them, the true meaning of the Church, which the Church itself had, in its institutionalized dogmatism, allowed to become obscure. All of them were reformers, wishing to transform the life of the clergy and of the faithful, to renovate the existing Church so as to bring Christians to a better understanding of the Christian message and to better conduct in accordance with the letter and spirit of that message. This will to return to a practice purified and made new found expression well before 1500 in certain ecclesiastical circles, under the name of *devotio moderna*, and this 'modern devotion' was given a considerable impetus as the numbers of scholars and humanists increased and groups of friends engaged in discussing problems of exegesis and theology.

The movement was governed by a twofold logic: that of

the critical method of the philologists, exercised upon the sacred texts, and that of the critical reconsideration of institutions which had been overwhelmed by the uncontrolled (and uncontrollable) diffusion of the new learning. It became focused, in the last decades of the fifteenth century, upon reform of the Catholic Church, upon that 'good discipline' to which many efforts were directed; as various in approaches and methods as they were unequal in effectiveness: preaching, monastic reform, appeals to the Pope and to the Roman Curia, translations of the New Testament, commentaries on St Paul, reform of the episcopate, praise of the religious life. This seething of more or less clearly formulated projects and unfurling of innovatory ideas, which makes it hard to read in its proper context the least important work of a reforming tendency unless we know the precise date when it was published, kept on increasing during the first decades of the sixteenth century. But the enthusiasm and serenity of the reformers gave way in 1515–18 to a vague disquiet. Did Erasmus, who was more often apprehensive than others, have a presentiment of the coming break-up? 'I am afraid', he wrote in September 1517, a month before the Wittenberg thunderclap, 'that a great revolution is impending.' When Leo X set about treating Luther as the heretics of the Middle Ages had been treated, through the violent suppression of his heresy, the first revolution came – to be followed by several others during the next forty-odd years.

I. THE 'DEVOTIO MODERNA'

The expression *devotio moderna* is not without a certain ambiguity. It originated in the fifteenth century in an effort undertaken in the Northern Netherlands to overhaul religious life by reforming both the monasteries and the way of life of the laity. This reforming zeal, which preached by example and did not concern itself with doctrinal innovation, or even with getting permission from the hierarchy, assumed two inter-related forms. On the one hand, monastic houses open to the laity were set up, where the 'Brothers and Sisters of Common Life', living under one roof, submitted themselves to rules of living inspired by a serene and pious conception of Christian duty: simplicity in everyday life, purity in morals, frequent acts of worship, performed in a serious spirit. On the other, a congregation was created around the monastery at Windesheim, and recruited from among the Augustinian canons, which offered those who joined it a return to a strict monastic rule and an active 'piety directed mainly into teaching. This twofold movement, of 'the Common Life' and of Windesheim, began in the Yssel region, spread rapidly throughout the Northern Netherlands, from Friesland to Holland, and through the Rhineland. Houses of 'Common Life' were set up, monasteries adopted the Windesheim rule, schools were opened which, though the teaching given remained very traditional, soon attracted an extensive clientèle, from families of the bourgeoisie or the nobility. The Church authorities, though they quickly became anxious about these developments, which had taken shape without their explicit approval, nevertheless admitted that the move-ment was orthodox.

The *devotio moderna*, thus given recognition, steadily won over fresh religious houses in North-western Europe, and acquired new practitioners, especially among the laity, who found in this new form of piety an answer to the worries for which the wretched state of the times and the ills of the Roman Church had long given them cause. From Deventer to Windesheim the *devotio moderna* achieved expression in the lives of men and women, and it was also expressed in a book, said to have been written by a canon of Zwoll, Thomas à Kempis, *The Imitation of Christ*, which enjoyed growing success at the end of the fifteenth century. Presenting an apologia for renunciation of the world and rigorous observance of religious duties, the *Imitation* delighted and uplifted generations of Christians, including Loyola himself, during the time when he was troubled. Thus, the manifestations of the *devotio moderna* spread wider and wider. The movement founded new communities or won over old ones, which rallied to the pioneers, and all across Western Christendom the need came to be felt for a movement of renewal for which these northern communities furnished the example, by showing that it was possible to bring about an immediate transformation, effected step by step, with the agreement of the hierarchy, and without waiting for orders from Rome or from a Council.

In the second half of the fifteenth century, in which this movement developed, the name *devotio moderna* came to be given more broadly to every tendency working in the same direction, without concern for any formality of filiation or dependence. This was understandable, since the reformers' statements and plans had long since overflowed a framework limited in space and in source of recruitment. In the Netherlands, where the new piety had taken shape, at the beginning of the fifteenth century only the Augustinian canons had advanced along this dangerous path, while the mendicant orders continued with their preaching as before. By the end of the century, however, some of the Franciscans had in their turn undertaken to reform their houses and had even overhauled their preaching. For all who could no longer remain satisfied with Catholic religious life in the form in which Rome had petrified it, and with all its worldly cravings, the *devotio moderna* became the model by which to conceive and make concrete every innovation that could help to bring about, within the Church itself, the renewal that was everywhere being called for. Erasmus received part of his education from the Brothers of Common Life. Luther did not conceal his admiration for their movement. The spirituality and observance of these Netherlanders offered a first response to the demands of faith, and the greatest of the Christian humanists made it their task to enrich and clarify this response, in the years between 1490 and 1520. Better equipped than the official theologians, imprisoned in their doctrine, the active exegetists of Holy Writ provided the *devotio moderna* with a body of theology and a content of 'true goodness', in a period when final, irrevocable choices had not yet been made, and every hope seemed justified.

One of the most brilliant witnesses to this aspiration to a renewed faith was Jacques Lefèvre d'Etaples, in the course of his long career which began at the Collège du Cardinal Lemoine, where he taught Aristotle's philosophy, and ended in 1536, on the eve of the Calvinist Reformation. A humanist of high repute, who had studied both in Paris and also in Italy, under Pico della Mirandola, he published Aristotle, with commentaries, and translated both the *Introduction to Metaphysics* and the *Nicomachean Ethics*. In his first college he taught astronomy and mathematics as well as Greek philosophy. A Platonist rather than an Aristotelian, he drew around him a number of students who became teachers in the opening years of the sixteenth century: Josse van Clichtove, who was later to teach Lefèvre's philosophy at the Sorbonne, Charles de Bouelles (Bovillus), Guillaume Budé, and Guillaume Briçonnet the younger, the future Bishop of Meaux. At the same time, Lefèvre was working on the sacred texts, and after his visit to Rome in 1499, to obtain the plenary indulgence accorded to pilgrims on the occasion of the fifteenth centenary of the Saviour's birth, he applied himself to theological studies with greater deliberation. He proceeded from Dionysius the Areopagite (*Theologia vivificans*) to John of Damascus, then to the Psalms (1509) and, especially, to the Epistles of St Paul, an edition of which he published in 1512. Then he got down to his major work, the translation of the Bible: his New Testament appeared in 1524, his Old Testament in 1530, and his version of the complete Bible 'in French, translated in accordance with the pure and complete version by St Jerome', was published in 1534, not long before his death. This indefatigable commentator and translator of the sacred texts found, towards the end of his life, the setting in which his desire for reform of the Church from within could blossom, when he was called to the side of his former pupil, Guillaume Briçonnet, at Meaux. This ecclesiastic's father, a great financier who became, after his wife's death, a cardinal (and the first cardinal to be a French king's minister), had introduced him to the Curia in the time of Julius II. He returned to Italy in the days when Leo X was letting it be thought that he might set going the renewal which was desired by all, and accepting the dedication to him of the most audacious works – Reuchlin's *De arte cabalistica* and Erasmus's New Testament: the days when Gian Matteo Giberti, Bishop of Verona, was carrying out reform in his diocese, dismissing incapable parish priests, overhauling somnolent monasteries and restoring hospitals. Guillaume Briçonnet, having been translated from Lodève to Meaux, and enjoying the protection of Marguerite, sister of Francis I, undertook a programme of reform that was strikingly similar to that carried out in Verona. Jacques Lefèvre went to Meaux in 1521 as administrator of the hospital, and soon became Vicar-General. He was joined by Gérard Roussel, Vatable and Martial Mazurier, and the bishop even set up a press in order to make available for distribution good texts of the Gospel, those which made Lefèvre's name. At the very time that the Lutheran storm was about to break, hope of reform was gaining strength and consistency there, at the gates of Paris. But as Lutheran writings began to arrive in France, the Meaux experiment, coming under attack from the upholders of tradition, was revealed as increasingly threatened and fragile. Nevertheless, Lefèvre d'Etaples stayed loyal to this hope to the end of his life, refusing all invitations and temptations to join the new Church that was being formed. And this was certainly due to conviction, and not to prudence, as was soon to be insinuated by adherents both of the Reformed Church and of Catholic traditionalism.

More remarkable, perhaps, as a figure characteristic of this aspiration for reform from within, was Jean Vitrier, warden of the Franciscan friary of St-Omer. For long known to us only from the admirable portrait of him drawn by Erasmus in a letter to Justus Jonas (Jodocus Koch), he is now more accessible since a young French researcher has recently attributed to him an anonymous collection of sermons preserved at St-Omer. Jean Vitrier was not only the notable scholar who taught his friend Erasmus a pertinent reading of the Epistle to the Romans, led him to discover Origen's polemic against Celsus, and introduced him to the Hussite teachings (which had made their way to the Netherlands, and been preserved there, by some unknown means) – the Jean Vitrier whom we can glimpse through Erasmus's correspondence. He was also a reformer of religious houses and one of those preachers who were able, at the end of the Middle Ages, to draw great crowds. An exact contemporary of Lefèvre (born in 1454), this Franciscan cherished a similar enthusiasm for St Paul, whose preachings he worked over line by line, but to which he added the homilies of Origen, to form an equally important element in his inspiration.

Jean Vitrier, mystic and reformer, Franciscan of strict observance, did not enjoy, any more than Lefèvre, an entirely even career. In 1498 he preached in Tournai, thundering against morally decayed monasteries, canons and clergy lacking in virtue, the cult of saints carried to the point of superstition. His words caused offence, and the bishop of the city extracted from them sixteen propositions which he submitted to the Faculty of Theology at the Sorbonne, which censured them. In 1500 he was warden of his order's house at St-Omer. There he managed the friary's property in his austere way, refused to preach the papal indulgence of 1500

(which he declared to be simoniacal), rejected the hundred
florins offered to him to avoid a fresh scandal, and was the
object of a suit pressed with zeal by the Bishop of Thérouanne's
suffragan, a fiercely orthodox Dominican divine – who
proved unable, however, to carry the case through to the end.
In 1503 Vitrier, having been removed from his post as warden
and reduced to the ranks, devoted himself to preaching, which
he practised to the end of his life in a nunnery in Courtrai to
which he had been relegated.

This career clearly reveals, in itself, the conflict between
oppressive church tradition and the desire for reform – which
turned into prophesying and came to naught (though Vitrier
did have some disciples, both lay and clerical, of whom trace
has now been lost). The discovery of his book of homilies
enables us to understand better what the intellectual and
spiritual demands of a man like Vitrier were, and also the
unusual reception his preaching met with. Jean Vitrier's
sermon reflecting on 'the faith that justifies' defines, on the
basis of Scripture, 'the place and sacrament of faith', prayer
and the sacraments, as they contribute to the making of good
Christians: for he distinguishes between the good and the not
so good – the true Christians, in accordance with the Gospel,
are the little people, whether clergy or laymen, who are concerned above all to improve their religious observance,
mounting gradually higher by virtue of humility and long-
suffering. In doing this, Vitrier defines also, in his own way,
the 'pure philosophy of Christ', that is, by teaching a whole
vision of the world and of mankind: the four constituent
elements of the world 'which will pass away', the senses of
the body and the soul, and also man's heart, which he
frequently mentions, with a variety of significances, as the seat
of physical life and of feeling, the organ of all religious life,
the vital place wherein man perceives the Truth, for none but
God 'can content the heart of man'.

The themes, if not the accent, of the Franciscan preacher

are those of Erasmus, in his *Enchiridion militis christiani*, published in 1504, when the two men had just formed a friendship which time was not to undo. The accent differed because Jean Vitrier was a man of the pulpit who spoke to and knew how to make himself understood by a motley public in which bourgeois citizens mingled with craftsmen and clergy, whereas Erasmus, a man of the study and of discussion, wrote for a vaster and less definable public. Yet their intentions were the same. Erasmus wrote the *Enchiridion*, he told Colet, 'solely in order to counteract the error of those who make religion in general consist in rituals and observances of an almost more than Jewish formality, but who are astonishingly indifferent to matters that have to do with true goodness'. For the definition of 'true goodness' Erasmus always came back to formulations which simply extolled the teaching of Christ, that is, 'the virtues that he preaches: charity, simplicity, long-suffering, purity' (*nil aliud quam caritatem, simplicitatem, patientiam, puritatem*). But the parallel can be taken further, for the same approach is found in Erasmus, more clearly expressed by him than by many others, who were less apt than he to indicate where they agreed and where they disagreed with the actions of theologians and other preaching clerics.

In the professions of faith which he set forth in the period preceding the great crisis, two phrases echoed immediately the teachings of Jean Vitrier. In the *Praise of Folly* Erasmus ridicules the theologians, both for their style 'abounding in newly coined expressions and strange-sounding words' and, even more, for their absurd preoccupation with the solving of futile problems: 'What was the exact moment of divine generation? Are there several filiations of Christ? . . . Could God have taken on the form of a woman, a devil, a donkey, a gourd or a flintstone? If so, how could a gourd have preached sermons, performed miracles, and been nailed to the cross? . . . Shall we be permitted to eat and drink after the resurrection?'

And yet, in the same work, Erasmus is no more tender in dealing with popular beliefs and cults, which he condemns sweepingly because this multiplication of patron saints seems to him to threaten truly Christian faith: 'It is much the same when separate districts lay claim to their own particular saints. Each one of these is assigned his special powers and his own special cult, so that one gives relief from toothache, another stands by women in childbirth, a third returns stolen objects, a fourth will appear as a saviour for shipwrecks, another protect the flocks, and so on ... There are some whose influence extends to several things, notably the Virgin, Mother of God, for the common man comes near to attributing more to her than to her son.' It would be idle to speak of the 'Reformed' tone of such criticisms, for that would be anachronistic. It is more appropriate to point to the proposals for reform which are implicit in these severe views, expressed thus without passion: they aim at correcting the sterility of Scholastic teaching imprisoned in its own rhetoric, and the practices encouraged by the secular clergy, the multiplying of devotions to and cults of intercessors who were as numerous as the ills of suffering mankind could engender.

True goodness, according to the promoters of a restored devotion, does not lie in that kind of thing but in a return to the sources, as Erasmus explains a few years later, in the dedication of his New Testament to Leo X: 'Our chiefest hope for the restoration and rebuilding of the Christian religion ... is that all who profess the Christian philosophy the whole world over should above all absorb the principles laid down by their Founder from the writings of the evangelists and the apostles, in which that heavenly Word which once came down to us from the heart of the Father still lives and breathes for us.' Erasmus claims to have 'perceived that that teaching which is our salvation was to be had in a much purer and more lively form if sought at the fountainhead', and therefore to have 'revised the whole New Testa-

ment . . . against the standard of the Greek original, . . . calling
in the assistance of a number of manuscripts in both languages,
and those not the first comers but both very old and very
correct'. Later in his presentation of his translation, Erasmus
comes back to the need to put the sacred text at the disposal
of all believers and not of the clergy alone, 'who make up the
smallest part of Christendom' and who, moreover, often
'concern themselves with earthly rather than godly matters'.
The Scriptures, translated into the vulgar tongue (and, in the
first place, into good Latin), must be made available to all
Christians: the tenets of Christianity are not to be the privileged
possession of anyone, be he scholar or syllogist, any more than
baptism and the other sacraments. 'I wish that the humblest
woman might read the Gospels and the Epistles of Paul . . . I
would that the countryman might sing some parts of them
at the plough, the weaver chant them at his loom, the traveller
lighten with them the weariness of his journey.' In so saying,
Erasmus came close to Vitrier, preaching for the benefit of all
his parishioners, and was far from the position of Lefèvre,
who had never yet contemplated, at that same period, putting
the Bible into the hands of ordinary believers.

But, above all, Erasmus defines the modern Church of his
dreams: an institution capable of returning to that primary
Christian philosophy which had been obscured by tradition.
Life and inspiration, a feeling more than anything else, this
faith is sustained by the Word, by the practice of those virtues
of which Christ himself gave the example. The *devotio
moderna* which is defined by this elegant and precise pen is an
act of faith ceaselessly renewed, it is justification by faith –
which, much more than adherence with mind and heart to a
creed formulated in a few well-docketed articles, much more
than membership of the Church, means for Erasmus (as for
Lefèvre, Roussel and others) trust in the truth of God's Word,
which gives the Christian security and hope down to (and
including) the day of his death. Less mystical than that of

Lefèvre d'Etaples, Erasmus's message of the faith that sanctifies was heard throughout the learned circles of Europe, where these aristocrats of the spirit recognized in each other true Christians who were advancing along the path of renewal – until the 1530s. In Italy there were Cardinals Contarini, Morone and the Piedmontese Gattinara; in Spain Juan de Valdés and Vergara, men with influence at court; not to mention the many Erasmians who were to be found all over Northern Europe, with the Amerbachs at Basle, and also in the entourages of sovereign princes, the Queen of Navarre, Renée of Ferrara, and many others of less renown. The *Philosophia Christi* of Erasmus, that primacy of Christian morality which for a long time he hoped to have adopted by the princes of the Church in order to transform a Church that had been ill-used, and the argument of which runs continuously from the *Enchiridion* through the *Colloquies* to the *Praise of Folly* and the *New Testament*, was the sustenance of that reform-seeking Europe, which was in torment from 1520–21 onward, though never abandoning its hopes, until the Council which, announced as early as 1532, was to deliver its verdict thirty years later.

Reviewing these three figures of ecclesiastical and Christian renewal who laboured during the first decades of the sixteenth century does not suffice to evoke adequately the scope of the movement and the multiform proliferation of its projects. and of the resistance thereto. True, Erasmus polarized around himself much of this gestation of thought, if only through his copious correspondence. To take England alone, his profound accord with John Colet and Thomas More shows the terms in which these important figures at the court of Henry VIII themselves conceived the transformation of the Church. Too many bonds were knit between them and Erasmus for there to be any room for doubt on that score, while the whole correspondence of Erasmus gives proof of the enthusiastic and sincere mutual approval that accompanied each publication

by Colet and More or by Erasmus himself. The religious life
described by Thomas More in 1516 in the island of Utopia
was as 'evangelical' as Erasmus could have wished, and more
tolerant than he required (to the point of being content with
expelling Epicureans and atheists only); the Erasmianism of
the English humanists is beyond dispute. But we must look
elsewhere, too: from Basle, home of the Frobens and
Amerbachs, to Strasbourg, where Wimpfeling, Brandt, and
Geiler von Kaisersberg were at work, and down to Mainz
and Cologne, in all those lively and bustling Rhineland towns,
where teachers and new-style scholars were numerous and
communicated the more easily with each other because
relations between them formed part of their everyday life:
that Rhineland world where the Reuchlin affair had exploded
in the first years of the century.

Another great figure was Johann Reuchlin: once a pupil of
Robert Gaguin in Paris, a loyal friend of Sebastian Brandt, the
author of *Stultifera navis*, linked with the Platonists of
Florence, introducer of Hellenic studies into the schools of
Stuttgart and Heidelberg, he was an enthusiast for Hebrew
literature and the Kabbala. His *Rudimenta linguae hebraicae*,
published in 1506, was used by all who sought to add to their
knowledge of Greek and Latin a knowledge of the third
sacred language. His *De verbo mirifico* (1496), an introduction
to the Kabbala, also excited wide interest. The quarrel in
which Reuchlin was involved in 1509–10 was stirred up by a
converted Jew named Pfefferkorn, backed by the Dominicans
of Cologne, who obtained from the Emperor Maximilian an
edict for the surrender of all Jewish books suspected of containing anti-Christian interpretations of the Bible. The
polemic between Pfefferkorn, who aimed at getting all Jewish
books burnt, and Reuchlin, who declared Jewish exegesis to
be indispensable for the understanding of the Bible and called
for the introduction of Hebrew teaching in all the universities,
became very acute. Reuchlin, having been accused of

plagiarism and condemned by the Dominican theologians of Cologne, appealed against this treatment to all his learned friends, denounced the low tricks of his opponents and the ignorance of the university teachers, and, when eventually summoned to appear before the inquisitor in Mainz in 1513, appealed to Rome. Reuchlin's condemnation by the Mainz tribunal, though suspended by the Curia on Leo X's order, shook all Europe, dividing opinion in the universities; this happened all the sooner because the Cologne Dominicans decided to submit the case to the Faculties of Erfurt, Louvain and Paris. This was a fine opportunity for the traditionalists to attack 'the friend of the Jews' and with him the modernists in general. At Erfurt Mutianus Rufus (Konrad Muth) and Eobanus Hessus sided with Reuchlin. In Paris Boussard, Duval, Guillaume Petit (although he was a Dominican) and Lefèvre d'Etaples pleaded Reuchlin's cause in vain. All the same, he went on with his teaching and his work of publishing the writings of Nicholas of Cusa. At least the Reuchlin affair did force out into the open the resentment felt by the established theologians against the innovators, providing the occasion for a clash which was seen as aggression by the new-style scholars and as a counter-blow by those whom criticism inspired by Erasmus had not spared for several years before this event.

To appreciate properly the growth of the reform movement we need, further, to turn, for a moment at least, to the Rome of Leo X, on the morrow of the Lateran Council in the spring of 1517. That city where Julius II and Leo X employed the greatest masters of Italian painting at the beginning of the sixteenth century, where, on the ceiling of the Sistine Chapel and in the rooms of the Vatican, the Romans had been able to admire, since 1512–14, those extraordinary compositions in which pagan Antiquity was reconciled with Christianity, Michelangelo painting man's expectation of the Redeemer since the Creation, Raphael multiplying his symmetries: the *School of Athens* and the *Dispute about the Holy Sacrament*, Plato, Aristotle and the Fathers of the Church ... In that Rome, which was less dedicated to paganism than many historians have alleged, Leo X was surrounded by prelates who understood the need for an overhaul of the Church, men like Sadoleto, whom he made Bishop of Carpentras. The Pope intervened to block the bellicose moves of the Dominicans against Reuchlin because he favoured using the most pacificatory measures in dealing with the conflicts which set the defenders of order against the modernists. He allowed reforms to be undertaken in Rome itself such as others had attempted elsewhere. Clergy and laymen together, the brethren of the Oratory of Divine Love (*Oratio del divino Amore*) gathered in a little church to carry out a reform which, though only partial, no doubt, was immediate, in their way of life and in their faith. Sadoleto, from time to time, Gaetano da Tiene (St Cajetan), Giovanni-Pietro Caraffa, Bishop of Chieti, Lippomano, all envisaged a reform that would affect the secular clergy, and the bishops first and foremost, in order to ensure a better administration of dioceses and a better pastorate.

These men, who were in touch with the modernist scholars (Caraffa with Erasmus and Ximenes) and who were soon to recruit model bishops from the Order of Theatines, founded by Gaetano da Tiene and inspired by the same spirit, preached first and foremost by example: Caraffa, when not engaged on the diplomatic missions entrusted to him by the Pope, spent most of his time in his mountainous diocese, visiting the parishes, reorganizing his clergy, reforming practices that seemed to him worthy of blame. So far as this group was concerned, at any rate, the Rome of Leo X showed a community of concerns and sentiments with the modernists which ought not to be overlooked. Nowhere, in those first decades of the century, were positions finally decided or choices definitively adopted by all. Just as Vitrier, in his preaching zeal, did not shut the door on the bad Christians whom he denounced, so Guillaume Petit, the Parisian Dominican, did not shrink from taking up the defence of Reuchlin against his brother Dominicans of Cologne.

All these clerics, who were first and foremost men of the Church, were, in general, aware of how many mansions there are in the Church, how many opportunities could be offered to those who wished to innovate. The sclerotic state of institutions established in a different epoch and unadapted to the new world that was being transformed was no secret even to the most hardened of the clergy: but, in the crisis, more than one stout spirit hesitated as to the remedy to be employed. All who had pleaded for reform had declared themselves, for a quarter of a century at least, in favour of a transformation of men and institutions from within. That was true of the young Augustinian of Wittenberg no less than the others – until 1518, at any rate. All the personalities we have been discussing remained in the Church, convinced that change could be expected to come from within. Some preached by example, on the scale of a diocese. Others taught, persistently, slowly, and without hope of sudden changes, the true doctrine that they drew from the only valid source, the Scriptures. Yet others tried to persuade the princes of the Church to take the lead in the movement to restore both the Church and men's faith. Between these different paths, that of reform and that of the clenched defence of Tradition, of the Roman heritage congealed in its orthodoxy for centuries, what hesitations and scruples there must have been, of which neither letters nor works written to persuade or to comfort men in a choice they had already made can tell us! But in this fever for reform, temperaments and doctrines asserted themselves. Neither Vitrier, nor Lefèvre, nor Erasmus, whatever attacks they suffered or insults they had to endure, ever thought of leaving the Church – neither after the worst moments of disruption that followed 1520, nor before that date. For them the line was drawn: to make new the men and the institutions that were in being, within the framework of that Church of Rome which was theirs, to fight with all their might and to their last breath for this renewal, but certainly not to create a new apparatus, a new institution, alongside of and opposed to the old one. No doubt this was only a dream, as shown by events after 1520. But there were many in the group of humanist scholars who persevered to the end in this hope, and more than one paid with his life for this loyalty to their faith so defined, when times became difficult, as happened in the case of Fisher and Thomas More. The condemnation of Martin Luther opened a new epoch.

2. NEW CLERICS AND NEW CHURCHES: THE DISRUPTIONS

And yet Martin Luther had started out just like the rest. The Augustinian who went to Rome at the beginning of the century and who gave most of his time to reading the Scriptures was not, before 1517, a man whose career was out of the ordinary. He was deeply shocked by the trivialities of the Roman Curia and by the atmosphere of the city, as were many other visitors, taken aback by this capital of the Western Christian world which was more Italian than they had realized: but when he returned to Germany he did not at once give outward expression to the exceptional indignation that he felt. As a great reader of the sacred texts, which he annotated line by line, and anxious to find through this reading the answers to his misgivings about salvation – one of the principal features of religious sensibility both in Germany and elsewhere – the young monk was in no way unusual, but shared with many clerics, regular and secular alike, throughout the Empire, that disquiet which moved the world of scholars, whether theologians or not, at the opening of the century. A hard worker, he applied himself to the most difficult passages, striving to interpret them. At Wittenberg in 1515 and 1516 he gave a noted series of lectures on the Epistle to the Romans. Though a scholar of high quality, as he proved while a member of his community in 1513–17 and still more impressively later on, when he translated the entire Bible into German, Luther was hardly exceptional in a country where biblical researches and studies were further developed than anywhere else in the West. On the very eve of his public outburst in October 1517 he was stirred and scandalized by the campaign for the sale of indulgences organized by the Pope's commissioner in Germany, the Dominican Johann Tetzel, with the backing of Jakob Fugger, in order to provide Rome with the funds needed for the great works undertaken by Leo X. It is certainly easy, above all with the benefit of hindsight, to see the role played in this situation by the monk's pugnacious temperament, his spiritual needs, and the constraints to which he was subject in the monastic milieu he inhabited at Wittenberg. A visionary endowed with a powerful imagination, like so many men of his time, there emerged from the depths of his personality that bold reaction of revolt which decided him to draw up, at the end of October 1517, the Ninety-Five Theses in which he defined what he desired and what his criticisms were of the actual practices of the Roman Church.

It was then, in those last weeks of 1517 and during 1518, that the major event took place, the one that made of Martin Luther the inspirer and standard-bearer of the German reformers. The protest represented by the Ninety-Five Theses, a public appeal for a thoroughgoing reform of the Church in the name of justification by faith, was heard more widely than, and, above all, understood quite differently from, all the learned works that were being published at the same time, ornamented with cordial dedications and aimed at the restricted public of readers familiar with 'good letters' and the subtleties of translations full of cross-references and notes giving all known versions of the correct text. Within a few months the Ninety-Five Theses – first transcribed, then printed – had spread all over Germany, becoming matter for discussion among advocates of reform, and even for comment by the common folk, the craftsmen, printers and others, in the great cities of that country.

All through 1518 the monk of Wittenberg received proofs of the interest aroused by his initiative. From the summer of 1518 onward, preachers who had hitherto lacked a guide set out to meet Luther in his Saxon monastery, while others sent him their approval and encouragement in writing, or asked for his advice. The Roman Curia had not yet found time to take cognizance and assess the seriousness of the monkish rebellion when the event acquired a new dimension, becoming national in scope, and ceasing to be an affair between clerics, to be settled within the Church. By the autumn of 1518 Luther himself was able to measure the actual consequences of his deed. His appeal to the ecclesiastical authorities had become a political act no less than a religious one, for he had stirred the consciences of the German princes, and not only the Pope but the Emperor too was paying attention to him. It was printing that had helped to bring this situation about, by multiplying thousands-fold that mere sheet of paper of his which was, of course, more accessible than any fat book could be, discussing indulgences and the part to be played by works in the justification of a Christian man. Also important was the fact that, throughout the Empire, an extensive public made up of humanists, students and burghers had long been made aware of these problems of Church reform, of clerical life and of the role to be played by the laity in Church affairs, problems on which so many writings had already long since been put into circulation. Luther came on the scene in 1518 bringing an answer to a widespread vague uneasiness which had never before been expressed with such clarity and vehemence. Soon, in 1518–20, he was flanked by disciples: Karlstadt, Thomas Münzer, and later Schwarzerd, known as Melanchthon. Luther had within a few months become the leader of the reform movement among the Germans. A little later Crotus Rubeanus was able to confer on him his famous title: *Ego te, Martine, saepe patrem patriae soleo appellare.*

The second decisive stage, which belongs to a quite different field of analysis, was the break that took place at Worms in 1520-21. During the three years in which the monk of Wittenberg had begun to preach, together with his disciples, all over Northern Germany, with the princes showing interest in, and in several cases frankly encouraging, his harsh criticism of Catholic practice in temporal affairs, the 'case of Martin Luther' had been brought to maturity at Rome and in the Imperial Chancellery. The Roman Church, insistently appealed to by Charles V, could not look with disapproval upon an intervention that would put a stop for a considerable time to those speculations about reform which Pope Leo X had been encouraging not so long before. According to the logic of an institution which unremittingly affirmed its stability and continuity, condemnation of the heretics, following a technique long since perfected, offered more than one advantage. The fate of the heresiarch – either handed over to the secular arm or immured for life – mattered less than the disciplinary effect to be expected on all those others who might be tempted to stray from the strait path of orthodoxy. For everyone who had followed Luther, whether they had gone far or not so far, the Catholic Church possessed an arsenal of well-graded penances which would contribute effectively to restoring the wished-for calm. The fact that the same Leo X who a few years earlier had smiled upon the innovators now resolved to apply to Luther the remedy once imposed upon Hus does not require much explanation: the repressive machine of the Roman Curia carried the Pope painlessly over any hesitations or scruples he may have felt.

The summoning of the rebel to Worms corresponded to the appearance of Hus at the Council of Constance: there, however, the similarity of the situations ended. Luther arrived at Worms, escorted by a great crowd of people, after a triumphal progress which testified eloquently to the success his protest had achieved in the previous four years. Though he entered into discussion with the areopagus of theologians assembled in order to confound him, he refused to bow to their arguments, but stood by the theses which Rome held to be heretical. And though when he left Worms he was under the ban of the Empire, imposed by Charles V, he was well protected by the Elector of Saxony, who installed him in the Wartburg, out of anyone's reach.

Thereafter, with the Church of Rome checked in its anti-heretical procedure, Luther took the decisive step. As founder of a new Church, he abandoned the Erasmian path of reform from within and created a new set of institutions, with all the consequences that the establishment of a Church entails by way of definition of discipline and orthodoxy: not to speak of the inescapable struggles needing to be waged on the borders, geographical and spiritual, of adherence to this Church. The new faith and worship were defined explicitly in accordance with the lines traced out in the preceding years by Luther and other reformers: simplification of ritual, participation of the laity in services, reduction of the number of sacraments, proclamation of justification by faith (the famous *crede fortius*), suppression of the cult of saints and restriction of the cult of the Virgin Mary – all of them features that were to be found sporadically in the preaching of reformers from the end of the fifteenth century, and even earlier, in the writings of Wycliffe and Hus. Luther, however, carried along by his first associates, such as Andreas Bodenstein (Karlstadt), who introduced many liturgical innovations after 1520 (reading and singing in German, communion in both kinds, abolition of images), quickly formed these features into a coherent doctrine between 1521 and 1524, while organizing his Church, and modifying doctrine and discipline in accordance with the dramatic circumstances in which he was promoting the building of this new institution.

Three points are essential to the definition of the Lutheran outlook, which was to become firmly established in the next few decades. Luther did not understand that the reformers scattered through all the states of Western Europe would not in every case rally to his Church and espouse his struggle against the Roman Antichrist. Above all, he failed to appreciate the gulf separating him from the Erasmians, since he considered that no human philosophy could serve as man's guide in the right path (*nulla prorsus doctrina sive philosophia et quocumque modo humana potest hominem dirigere et rectum facere*), whereas the Erasmian reformers were moralists who constantly invoked charity, patience and examination of conscience. Luther's polemic with Erasmus constituted the most dramatic moment in this failure of comprehension, when Erasmus, appealed to both by Luther and by Rome to take a stand on the schism and refusing to approve Luther's disruption, yet having no wish to give satisfaction to the Curia, decided to write his treatise on free will (*De libero arbitrio*), so as to explain just where he stood. Luther replied with a furious and vindictive treatise on 'the slave will' (*De servo arbitrio*), consummating the split between the Catholic evangelicals and the promoter of the new faith, whose shouting, inconsiderate and indiscriminate impetuosity, and, soon, lack of humility were long to scandalize those men of learning who followed the Erasmian line.

On the other hand, Luther did not welcome without misgivings a number of German sectaries – reformers inflamed by his words, monks who had fled from their monasteries – who joined him in the wave of fervour following 1518. Some of these left him quite soon, when they saw taking shape an ecclesiastical institution which seemed to them dangerous *per se.* Many stayed, however, offering their services and contributing their aspirations and their knowledge, which was drawn from the same sources as Luther's, and these had to be disciplined and guided, step by step. For one Melanchthon, a disciple who was at bottom more Erasmian than Lutheran, who for years served the master in the roles of accompanist, secretary and drafter of documents (he it was who was responsible for the Wittenberg Articles, which were destined to be discussed all over Europe) and who undertook the hundred and one indispensable tasks involved in the day-to-day organization of a Church deliberately intended to be different from the old one – for one Melanchthon, there were numerous undisciplined petty prophets who repeated, and sometimes distorted, the lessons of the founder, and soon distracted him far from his vital concerns with the faith and salvation of men. There were those like Thomas Münzer, nourished upon the teachings of Hus (to the point of going to Prague in 1521 in order to summon his 'dear brethren of Bohemia' to resume the good fight that Hus had fought), who stressed the social aspect of evangelical preaching – the denunciation of the rich and powerful, the egalitarianism to be found in some passages of the Gospel. The Peasants' War which broke out in Germany in 1524, sweeping over Swabia and Thuringia, took Luther by surprise (although in 1521 he had laid claim to the whole heritage of Jan Hus), whereas it seemed inevitable to other prophets of the new Church who linked closely together reform of the Church and transformation of society.

Luther had very quickly reconciled himself to the fact that the princes who had rallied to his cause were secularizing for their own benefit the property of the Catholic clergy, who had been stripped of all power: now these other adherents of his were pushing on and going further than the founder could allow. For him, what mattered essentially was the definition of faith. Even if the abuses sanctioned by the Church when it engaged in judicial operations (through monitory letters, for example) were notorious, Luther did not go as far as to approve of a social revolution which would correspond to the revolution in religious life he had initiated, and would provide the latter with different foundations, sociologically speaking. A man of order, who wished to maintain relations between men just as they were, he called, in the midst of the civil war, in a frenzied pamphlet (*Wider die räuberischen und mörderischen Bauern*), for the extermination of all the rebels: he allowed full authority to the princes to crush these revolts in blood so as to restore the order established by God. After the battle of Frankenhausen, in 1525, Thomas Münzer, repudiated by Luther, died under torture, but his influence persisted for a long time, especially in Thuringia. The Lutheran Church, with its simplified hierarchy of bishops and pastors, was placed in the princes' charge, and they became its masters as Church organizations were formed in each of the principalities where the new religion took root. It is true that these decisions, which were essential to the discipline of the Churches that were multiplying in Northern Germany, and were soon to spread across the Baltic and even into Northern Poland, do not throw much light upon the Lutheran view of religion. All the same, submission to the constituted civil powers was indeed an element in that view, no less than the new catechism which Luther published in 1529 and the articles of faith drawn up in the Confession of Augsburg and recited thenceforth by generation after generation, just as they sang hymns in which Luther proclaimed his most fundamental principles, such as: 'A safe stronghold our God is still' (*Ein' feste Burg ist unser Gott*), a graphic affirmation of justification by faith, the doctrine dear to all the reformers.

Nevertheless, these decisions taken by the Lutherans help to explain the disarray in which Christians of all allegiances found themselves in 1525–40, the multiplication of Churches and sects all across Europe, the significance of the various new foundations which gradually appeared, down to and including Calvin's. Pamphlets and articles of faith inspired by Lutheranism spread over Europe with all the greater success because the soil had been prepared long beforehand. As early as 1521-3 groups of 'persons of unsound belief', as the law-courts of the King of France were soon to call them, were reported in the north-east, in Picardy and Champagne. The enemies of Briçonnet's circle at Meaux were not slow to accuse these reformers of being Lutherans. In the same period, 1521 and after, Henry VIII's councillors, with the advocates of reform at their head, took a stand against the declared Lutherans, who were expelled outright from the kingdom.

But it was in the Rhine valley that the message of Luther found its most remarkable echoes. From Basle, a city cut out to be a centre of reform, excellently furnished as it was with courageous printers, to Zürich, in the heart of the Swiss cantons, an independent variant of the reform movement quickly emerged, under the firm leadership of Zwingli, aiming to subject itself neither to Rome nor to the new Rome at Wittenberg. Ulrich Zwingli, master of Zürich from 1520-22 onward, a man trained in the Erasmian spirit and an admirer of the earlier Luther, defined a kind of reform that was strictly evangelical, directly inspired by Scripture alone, with the sacraments reduced to mere symbols, and services to readings from the Bible. With his great power of conviction Zwingli won over to his way of thinking Berne in 1528 and Basle in 1529, thanks to the aid of Oecolampadius (Hausschein), and inspired the creation of a little Church of the Upper Rhine that was subsequently led with a firm hand by Bullinger, his successor at Zürich, an assiduous correspondent of Calvin's during the persecutions launched by the King of France. Further north, at Strasbourg, a lively Imperial city situated at the heart of continental communications, two great reformers were active – Johannes Sturm and, especially, Martin Bucer, another German genius of religious controversy: an indefatigable polemist whose career culminated at Cambridge. Soon, the 'four cities' of Strasbourg, Lindau, Constance and Memmingen constituted a distinct religious persuasion (which, however, was close to Zwingli's) known as the *Confessio Tetrapolitana*. On the Upper Rhine the reform movement thus became 'municipalized', escaping from even the distant tutelage of the founder: at the Diet of Augsburg assembled in 1530 on the initiative of Charles V in order to try bring about reunion, Melanchthon represented Wittenberg, Zwingli represented Zürich, Berne and Basle, and Bucer represented the 'Four Cities'.

A little later, on the other side of the Channel, Henry VIII undertook, from 1530 onward, the reform of religion in his realm, carrying this out in his own way, neither Lutheran nor Roman. As against Rome, he proposed to secularize Church property on a grand scale, for the benefit of the Crown, and soon he set about ending the ties of dependence between 'his' Church and Rome. Nevertheless, he was no Lutheran: he persecuted the followers of the German monk and did not adopt the definitions of doctrine or of liturgy that had been established beyond the Rhine. The Anglican Church, retaining the Roman rites but without allegiance to the Papacy, might constitute an independent national Church provided that the bishops and reformers in England accepted the King's decisions. In February 1531 the English episcopate, despite the opposition of Fisher and More, recognized Henry VIII as supreme head of the Church of England, 'so far as the law of Christ allows'.

We must not omit to mention the revival in Central Europe of the dissident sects which had been silenced for a hundred years but which now, in the effervescence stirred up by the Lutheran explosion, found an audience, and scope for boldness: first and foremost the Hussites, both Calixtines and Taborites, who had survived in Bohemia, Moravia and Poland, with the tenacious vitality of dissenters long ill-used.

Further west there was the spread of the Anabaptist movement, which is difficult to trace in its earliest phases, at Zürich, St Gallen and Strasbourg in 1524–7 (under the inspiration of Münzer, whom they honoured as a prophet), and which triumphed for a year in Münster in 1534–5 under the leadership of two Dutchmen, Jan Matthyszoon and Jan of Leyden.

Above all, though, it is necessary to appreciate the spiritual consternation caused by the Lutheran breakaway, as the new Church became consolidated: so firmly had the Catholic Church caused credence to be given to the idea that outside its fold there could be no salvation. For political leaders in particular, the spread of Lutheranism in their states appeared a highly dangerous calamity. Charles V began an armed struggle against it at the beginning of the 1540s. Francis I, who was still benevolently disposed towards the reformers even after 1530, hardened his heart against them after the 'affair of the placards' in 1534: he resolved to suppress printing by a decree that was as senseless as it was inapplicable, looked glumly upon the humanists whom he had been flattering for twenty years, ordered that Lutherans be hunted down, and erected the first stakes for burning heretics. In Spain the swing-round was equally abrupt: Erasmus's writings were soon banned, and the *illuminati* confounded with the Lutherans in an amalgam which it was not difficult to justify. All Europe turned away from the open-ended discussion of the century's first decades and fell into disorder: resort to arms and persecution became the rule everywhere. In 1535, when John Fisher and Thomas More stood out for the concept of a reformed Anglican Church retaining its allegiance to Rome, Henry VIII showed them no mercy, despite the services they had rendered to him, and they were executed.

It was then, in this atmosphere of anxiety when many distressed Christians had lost hope of a Council that would reconcile and appease – a Council that Rome failed to convene, despite the urging of some of the cardinals: Caraffa, Contarini,

Sadoleto – that Jean Calvin came on the scene with his *Christianae religionis institutio*, and what it has become conventional to call the French Reformation began. A good humanist (author, at the beginning of his career at Bourges and Paris, of a commentary on Seneca's *De clementia*), Calvin was soon drawn into reform-seeking circles in Paris, frequently visiting Gérard Roussel and the others and taking part in their meetings. He was soon well enough known to be thought to have written in 1533 the eulogy of the 'Christian philosophy' which the rector, Guillaume Cop, pronounced before the four Faculties of the University of Paris. Under suspicion and sought for, he then began a wandering life which lasted several years, until he established himself in Geneva. It was while staying at Strasbourg and Basle that he wrote his *Christianae religionis institutio* (published at Strasbourg), dedicated to Francis I in a remarkable prefatory letter, in which he appealed to the King's reforming sentiments and to the justice that he owed to all his subjects; trusting in the truth of his cause and at the same time affirming his loyalty to the King and the kingdom.

Even before this work had produced its full effect and rallied to his side many of those potential reformers who were not attracted either by Luther or the founders of the little Rhenish Churches, Calvin had made two experiments *in vivo* which had a great bearing on his career as the founder of a new Church. Between 1536 and 1538, in company with Guillaume Farel, another innovator who had passed through Meaux, Basle, Paris and Strasbourg, he tried to convert Geneva, a city of merchants fond of good living who were not impressed by Farel's blustering style. After this unsuccessful attempt, Calvin was summoned by Martin Bucer to Strasbourg, where he remained for three years, between 1538 and 1541, sharing in the reformed religious life of this city where at that time many French innovators in flight from the prisons of Francis I were gathered, seeking a refuge in which

to pursue their evangelizing unmolested. It was in this circle
of refugees, and while participating in the ceremonies of
Strasbourg, that Calvin prepared for his future work at
Geneva – composing French versions of the Psalms, studying
the liturgy of the Strasbourg Confession, publishing at Basle
in 1538 a new catechism in Latin, and translating into French
his *Institutio*, which was destined to bring about the rise of a
new form of Christian life. This latter was more definitely
remote from Catholic faith and feeling than Lutheranism had
been, not only because, in the very manner in which he
defined his Credo, invoking the honour and glory of God
rather than the faith of a Christian, Calvin emphatically
distanced himself from Catholicism, but also because, over
and above his sweeping away of adventitious practices and
cults, in full conformity with the reform programme, Calvin
went further, calling in question some of the essential
mysteries of the Church, starting with transubstantiation in the
Eucharist: and, most important, he based his faith, in an
impulse of profound psychological significance, upon predestination, that definition of Divine Grace as wholly arbitrary,
which Catholic theologians had striven so hard to refute, over
decades and even centuries.

Definitively established at Geneva from 1541 onward,
Calvin built up his Church in accordance with a discipline
quite different from that of Rome or that of Luther. As a
community subject to a Consistory of Pastors and Elders,
assembled in plenary session whenever necessary, and
governed by a severe law dictated by respect for God and the
honour of the Christian serving his God, Calvinist society
(which was certainly no freer than any other of intolerance
and persecution) was a collegiate body. By its very definition
it distinguished itself from the hierarchical society, organized
as a monarchy, which prevailed everywhere else in Europe:
on this plane Calvin certainly took a step forward in a
direction where Luther had never for a moment thought of

going. The Calvinist Geneva of the first years following the installation there of the man from Noyon was a much sought-after place of refuge, especially for those in trouble in France for their religious 'unsoundness', though Strasbourg was still the capital of the French reformers in exile, where new arrivals from France could find each other. Until 1545, the year when Calvin banished the good Sebastian Castellio and began to tighten up his regime, Geneva had the reputation of being a city of freedom. Marot found shelter there in 1542, when Francis I resumed his persecution of Lutherans and Psalm-singers; Bernardo Ochino, an Italian preacher persecuted by the Inquisition at home, also came to Geneva; and there were many others for whom the author of the *Institutio* was a protector while elsewhere the faggots were starting to blaze and the prisons to fill up. Thenceforth the Reformation of France had found its matrix: another Church was taking shape and would soon, in its turn, begin to 'swarm'.

Thus, within twenty years, the Christian unity of Western and Central Europe had been shattered: the dream of the Erasmians had collapsed and new Churches had been founded, winning to themselves a section of the Catholic laity. This was a battle of ideas, but above all a struggle between men, as can well be appreciated. What courage must have been possessed by those men of the years between 1520 and 1540 who chose to abandon the traditional framework in which their lives, like those of their ancestors, had been passed, and to challenge all or part of that Church's teaching, in order to follow another Church, which would in its turn declare that it alone possessed the truth, in so far as it preached the Gospel restored to its true meaning, and could ensure better than any other that the believer would enjoy eternal salvation! In order to take upon himself this mission of fundamental importance, each innovator was obliged, as soon as he had given up all hope of reform of the Roman Church from within, to settle himself within a new institution, quickly put together, but just as solid (or so it was hoped, at any rate), as the old one. But not everyone saw the matter in that light in the first half of the sixteenth century, or even for a long time afterwards.

This was so especially in Germany, where the long cohort assembled by Luther while he was waging his fight against Rome was suddenly broken up after 1524-5, when the Lutheran Church took shape and began to function as such; all the more formidably for having been placed in the princes' charge. The first victims of the new order, after Luther had published his treatise on the duty of obedience to the temporal authority, were his early disciples, Karlstadt and Münzer, who were objects of all the greater fear on the part of the founder because they preached with success right up to the gates of Wittenberg. The path to be followed was clearly defined, and the Lutheran persecutions were not slow to develop. All those who refused to let themselves be enclosed within the new institutional framework had then to scatter about the Empire in order to pursue their quest and preach the truth as they saw it. Soon hunted down, they were driven from the north by the Lutherans and from the south by the Catholics, but were saved by the weakness of police organization in a country where political fragmentation was added to the general inadequacy of means of identifying individuals. Well known is the tale of protracted wanderings of Thomas Münzer, who was given shelter in monasteries and inns all over Germany, preaching one day and sleeping the next, always pursued, but recognized too late, welcomed with kindness and protected by the common folk, who were eager for the good word and accustomed to seeing arrive among them these clerics without label or organization, these preachers without a Church who were continuing their journey beyond the bounds of the Lutheran 'solution'. German history knows as *Schwärmer* and *Erzketzer* (fanatics and arch-heretics) these men of the first wave of the reform movement who perseveringly refused to be regimented, despite all the risks they faced: they were founders of small sects only to the extent that sometimes they let a few disciples gather round them, men who recorded what they said and spoke as they did, but were bound by no obligation or Credo.

One such, the earliest, was Sebastian Franck, who founded no sect or 'religion' of his own making and did not 'prophesy' as so many others did, but who explained better than anyone else why he rejected every kind of Church: because the spirit bloweth where it listeth, and all ceremony, even all dogma, is merely symbolic, the spiritual community of the true believers is recruited from every epoch and every milieu, without regard to the definitions laid down by outwardly existing Churches (which in his view were the *real* heresies, the Lutheran Church no less than the Catholic). The only Church he recognized, in that wretched age when excommunications and exclusions rained down, was the one that he described in his *Ketzerchronik*, the Church invisible and everlasting which embraces Socrates as well as Origen – all men, in fact, of personal religion and spiritual freedom. Such also was Karlstadt, and also Paul Lautensack, the minor prophet of Nuremberg who, after teaching in that city for four years, was forbidden to publish his writings and banished by the Magistracy in 1542 for having propagated 'enthusiastic' doctrines: they too were contemporaries of Luther, born in the last quarter of the fifteenth century and dying in the middle years of the sixteenth.

But the best example of these enthusiasts and visionaries is, perhaps, Kaspar Schwenkfeld, who, having once been a pupil of Luther's, opposed him bitterly when he became convinced of the 'betrayal' committed by the Master of Wittenberg. To the 'new Popery' Schwenkfeld counterposed his conception of an inward religion, based upon the reading of the Gospels, plainly arguing along the same lines as Luther, but turning these arguments against his former teacher, in the name of the freedom of the individual Christian and of evangelical piety.

A mystic and *illuminatus*, this Silesian gentleman, a self-taught theologian mocked by Luther in his *Table Talk*, clung firmly to certain definitions which marked out in a fundamental way the distance separating him forever from the Lutheran Church – that human creation, stained, after all, with sin, like everything that was done by man in his sinful state (*Sündenstand*). Schwenkfeld, who was not sparing of sarcasm about the Augsburg Confession, kept coming back to the same set of arguments, which were incomprehensible to the Lutherans. Only a personal spiritual illumination enables one to understand the Scriptures: the real presence of Christ in the Eucharistic species is a nonsense, as Christ's own words make clear: participation in the sacraments is meaningless when there is no guarantee of the faith of the officiating priest: besides, baptism, communion, ordination are only rites, ceremonies of outward religious life which have no bearing on what is essential. These are so many points in dispute that reveal two religious attitudes which are absolutely irreconcilable – as Luther himself, a better theologian than his opponent, understood quite well, looking beyond the Silesian's bold polemics on partial questions. Kaspar Schwenkfeld was certainly an 'enthusiast' of the purest stock, since the ultimate conclusion of his spiritual doctrine is an affirmation of the superiority of the spirit over the letter, of the regenerating power of man's faith: faith, as he defines it, is 'the immediate possession of God'.

Outsiders, cut off from the official Churches, not often getting into print and even then finding few readers, better known after their deaths than they were to their contemporaries, these visionaries nevertheless founded a real tradition. In the subsequent history of the German sects, other men appear who reveal the same state of mind, men such as the Lutheran pastor Valentin Weigel (1533–88), who performed his duties for twenty years and agreed without hesitation to sign in 1572 the Lutheran formulary drawn up with the purpose of separating the wheat from the tares (*Konkordien-formel*),yet preached in his own way, which was visionary to the point of sometimes upsetting some of his flock, and left at his death a quantity of writings, undoubtedly heretical from the Lutheran standpoint, in which the essential themes of the 'enthusiastic' spirit appear: spiritual rebirth through personal reading of the sacred texts, primacy of inner reflexion over any and every institution, direct relationship between the believer and God.

The same phenomenon, in its twofold aspect – the call for a personal, intimate religious life, and the absolute (instinctive, so to speak) rejection of any sort of Church-like institution – was manifested in the middle of the sixteenth century in all parts of Europe where the reforming spirit had found vigorous expression: in Basle, which continued, like Strasbourg, to be a meeting-place and refuge for those who were in need of asylum and somewhere to work; in the Netherlands, both in the south and in the north, where Lutherans, Calvinists and reformers coexisted in the little, slowly-expanding towns beyond the Rhine; finally, and above all, in England, where the dissenters of all varieties, reduced to silence while Henry VIII was enforcing his will, gradually came to recognize each other. There were Lutherans of strict obedience who would not go along with Thomas Cranmer and the Prayer Book of 1539, and soon these men who, though opponents of the regime of the Anglican Church as desired by Henry VIII, remained attached to the concept of a Church were joined by dissenters of the German type, who were to found a tradition of their own, with a notable posterity ahead of them at the end of the sixteenth century and in the seventeenth, in the Levellers, Diggers and Fifth Monarchy Men.

Nevertheless, all was not settled when this swarming of sects and these fundamental disruptions in the religious life of Western and Central Europe had taken place. In this period, which knew nothing of the virtues of peaceful coexistence and pluralism, open war, launched by the princes and encouraged by the Churches which had become established, entered very soon into the action. This hardened antagonisms and gave rise to doctrinal changes of far from negligible significance. The polyphony of the Reformation lost its exuberant creativity as antagonisms stiffened in armed conflict. This was the third panel of the triptych, the third epoch in the evolution of the reform movement.

3. PERSECUTIONS AND FIRST RELIGIOUS WARS

War and persecution were one and the same in an epoch when political power existed only with the sanction of a Church and when secular and ecclesiastical institutions lived in constant symbiosis with the initiative for legal repression or for armed action coming both from sovereign princes and from Church authorities who felt threatened, dispossessed or repudiated. Nevertheless, a distinction needs to be made. The Catholic Church had long possessed its own militias and its independent organization for keeping watch on breaches of doctrine or discipline – forces which had proved inadequate to their task, beginning with the Inquisition which the Dominicans had operated for such a lengthy period. Two forms of direct struggle against heresy thus stood ready for action in lacerated Europe. On the one hand, the secular arm, intervening against individuals by means of the judicial organs directly subject to the sovereign's authority, or inspiring an armed fight against heretical groups, when the scale of dissent did not call for a more substantial form of intervention, as in France and England, and in Germany at the time of the League of Schmalkalden. On the other, the Catholic Church, after being thrown off balance for a dozen years by the upheaval, discovered fresh resources adapted to the new situation and created new orders, additional to those inherited from the Middle Ages, which undertook the battle to recover

lost ground. All this was done not in a calm, orderly atmosphere in which tasks were distinguished and assigned with a
view to all contributing to the same end, but in the com-
parative precipitancy and confusion of men who realized what
a great responsibility they bore and who had seen the familiar
horizon of their everyday lives shaken by successive disruptions. The latter did not wholly spare any province of the
Catholic world. Even Italy and Spain had their heretics and
were obliged, like the rest, to fight for the maintenance of
orthodoxy. M. Bataillon and D. Cantimori have amply
proved this, for Spain and Italy respectively, while also
indicating the limits of the problem in those countries.

The major event which struck contemporaries most
forcibly, and thereby played the biggest role in solidifying the
doctrinal antagonisms between the men of 'Reformed'
beliefs and the 'Papists', was undoubtedly the war waged by
the Emperor Charles V against the Lutheran princes who were
subject to his authority – the first religious war (and a protracted one) to be endured by a Christian Europe now torn
apart. Charles V declared war on the 'Reformed' after the
setback he suffered at the Diet of Augsburg, in 1530, when the
bases of agreement proposed by the Catholics were rejected
by the delegates belonging to other confessions. The struggle
ended in 1555 in that same city of Augsburg, when the
Emperor's representative acknowledged the existence of the
'Reformed' in Germany (a quarter-century earlier they had
been given seven months to return to the Roman fold) and
agreed that every German prince should have the right to
choose the religion of his own state. These twenty-five years
of conflict (which it is not our business to narrate) were not
actually years of unremitting battle. On a number of occasions,
from as early as 1532, Charles V, who was inadequately
equipped to impose his will, struck his flag and postponed the
application of the decisions which had been taken at Augsburg
in 1530. Furthermore, the struggle between Charles V and

the princes rapidly acquired an international dimension, with the King of France, Francis I, in pursuit of a contest which ended only with his death, intervening many times to help the Protestant princes and towns – even while persecuting the 'Reformed' within his own realm.

The aspect of this long war which, rightly, made most impression on contemporaries was the fact that the two sides resorted to force with such light hearts. The Emperor sought to safeguard the spiritual unity of his Empire and felt confident that right was on his side, since he aimed to ensure precise application of the Edict of Worms, restoring bishops to their jurisdictions and recovering church property that had been secularized. The Protestant princes, headed by John of Saxony and Philip of Hesse, brushed aside Luther's scruples in the name of the nobles' right to revolt against Imperial injustice, and assembled the defenders of the Gospel at a gathering held near Gotha in December 1530, uniting beneath one banner all the Reformed princes and towns, with the exception of the Zwinglian cities. No doubt the mixing up together of defence of the particular rights of each principality and protection of the new religion lent itself to misunderstandings. But it is none the less true that, in the contrast it made to peaceful methods of discussion and compromise, the step taken was an important one. The adherents of the Reformed religion were obliged, and were able, to organize themselves militarily, and therefore politically, in order to ensure the survival of their faith.

This circumstance did not fail to strengthen the control exercised over the new Church structures by the lay authorities, and in the case of the Lutheran Church such a development was, despite the powerful personality of the founder, quite logical. There was nothing surprising in the fact that, in 1537, it was a prince, Philip of Hesse, who proposed the convening of a Protestant Council to counter the Catholic Council which was continually being promised by Rome. In the little Churches of Switzerland and the Upper Rhine it was, similarly, the municipalities of the Reformed cities that urged on the religious leaders, drawing up the instructions that Martin Bucer and the Swiss preachers took with them to Wittenberg in 1536, and thereby helping to decide the politico-religious option chosen. When, in 1539, the League of Schmalkalden held its assembly in Frankfurt, Philip of Hesse presided, and negotiated with the Emperor, in the name of all, a renewal of the truce for fifteen months. Luther, when consulted on political questions and external alliances, no longer succeeded in making his views prevail, any more than Melanchthon, the peacemaker, or Bullinger. Princes and ordinary laymen played, in this difficult game, in which the two halves of Germany confronted each other in arms, a role which it is important not to minimize. The Evangelical Reform was an affair of laymen no less than of clerics. When the papal legates Morone and Contarini came to negotiate an agreement once more, at the Diet of Regensburg in 1541, Melanchthon and Bucer answered them on the questions of the sacraments and of grace, but the limits to their acquiescence – and so the failure of this new attempt at reconciliation – had been defined beforehand, in the resort to force which was taken for granted by everyone concerned.

This important role played by the laity did not contribute to greater comprehension within the Reformed camp itself. While the Reformed theologians continually made contact with each other, exchanging letters between Zürich and Wittenberg and Strasbourg, the princes and municipalities took their stand very quickly and very strongly, when the Anabaptists made their appearance in Germany: from the Swiss cantons to Alsace and Westphalia, the sectaries of adult baptism were hunted down and driven out, or, more usually, executed. When, in 1534–5, they seized the episcopal city of Münster and won a following all over Northern Germany, as far as Lübeck, which for a moment rallied to this new variety of the Reformed faith, Münster was besieged by the bishop's troops, soon reinforced by soldiers despatched by the Catholic princes. But the Protestant princes too discussed a proposal made to them by Luther, pitiless towards everything that might recall the memory of Münzer and a social revolution, that they help the Roman party to strike down these new reformers. At the same time, this control achieved by the laity provides to some extent the key to the surprises of the war. Changes of side contemplated by the princes of Central Germany filled up the chronicle of those years in which the war amounted to no more than local persecutions and raids of limited significance. Family rivalries intersected grand designs: Maurice of Saxony changed sides soon after Luther's death, fought against the Reformed party, and, after Mühlberg, received the Electorate from the Emperor's hands as his reward. The battles of autumn 1546 along the Danube, from Regensburg to Donauwörth, brought about capitulations as sensational as that of the Duke of Württemberg.

In the spring of 1547, with Saxony invaded, the army of the League beaten at Mühlberg, and Wittenberg captured by the Imperial forces, the League's cause seemed lost indeed. Eight years later, the peace of Augsburg consecrated the religious partition of Germany: this was a treaty between the Lutherans and the Roman Church, excluding all other forms of Protestantism, whether Calvinist, Zwinglian or Anabaptist. The sovereign princes and free cities were permitted to choose only between the two recognized religions. Wittenberg, seat of a university and capital of Lutheranism, became a 'mother-city', like Rome for the Catholics. The most obvious consequence of this long war had been to impose the discipline of a Church that was kept under the thumb of the state in all parts of the Holy Roman Empire. The road traversed since Luther proclaimed the freedom of the individual Christian is striking: within half a century the new orthodoxy had forced the old one to recognize it, but at the cost of total submission to the political order, and this submission had been intensified since the death of the founder. In Central Europe, at a time when the old, persecuted Hussite church was giving ground in Bohemia itself to the new confessions, Lutheran and Calvinist, religious war was ratifying for centuries to come that process of subjection to the political state which had been entered upon in 1524–5, with the result that Church institutions became more and more rigid.

In England a comparable process subjected the clergy and all the dignitaries of the Church to King Henry VIII. Between 1531–2 and his death the bloodstained King caused heads to fall by dozens – as his sexual whims dictated, so say the chroniclers: according to his own frequent explanations, however, it was in consequence of the intention he vigorously proclaimed to create a national Church, which, though schismatic, should be orthodox. Yet the hesitations of Cranmer and Cromwell on this matter, their negotiations with Wittenberg, the re-touches applied so often to Anglican dogma, offer no justification for that claim to concern for orthodoxy. Henry VIII and his men certainly showed on many an occasion their desire to mark themselves off from the Lutherans, even while separating from the Church of Rome, despite all the resistance put up by the Catholics, Erasmians included. But so many heads fell and so much property of the religious communities was confiscated, in order to consolidate a religious unity defined by the state – that is, by the King and by a Parliament devoted to the monarchy. The Six Articles Act passed by Parliament in 1539 might determine those points of dogma that were to be distinctive to the Church of England, but what was essential was, nevertheless, the repressive aspect of this 'Act abolishing diversity in opinions', which organized the struggle against every form of dissent, with the death penalty for anyone who denied the reality of transubstantiation, and so on. Down to the death of Henry VIII in 1547 the persecution of heretics was carried on unrelentingly. It was a King's matter and made manifest the subjection of the Church to the political ruler.

This fact was illustrated, too, by the decisions of his successor, Edward VI, who (with Cranmer still at the King's side), accentuated the turn towards Lutheranism, decreeing communion in both kinds and permitting priests to marry. Calvinist influence, noticeable in all the measures taken between 1549 and 1552, hastened the progress of the reforming trend. The Prayer Book of 1549, imposed by the Act of Uniformity, provoked popular resistance that was repressed by the Government, now persecuting both the supporters of Henry VIII's reform and the Catholics. There were imprisonments and executions. This new Anglican dogmatism claimed fewer victims than the first variant only because Edward VI did not reign for long, but it contributed substantially to promoting confusion among believers and opening the way to new varieties of nonconformity. The complexity of religious developments in England contrasts with the simplicity of the transition to Lutheranism that was carried out in the Scandinavian countries on the initiative and by the authority of their kings, who had been won over to the faith of Wittenberg. To be sure, reform-seeking humanism had not made much headway there, among either clergy or laity.

In a country which remained officially Catholic, such as France, where the princes, unlike those who defied Charles V, had lost most of the attributes of sovereignty, persecution remained an entirely one-sided affair for about fifteen years. Francis I, followed by Henri II, pursued the same tireless hunting down of those heretics, Lutherans and Calvinists alike, who revealed their presence in the kingdom. Helped in this task by the repressive ardour of the Catholic theologians who were responsible for meticulously censoring all printed publications in which scriptural matters were discussed, the French kings even allowed ample scope to suspicions based on the presence in books of expressions that were habitually used by those of the Reformed faith, or even merely on the *other* publishing activities of the printer-publisher who had produced a certain work. The worthy Rabelais, with his imprudent pen, was troubled in this way, and obliged to seek refuge under the wing of a prince of the Church, Cardinal du Bellay. Worse was the fate of Etienne Dolet, printer to Erasmus, Lefèvre, Marot and Rabelais, whose fault it was to have published in and after 1542 a number of books that seemed to fall into the category of heretical propaganda. After many misadventures he was condemned to death for blasphemy, sedition and publication of banned books, and burned in the Place Maubert on 3 August 1546.

Sedition was the key word here: it was to this offence that Francis I had referred already when the German Evangelicals reproached him for carrying out such persecutions and executions while he was supporting their party against Charles V. For this French monarch and his successor, who were indifferent to Calvin's protestations of loyalty, embracing heresy meant breaking up the religious unity of the kingdom and endangering its security. Brutal repression was legitimized by a religious definition of the state, in which the sovereign's personal faith was held to coincide with the interests of the monarchy as so understood. In the case of Francis I, who had over a long period shown sympathy with the humanist reforms and given ear to his sister Marguerite, patroness of the Meaux group, the ardour with which he repudiated these relations, and handed over to the executioner the suspected heretics he now gathered in by dozens with each cast of the net, has presented historians with a problem – on the plane of individual psychology, though, rather than that of the logic of monarchy. In the case of Henri II the question was simpler and the repression more severe: increased persecution, establishment in 1547 of a *chambre ardente* to try suspects more expeditiously, adoption in 1557 of an edict intensifying suspicion, all signified an ascent to a climax in the fight against heresy which had no equivalent in the struggle being waged simultaneously in Italy and Spain.

In the decade preceding the Wars of Religion in France persecution mounted to a level that provoked a veritable exodus from the kingdom. Hundreds of townsfolk, craftsmen and merchants especially, left France to seek refuge in Geneva, Calvin's city, where they were received as hospitably as possible. Persecution thus consistently attained its purpose by two concurrent paths: whether the victim went to the stake or into exile, the result was the same – his expulsion from the community. *A contrario*, as soon as the moment came when, here and there, in Normandy, in the Paris region, or in the Rhône valley, the 'Reformed' felt strong enough to resist the King's archers and men-at-arms sent to arrest them, the first clashes occurred, with armed resistance and civil war. Merciless slaughter took place, strengthening convictions on both sides, in unappeasable hatred. The consolidation of doctrines and 'religions' was sealed, in France as elsewhere, in human blood.

However, the Churches felt obliged to respond on the intellectual plane to the requirements of the struggles and aspirations of their followers, who, throughout Europe, were demanding definitions of doctrine and coherent explanations of the major problems posed by the Reformation: the relation between Scripture and the Tradition of the Fathers of the Church, justification by faith and by works, the number and meaning of the sacraments, the cult of saints as intercessors, and the cult of Mary. Luther devoted part of the last ten years of his life, in the midst of the War of the League of Schmalkalden, to this work, while Melanchthon was ceaselessly busy republishing and revising his *Loci communes rerum theologicarum* and reorganizing the University of Wittenberg, whose theological faculty had the task of training Lutheran bishops and pastors. Calvin, installed at Geneva, presided with the utmost rigour over the recruitment of ministers. A Consistory of these ministers was the real ruler of the city: it expelled Anabaptists and 'the Freethinkers who call themselves Spirituals' and gave special attention to organizing the College of Geneva, at which the two basic subjects of instruction were the classical languages (as a necessary preparation for theological studies) and critical exegesis of Holy Scripture. Calvinist orthodoxy, now firmly established, made its severity known throughout Europe when the General Council of the city condemned to the stake Michael Servetus, author of a work, *The Restoration of Christianity*, which denied the divinity of Christ. The sentence was executed on 28 October 1553, and justified a month later by Calvin in his *Defence of the Orthodox Faith against Michael Servetus*.

But the most remarkable effort of the time was the work carried out, from several different angles, within the Catholic Church. While the orders created in the later Middle Ages continued to fulfil their primary tasks – the Dominicans (with a few individual exceptions, such as Guillaume Petit in Paris) activating the inquisitorial persecution of heretics, and the Franciscans pursuing their business as preachers, denouncing the errors of the innovators and reasserting the truths of Catholicism (this was done also by their new community, the Capuchins, founded in Italy in 1526, who soon became celebrated for the effectiveness of their popular preachers) – fresh initiatives were undertaken which were to play a vital role in the development of religious thinking in the West. In Rome, as we have seen, the foundation of the Oratory of Divine Love, and, especially, of the Order of Theatines, formed in 1524 as a body of canons regular devoted to study and teaching, was aimed at improving the education of the clergy, and, in particular, of the Italian bishops: Pietro Bembo and Reginald Pole were for some years the leading figures in this first oratory inspired by Erasmian ideas.

The most original initiative, though, was the founding of the Society of Jesus. The career of Ignatius of Loyola – a soldier compelled to give up his military occupation; a pilgrim sent back from the Holy Land as soon as he arrived there in 1523; a Spaniard of good family who wrote at the age of thirty-five his own manual of religious life, the *Spiritual Exercises*, and was driven from his own country by the Dominican-controlled Inquisition, which saw in him an *illuminatus*; a belated student at the colleges of Paris who swore an oath on Montmartre, in 1535, along with six comrades, to practise the monastic vows, to make the pilgrimage to Jerusalem, or to place himself at the service of the Pope – that simple and straightforward career which reads like one of the Lives of the Saints concerns us here less than the Society created in 1539–40 in Rome, with the approval of Pope Paul III. The Bull *Regimini militantis Ecclesiæ* sanctioned the constitutions drawn up by Ignatius, which added to the three regular vows a vow of obedience to the Pope (through the head of the new order, who was accorded unlimited power). It confirmed the chosen title of 'Society of Jesus' and placed the new order under the direct protection of the Holy See.

The most notable feature of this creation was not so much the subjection of the Jesuits to a strict military discipline as the intention affirmed from the outset to recruit to the new order only men of high culture, capable of writing, teaching and preaching, that is, of defending openly and firmly the doctrinal positions of the Catholic Church. During the ten years in which the order was being organized, between 1540 and 1550, the standards of these intellectual requirements were defined and approved afresh by Pope Paul III, in 1549. Loyola imposed on future members of the Society a long training in which study played a very large part, such as no other religious order had ever before insisted on. At the stage of novitiate the Fathers selected those candidates who appeared capable of following the career of a Jesuit, and sent them to the Society's schools, where they received a humanistic education lasting four years. Study of the languages of

Antiquity and of philosophy were the main items in this first stage, and the most advanced students were called upon to teach grammar and philosophy to the younger ones. Four years of theological study then equipped them to become priests, renewing the three regular vows which had already been taken at the end of their novitiate. After that, two more years were spent undergoing various tests, in preaching and the teaching of theology, and at last the professed were allowed to take the fourth vow and become members of the Society.

The duration and rigour of the training of a Jesuit provides explanation enough of how it was that the Society of Jesus (which soon recruited more than the sixty members authorized in 1539) was able so soon to establish a strong position in the Church of Rome, and, in particular, at the Council of Trent. It explains also how the system of education for laymen which the Society grafted upon its own internal schools was able to take over the humanist heritage, as urged by the reformers inspired by Erasmus, while at the same time insisting on defence of the Catholic tradition in its entirety. The Reverend Fathers of the first generation found themselves in the forefront of this new fight for the defence of orthodoxy, in which the solidity of their theological training enabled them to encounter the enemy armed with weapons that were all the more effective because they incorporated everything that was 'useful' in the heritage of Antiquity. Efficient fighters for the reconquest of the ground lost by Catholicism, the Jesuit Fathers at the same time promoted the diffusion of classical studies through the schools. The *Ratio studiorum* of their colleges, which were soon to spring up all over Europe, laid down the norms, and the prudently defined limits, of these studies. In the second half of the sixteenth century the Roman Church found in the Jesuits not only a militia which soon made itself feared, but also bearers of a doctrine which ensured the maintenance of the Tradition while at the same time embracing that critical knowledge of Antiquity in the name of which the Erasmians had called for 'reform from within' of the Church's dogma and discipline. While the disruptions of 1520–40 had already implied the defeat of the hopes of reform cherished by Erasmus, More or Sadoleto, the foundation of the Society of Jesus, armed with solid classical culture and with the mystical meditation of the *Spiritual Exercises*, meant in a certain sense a second defeat, in that it showed the possibility of allying together and maintaining *both* inheritances. The institutional immobilism of the Catholic Church had discovered, at the midpoint of the century, the means to justify itself.

All this was not, of course, perceived at once by contemporaries – by the cardinals of the Roman Curia who hesitated to advise in favour of the creation of the new order, or by the episcopate of the various countries, who were not pleased to have to deal with an order created by Rome and exempt from their authority, an arrangement which had long been a subject of dispute and which was long to trouble the ecclesiastical world: or, finally, by the heretical opponents of Rome. Above all, the enterprise developed in an atmosphere of struggles so complex and so furious that it could not facilitate perception of the significance of the most original initiatives. With excommunications and doctrinal condemnations, pamphlets written in reply, and restatements misconstruing the adversary's view, the whole religious polemic, which kept on breaking out afresh as the dogmatism of the different sides became more rigid, was refreshed with anathemas and vehement accusations. In order to obtain a correct notion of the climate that prevailed we need to be able to judge what impression all this made on the contending parties. We can at least note a few important coordinates, at the extremes of expression and behaviour.

First of all, where terminology is concerned, there is the paradox of atheism. No period in Europe's intellectual history had ever made such free use of the epithet 'atheist'. This charge, which should have been the most dreadful of all, was hurled by everyone at everyone else, along with formulations in which the Pope or the founders of the new Churches were treated as emissaries of Satan. 'Atheists', 'disciples of Lucian', these expressions which flow from the pens of all the polemists, great and small, did not mean very much, though. They were, so to speak, terrific oratorical exaggerations, as Lucien Febvre has shown, in the French cultural context, to have been the case with Rabelais: and exaggerations all the more indecent in that fundamental belief was so utterly unlikely in a world wherein, from the cradle to the grave, in their family and occupational lives alike, men found themselves in a setting determined by Church institutions. Rabelais, accused a hundred times of being a freethinker, was a Christian: certainly not a Calvinist (as his Fourth Book well shows); perhaps tempted by Lutheranism, and, more certainly, in his own way, an Erasmian. In the France of Francis I, on the morrow of the Affair of the Placards, one humanist alone dared to write a treatise which portended disbelief (and this was published anonymously in 1537): namely, Bonaventure des Périers, the author of *Cymbalum mundi*. Made up of dialogues in which the participants, bearing the anagrammatized names of Luther, Calvin and Erasmus, discuss the divinity of Christ, the *Cymbalum* makes use of Origen's debate with Celsus, following the argument of the Greek philosopher so as to reject the human incarnation of an eternal God. With Jesus reduced to a human dimension, the Passion becomes an historical event, exceptional no doubt, but in no sense the Revelation described by the Gospel authors. Condemned by the Parlement of Paris and the Sorbonne in 1538, and by Calvin a little later in his treatise *De scandalis*, the *Cymbalum* soon disappeared from the bookstalls, inspiring no school: it was a bold effort by a solitary precursor whom all the circumstances doomed to failure in his own time ... But

the charge of atheism (or of Epicureanism) persisted nevertheless, waiting to receive more solid justification in the first
half of the seventeenth century.

More difficult to define, at the frontiers of all the orthodoxies,
are the practices of Satanist magic, and the consequent repres-
sions which were organized by the new Churches as well as
by the old one. The fight against diabolic errors was organized
by the Catholic Church with increased vigour in the final
decades of the fifteenth century, after the publication of the
Malleus maleficarum, by the Inquisitor Sprenger. Any simplistic
explanation of this increased repression, for which there is
evidence so far as Germany is concerned for the whole period
of humanism and the Reformation, as also in England
(especially after 1542), Spain, Italy and France, fails to account
for a large part of an elusive reality, known to us only from
demonological writings and judicial sentences, which is highly
complex in character. Neither reference to the evil promptings
of poverty, nor allusion to the influence exerted by a book
of great prestige, nor the reconstitution *à la* Michelet of a
clandestine counter-society opposed to the social order can
validly account for the widespread character of the phenomenon and for the multiplying of persecutions, wave upon
wave, which make one think of those contagions most likely
to invade a country or a region.

At any rate, these epidemics of witch-hunting which
ravaged Essex as well as Franche-Comté, the Duchy of Cleves
as well as Friuli, can be seen, as regards both the magistrates
who conducted them and the rural populations that were
decimated by them, as a major symptom of a crisis of consciences and of religious practices. The fact that all the
descriptions of witches' sabbaths include the Mass turned
upside down, and acknowledgement of an authority symmetrical with that which the priest exercised in his parish,
does not merely recall those medieval festivals at which such
inversions were carried out once a year, but, still more,

testifies to the liveliness of a religious sensibility which, going far beyond the speculations and movements fostered by the humanist reformers, was dissatisfied with the practices imposed upon it and found outlets in conduct which the Church repressed with all the more vigour because the guilty ones were, in this case, poor old women, supposed to be dispensers of good and evil in their villages – who were certainly easier to condemn and send to the stake than those persons of quality, bourgeois and nobles, who might be surprised in some evangelical gathering. Johann Wier, a Rhineland physician who dared to publish, in 1563, a big book in which he discussed and condemned witch-hunts such as he had witnessed for many years in Western Germany, does not conceal either the pressure brought to bear on suspects by magistrates who were convinced that they were fulfilling a vital religious mission, or the social purgation constituted by the sentencing and elimination of witches, male and female, in tens and hundreds, scapegoats of a constraint and a dissatisfaction that affected both the Church and the social order.

Inevitably little-known and hard to reconstruct, since in many regions the magistrates had the trial proceedings burned along with the accused, these witch-hunts cannot be correlated, as would be desirable, with the methods and chronology of repression against heretics. The two phenomena coincide roughly in time, but the field of action and the methods of investigation do not have a great deal in common. It would be naïve to make much of such facts as that heretics, whoever they might be, were called 'hell-hounds' by the orthodox; that Luther, when shut up in the Wartburg, fought against temptation by the Devil and threw an inkwell at a shadow; that Rome was called, by reformers who broke with Catholicism, the Devil's City. In all these formulations there is an element of that exaggeration which caused a writer who ventured to discuss transubstantiation to be described as an atheist, together with an element, no less important, of intimate conviction that Satan is present in this world of ours and has many effective means of bringing mankind to perdition through his temptations – among these being the pride of a person who presumes to set up a new Church, or to defend the errors of the old one.

What is essential here is the behaviour of the principal personages involved: the secular magistrates to whom the Churches entrusted the task of tracking down those suspected of witchcraft, werewolves, magicians of all sorts, and those who had made a pact with the Devil, and who carried out this mission with diligence, helped by the availability of good manuals like Sprenger's, and also by the denunciations that these magistrates received from the rural communities, which were vital factors in these affairs. Personalizing the sins of the community in an individual suspected of witchcraft because of his ancestry, or of what he talked about at evening gatherings, or of whispered tales about him, these communities found a sort of release in handing over to the judge, and then to the executioner, the person, male or female, whom they had cast out by means of their denunciation and of a few testimonies. What these practices of denunciation and purging reveal above all is an anxious religiosity, marked by an unacknowledged Manicheism (God versus Satan), fostered by the particularly crude dogmatic outlook which made up the basic framework of these people's conception of the world. Expressing the deep confusion of the humble laity and of the magistrates, the witch-trials, those proliferating persecutions, belong indeed to the margins of the protracted crisis which reached its paroxysm in the second third of the sixteenth century. They also show us, in their own way, the degree of fervour with which all sections of society, in different registers, faced this crisis: the converts who were first to take the step of abandoning the cult and practices of their ancestors and embrace a new faith, or the humanists who were accused on the basis of a gesture or of something questionable they had written and who faced exile or the gallows without flinching; the martyrs who made their stand in thousands all over Europe as persecutions got under way, or the wretched rustic witches briskly consigned to the flames; in all were found the conviction and courage that demonstrate that ideas have struck root in those 'living stones that are men' (Rabelais).

Chapter 3

REGROUPINGS AND CONFRONTATIONS

(1560–1600)

THE second half of the sixteenth century is dominated by conflicts, with the sound of arms and the fury of embattled men spreading over the whole of Europe, in the East and in the West as well as in the Mediterranean, where Moslems and Christians were again at war with each other. These outbursts, in which politics and religion combined, forming alliances and multiplying encounters, have concealed behind their chronicles and their famous events the intellectual and spiritual developments which continued in this period more fruitfully than is obvious at first sight. Not everything in the history of these forty years in the life of Europe is to be reduced to wars, even in France, where the eight Wars of Religion were separated by periods of truce that were sometimes quite long. However, the secret life of the intellectuals, who were often persecuted and forced to take sides, is not so easy to reconstitute as in a more peaceful period, like the first half of the sixteenth century. On the other hand, situations of violence and desperate conflict caused the contending parties frequently to explain their attitudes, expounding the theory of their struggles or of their peacemaking endeavours. While this provided opportunities for doctrines to be re-defined – and sometimes to be enriched with contradictions which serve as excellent proof of how much their development was dependent upon the political and social context – it is clear enough, too, and was clear to contemporaries, that the recurrent dramas, the taking-up of arms and the bloodbaths that followed, had the effect of hardening hearts, and favouring a definite evolution (even though there were differences between countries in this respect) towards a hardening of political and Church institutions which broadly reflected a change in the intellectual climate that was even more pronounced than in the previous period, when the new Churches had been founded. True, groups of enthusiasts continued to wander about Europe proclaiming the approach of better times, and there were still many humanists, expressions of their movement's 'second wind', who continued to plead for unity or for peaceful reconciliation between the antagonists. But stubborn division prevailed, even in the truces that were signed at the end of each major crisis. A century which had opened (for the great ones, the rich and powerful of this world, at any rate) with the enchantments of the great discoveries, dispersing the melancholy of the late Middle Ages, ended in the passion of regroupings that could not have been harsher in their implications.

I. CONSTRAINTS AND DEPENDENCES

The changes which it is hardest to grasp were those affecting the professional activities of scholars and humanists. If it was the case that love of good literature and of the new sciences was a source of profit only for the major figures during the first decades of the century, it seems that this was even more so after 1550–60. Research in ancient texts and exploration of little-known areas of knowledge provided decidedly less sustenance than before, and those who persisted in Renaissance pursuits were obliged to ensure their livelihood by carrying on some remunerative activity at the same time, unless their social position guaranteed them a comfortable unearned income.

It was not that the typical occupations of the early Renaissance period had disappeared. That extraordinary species, the publishers who were distinguished connoisseurs of Greco-Roman Antiquity, had not completely vanished: the greatest names in this field were perpetuated from generation to generation – the Plantins in Antwerp; the Manutius family, transferred from Venice to Rome, to serve the papal press; the Estiennes no longer in Lyon or Paris, since persecution had driven them away, but in Geneva, where Henri Estienne published in 1572 his *Thesaurus graecae linguae*. This wandering printer-scholar, Henri Estienne, offers a good example of the difficult conditions under which such craftsmen had to work, since he later found himself in trouble with the General Council of Geneva and had to withdraw, ruined, first to Montpellier and then to Lyon, where he died. On the scale of Europe as a whole, it was a time of ebb-tide, for these men, since printers unable to live in the absence of orders had to shut up shop owing to the diminished market, disturbed by wars, even in the major centres.

As Montchrestien appreciated, somewhat later, when he meditated on these long-lasting troubles, which entailed unemployment for the workmen and ruin for their employers, the decline of the printing trade was due to several concurrent causes. There was the slowing-down of production due to the quality of the books that had been produced: 'Since the revival of letters, libraries have been furnished with books, so that many of these remain, even though, owing to the ravages of war, many have been destroyed. This is an article that does not wear out like a garment.' Then there was the tailing-off of production of classical works, with translation and commentary, as the resources in manuscripts possessed by the monasteries and libraries of the Middle Ages were exhausted. After dealing with the classics of Antiquity, the romances of chivalry, the *fabliaux* and the theological writings of the Middle Ages, the activity of reproduction in printed form came to a standstill. Plutarch's *Parallel Lives*, translated by Amyot, which was published in 1559 and soon reissued,

in 1565 and 1567, found a place on the shelves of many a
library: but thereafter silence fell for a long time.

Finally, the printing trade suffered from international
competition, which soon undermined some centres that had
been prosperous at the beginning of the century. In Germany
books are the principal commodity sold at fairs, and a highly
profitable one, says Montchrestien, and the Flemings employ
non-specialist workers for the minor tasks in book-production,
which enables them to sell more cheaply those books 'which
are in very wide demand and therefore sell very readily',
while the printers in Geneva shamelessly pirate first editions
(which at that time were not protected by any laws). A great
printing centre like Lyon, which in mid-century was publishing works that found a market everywhere in Europe, thus
fell rapidly into decline. In 1591 a Lyon publisher (quoted in a
recent study) deplored the disaffection of his clients in Paris:
'the booksellers are very irritated with us . . . and say they no
longer need books from Lyon.' The good old days when the
publisher of scholarly works could bring out a dozen books a
year and welcome famous men of learning to his workshops
as proof-readers were now over and gone. The trade became
harder and harder to carry on, bankruptcies were frequent,
hunting for regular and reliable orders more necessary. The
careful craftsman's approach gave way to new methods which
accorded a clearer priority to the economic aspects of this
still novel commodity, which was bartered as much as it was
sold, and which was given away, exchanged and, above all,
lent, so reducing sales still further.

In teaching, too, there were perceptible changes, due both
to the exceptional difficulties attending instruction in a period
when the suspicion engendered by the ideological conflicts
created around every teacher a constant risk of losing his job,
so careful were educational institutions to preserve themselves
from heterodox influences, and also to the meandering path
followed by the careers of individual intellectuals, since

scientific activity was being carried on in an unstructured ideological framework wherein everyone tried, with difficulty, to make his way, practising two or three disciplines at once, teaching one but not the other, without any spirit of specialization in the present-day sense of the word. The theologians themselves, watchdogs of orthodoxy in their own domain, were not immune, even after the conclusion of the Council of Trent, from deviations and waverings that revived the major debates of the first half of the century. We have only to note the time taken by the Roman Curia to establish the *ne varietur* text of the Catholic Vulgate (from 1561 to 1590), the conflicts between scholar-cardinals in the time of Gregory XIII, with some advocating minor corrections inspired by the work of Erasmus while others stood by the traditional versions, and, finally, the last-minute remorse which led to the first edition, published in 1590, being withdrawn and replaced by the definitive text that was given to the public in 1592.

In everyday practice, the fact that the content of teaching had become less certain caused careers to proceed unsteadily, even when tragedy did not intervene, as in the case of the most illustrious of the French scholars and humanists of this third generation, Pierre de la Ramée (Petrus Ramus), philosopher and mathematician. A Platonist, he became well-known through his strongly anti-Aristotelian *Aristotelicae animadversiones*, condemned immediately after its appearance in 1544, as a result of which the author was forbidden to teach philosophy. However, as he enjoyed the protection of Cardinal Charles de Lorraine, Ramus was able to continue his mathematical studies and even to obtain the headship of the Collège de Presles in 1545. Still better, a few years later, he joined the Collège Royal (Collège de France) as Professor of Rhetoric and Philosophy, and drew around him a number of disciples who worked with him in mathematics and logic. Then, in 1561, he was converted to Calvinistic Protestantism. Thereafter he came up against furious opposition from the theologians of the university. On several occasions during the civil wars he had to suspend his teaching, leave the capital and go into hiding, either near the capital (at the Abbey of Royaumont) or in the provinces. Eventually, between 1568 and 1570, he left France to visit the high places of Protestantism – Strasbourg, Basle, Zürich, Heidelberg, Geneva – and worked for a time with Bullinger in Zürich on theological problems, particularly the Lord's Supper. When he returned to Paris he was deprived of his chair at the Collège Royal, and in August 1572 he was murdered, in the Massacre of St Bartholomew's Eve, by one of his Catholic enemies.

There were many others who, though their fate was not as tragic as this, nevertheless suffered painful tribulations. Suspicion and threats made necessary travels that were very different from those of the humanists and scholars of earlier times – veritable exilings and transplantations, which had the effect of shifting the centres of French learning to Geneva, the Rhine towns and Holland. These 'graftings' abroad, easily effected, were propitious to new exchanges. Joseph Justus Scaliger, who fled from France in 1572 but returned later, settled at the end of the century in Leyden, where the municipality offered him an academic appointment – in that Holland which was beginning to play the role of hospitable place of refuge for such men. But the French were not the only ones driven to pursue a nomadic existence during the forty years when war raged all around, in Scotland as in the Low Countries. George Buchanan, the great Scottish Latinist who had studied in France, and taught for a time in Paris and in Bordeaux when Montaigne was a student, subsequently returned to his own country as tutor to Mary Queen of Scots and her son James. The diffusion of Ramus's anti-Aristotelian doctrines all over Europe took place partly as a result of this mobility of the scholars who, in this centre or that, found employment in teaching them. A Dane, Andreas Krag, published 'Ramist' works in Basle, Rudolf Snellius commented on Ramus's dialectic and arithmetic at Leyden after 1578, William Temple discussed Ramus's dialectic at Cambridge, and Thomas Hood was inspired by the same master in his teaching of theoretical and practical mathematics in London in the 1580s.

Two social groups took over the task, so to speak, of continuing the work of the humanists, and this showed how the field of recruitment of scholars had been broadened and how their way of life had changed. In the first place there were the courtiers, in the widest sense of the word, who made up the entourage of the princes and who manifested the same interest as their sovereigns in the world of science and letters. In the little courts of Germany and Scandinavia, where the frenzy of theological dispute had died down somewhat since the Peace of Augsburg, humanist and scientific traditions survived and, here and there, inspired the activity of well-born noblemen and of scholars generously paid by donors who were keen to display their intellectual interests. Tycho Brahe, a protégé of King Frederick II of Denmark, was able to build his observatory at Uraniborg, on the Sound, thanks to royal largesse, and when he found himself no longer in favour with Denmark's new king he transferred himself, with some of his instruments, to the Emperor Rudolf II's court at Prague, where he trained in astronomical observation his pupil the Swabian Kepler, who was to continue his work during the first third of the seventeenth century. Similarly, Pierre de Ronsard found Charles IX and Henri III dispensers of protection and pensions until his death in 1585. Henri III surrounded himself, indeed, with writers who formed a little academy of polite letters – Antoine de Baïf, Sainte-Marthe, Salluste du Barthas, Amyot – and their company was cultivated by gentlefolk who took pride in their knowledge of literature and wanted to participate in literary life, such as the Abbé de Paimpont (Vaillant de Guélis). In a different way, around Elizabeth of England, poets like Spenser (secretary to a bishop, and then to the Lord Deputy of Ireland) and Sidney set the tone for many minor writers, little-known today, who freely imitated them and helped to form a lively intellectual milieu: even, and especially, when Spenser criticized court life in his *Mother Hubbard's Tale* he continued to play this leading role.   ^

More important than the courtiers, though, were the group made up of jurists, magistrates and advocates who were able to devote the leisure allowed them by a not too busy profession to pursuing work of a scientific or literary order. This phenomenon was very marked in France, but seems to have existed all over Western Europe. The lawyers, who were the first beneficiaries of the humanist instauration, in so far as the re-establishment of Roman law meant extensive discussions concerning principles of law and differences between forms of jurisprudence and customs, gradually became the continuators of humanism – both through professional necessity and through their appetite for knowledge, which the crises did not kill. As yet there has been no complete listing of the lawyers who won themselves a name in the world of learning in the middle of the sixteenth century, in such countries as Germany, England and Italy. The foundation of the Accademia della Crusca in Florence in 1582 reflected the need experienced by the learned, magistrates and others, to meet periodically for discussion in common of their researches and their problems. The Chamber of Rhetoric called the Eglantine, which functioned in Amsterdam in the same period, served the same purpose. In the case of France the proliferation of humanistic works by men from these circles was extraordinary, as may be judged by their productions in 1560–80 alone. From the registrar Jean du Tillet to the *présidents* Christophe de Thou, his son Jacques-Auguste, and Claude Fauchet, and including the advocates Bodin, Versoris, and Advocate-General Du Faur de Fibrac (who ended his career as a Councillor of State, after representing the King of France at the Council of Trent), together with teachers of law whose fame transcended the frontiers of France – Cujas, François Hotman and Daneau – there was a whole long series of prolific writers who were not content to write in their professional domain alone. As polemists they took their stand during the Wars of Religion, forming the framework of the 'third party' of the Gallicanists and *Politiques* (except in those cases when, as Protestants, they had, like François Hotman, to flee the country). As lovers of history they competed with those writers of varied talents (also educated in law) who were re-writing the annals of the kingdom (Girard du Haillan and François Belleforest) and seeking in a new presentation of history a source of justification for their patriotism. Among them were Etienne Pasquier, the first volume of whose *Recherches de la France* appeared in 1560: it was reissued at the beginning of the seventeenth century, substantially complemented with further volumes and preceded by an admirable preface in which he spoke loftily of his task: 'Writing here not for myself but for my France . . .' and being inspired by the wish that 'this gift that I give to my France may bring her profit and contentment'. There was also Claude Fauchet, whose *Recueil des antiquités françaises* was published in 1579.

A considerable number of these learned lawyers had long been meeting at the home of Président Henri de Mesmes, who, especially after being disgraced in the reign of Henri III, devoted his life to 'the study of good books' and the assembling of 'learned minds', studying the sciences and comparing the works of different writers, as dedications and expressions of thanks amply testify. In the 1560s Henri Estienne, Jean Bodin and Michel de l'Hospital frequented his library, which was reputed to be one of the finest in Europe. Later on, these meetings were held at the home of Jacques-Auguste de Thou, another great collector of books and rarities, 'from which he did not gain so much for his own work as from the advice of learned men, especially Pierre and François Pithou, Anthoine Oisel', and many others. There took shape in this milieu of learned lawyers, renewing the *sodalitates* of the first humanists, a particularly fertile type of regular meeting at which exchange of information, reading of letters and lending of books were the principal activities: the initial form of a movement that was to take an almost institutional turn, and to dominate to a large extent the new scientific developments of the first decades of the seventeenth century. In general, this diversification of the social functions assumed by scholars outside the ranks of churchmen testified to the influence that these activities had acquired and the prestige they had retained despite all the risks associated with them.

The second factor which contributed to a partial renewal of intellectual activity was the rise of national literatures which the Reformation, in its striving to bring the laity closer to the forms of worship and to a more immediate understanding of Scripture, had been preparing long since: everyone knows how important were the translations of the Bible into the vernaculars and the impulsion they gave to writers in every country. In 1549, in France, Joachim du Bellay, taking up on behalf of French what Petrarch had said about Italian, published his *Défense et illustration de la langue française*, a plea for poetry and literature composed in the vulgar tongue. Fifteen years later, Henri Estienne resumed in a more subtle way the argument against the hindering primacy accorded to Latin, in his *Traité de la conformité du langage français avec le grec*. But these works by theoreticians, significant as they were, are less relevant to our present subject than the abundant production of books – literary even more than scholarly – which conferred prestige upon the national literatures to which they belonged, and enlarged the possibilities of expression open to writers. This rise of national literatures was certainly an all-European phenomenon, observable even in the central and eastern parts of the Continent, where it was encouraged by humanists who chose to deal even with traditional literary themes in their mother-tongue, as in the case of Jan Blahoslav, the Czech translator of the New Testament, who published in 1567 a work *Against the Foes of the Muses* in Bohemia, where many writings of religious polemic, satirical songs and evangelical texts were also published, notably by the Moravian Brethren. In Romania and Hungary it was religious writing – by the Calvinists especially – that made up the stock of publications in the national language. Poland, however, seems to have shown the greatest vitality, with political poems, comedies, religious pamphlets (Calvinist, Lutheran and Catholic), and a great lyric poet, Jan Kochanowski, who spent some years in the West. By a curious paradox, neither Italy, 'mother of arts and letters', nor Germany, where Luther had standardized the German language for the first time, were particularly rich in their contribution to *this* epoch.

Italy, which had possessed her own models since Petrarch and Dante, lived, so to speak, at a more advanced stage than the rest of Europe, and there a number of minor poets wrote in the manner of Petrarch, producing tales and *novelle*, while the first treatises on courtesy (like that by Guazzo, in 1574) carried on the work of Castiglione's *Cortigiano*, but no one genre was predominant in literature, as were elsewhere the theatre or the novel. In Germany, too, where scholarly and theological studies continued to fill the shelves of the bookshops, no clear-cut orientation was to be seen in the national literature. In Spain, however, where the romances of chivalry, especially *Amadis des Gaules*, drawn from medieval subject-matter and circulated in thousands of copies, enjoyed greater success than anywhere else in Europe, a specific novel-like literature developed, in the form of imaginary confessions, telling of the rogueries of the nomad population of beggars and vagabonds who were so numerous in that country. This was the 'picaresque novel', the original model for which was provided by the *Life of Lazarillo de Tormes, His Fortunes and Adversities*, published in 1554 at Burgos and Alcalá. The last years of the century saw the appearance of the *Life of the Rogue Guzmán d'Alfarache*, by Mateo Alemán. Both books, which were quickly translated and spread all over Europe, were the precursors of the flowering of the picaresque novel in the seventeenth century, in the time of Quevedo (*Don Pablos, the Sharper of Segovia*, 'pattern of vagabonds and glass of swindlers'), Cervantes (*Colloquy of the Dogs* and *Exemplary Novels*) and Francisco López de Úbeda (*La Pícara Justina*). There was, to be sure, the theatre, at writing for which Cervantes tried his hand as a young man – a popular theatre, distantly descended from the Italian *commedia* of the Renaissance, which public taste caused to lean towards the *farsas* and *comedias* that foreshadowed the successful works of Lope de Vega. But to a greater degree than this (and leaving mystical writings aside), it was the picaresque novel, with its vitriolic evocation of a society dominated by the *pícaro* and the *hidalgo*, that constituted the Spanish national genre in literature.

In France the situation was less clear-cut, since poetry and historical writing shared almost equally the favour of writers and of the public. On the one hand there were the historians who set themselves to reconstitute the monarchical continuity of the nation's past, and on the other the poets of the Pléiade, the oldest of whom, like Ronsard and Du Barthas, wrote during the civil wars discourses upon the woes of the time, so deeply did the Wars of Religion mark the generation that experienced them. The composition and publication of national histories based upon medieval chronicles and memoirs was, moreover, not something specifically French – far from that. The same trend was to be found, though perhaps less accentuated than in France, in most of the countries of Europe: in Hungary (Schesaeus, *Ruinae pannonicae*, 1571), Germany (Turmayer, *Baierische Chronik*, 1566), Scotland, (Buchanan,

Rerum scoticarum historiae, 1580), Bohemia (Prokop Lupáč z Hlavačova, *Rerum bohemicarum ephemeris*, 1584), etc.

The most powerful development of a national literary genre was manifested, it would seem, in Elizabethan England, where a slow flowering of the theatre went forward during the whole of this *fin de siècle*. In the law schools, the Inns of Court, the students performed plays; and the London of 1590 possessed eight playhouses where citizens and nobles, sailors and merchants gathered, their preference, loudly expressed, tending toward plays that evoked recent history, rather than far-off events, and touched on the problems of the age. Among the many authors who succeeded in getting their works performed to good account there stand out Christopher Marlowe, who, before he was thirty, had written, between 1587 and 1592, *Tamburlaine*, *Dr Faustus*, *The Massacre at Paris* (dealing with St Bartholomew's Eve), and, finally, a drama of English history, *Edward the Second*. The master-figure in this realm of the theatre was, of course, William Shakespeare, who produced, for over twenty years, between 1590 and 1611, his cycle of national historical tragedies, his dramas of madness (*Macbeth*), and his fantasies such as *The Winter's Tale* – a whole world in which the past and present greatness of England appears, with even, here and there, a eulogy of her remarkable ruler at that time. In his Globe Theatre in London, and also later, retired to Stratford, Shakespeare exalts, with unfailing success, English national feeling.

This affirmation of national literatures, which certainly cannot be separated from the conflicts that were tormenting Europe, was important in itself, because it created for intellectual life some relationships that the previous period had not known; or not to the same extent, at least. It meant, on the one hand, a creative opening offered to whoever wished to go beyond the stage that had been accomplished, in which the reading and interpretation of the works of Antiquity, the enrichment resulting from the discovery of Greco-Roman civilization, constituted the essence of the strictly humanistic conception. It meant, too, a change in the relations between the author and his public, in so far as the generalized employment of national languages implied an exclusion, enclosing the exchange between writer and reader within a restricted cultural area. Latin, the language common to all the humanists, had previously enabled the writer to communicate with anyone who had mastered the 'humanities', and the greatest travellers of that time have been legitimately described as 'European', or even *heimatlos*, beginning with Erasmus (whom J. Huizinga tried, not without some contrivance, to claim as a Dutchman). In the second half of the sixteenth century, literary nationalism entailed a new kind of dialogue, with a smaller audience on the plane of Europe, in so far as this 'aristocracy' of scholars and men of letters was not polyglot, but a larger audience inside the nation in which the particular idiom employed could be read by more sections than knew Latin. In this way a specialization of literary genres became defined, but at the same time a whole range of new themes was brought within the scope of intellectual activity, themes bound up with the native traditions that had been submerged for almost a century by the tide of classical studies. In the end this transformation inevitably led to attempts, which soon became numerous, to establish new lines of communication between these triumphant national languages: translations of recently published works became a new genre, and a new trade appeared, that of the translator, who took his place alongside those other labourers in the field of book-production, the printer-publishers. The frequency and importance of translations enables us to appreciate the play of cultural influence between one country and another – the influence of Spain, with her picaresque novel, upon France and England; of Italy upon those same countries, with her treatises on courtesy and good manners; and so on. It is in the light of all these changes that we can measure the distance separating

Budé, the commentator on Cicero, from Etienne Pasquier, the explorer of old Frankish chronicles; or even Colet, the master of the classics, from Thomas Hood, addressing his audience of merchants.

A third factor, and not the least important, which acted strongly to shape new conditions of existence for intellectuals in the second half of the sixteenth century was the series of religious and political wars which threw much of Europe into confusion, from the north-west of France to the Netherlands and Scotland. It is not sufficient merely to note that these conflicts compelled many a writer to keep silent or to observe a caution justified by the zeal of the combatants in exterminating both their opponents and those who seemed to be waiting to see who would win. The example of Montaigne, in no hurry at all to publish his *Essays*, and leaving his travel notes on Germany and Italy in a folder until after his death, is very well known. This aspect of the situation, however, hides a reality of greater importance, namely, the appearance of many writings which, though produced as occasional manifestoes and comments on current events, nevertheless contributed to introduce new subjects for reflection which had a serious future before them. The abundant production of this type of literature hardly slowed down even after the coming of peace, and it gave rise to many new vocations and some new genres: the admonition, the discourse in the form of a vindictive pamphlet harping upon treasons and dangers, either in booklets a few pages in length or else, where the writer had more to say, as an indictment sustained by powerful arguments and attaining the dimensions of a substantial book – the masterpiece of this genre being the *Satyre Ménippée*. As one war followed another in all that part of Europe that had been set ablaze, the same conjunction of religious and national antagonisms determined a single ideological battlefield for Protestants and Catholics alike. To be sure, the most dramatic events in each theatre of conflict played a decisive role, giving a distinctive tone to the writings published in each country: the Massacre of St Bartholomew's Eve and the excesses of the League in France, the execution of Egmont and the atrocities perpetrated by the Duke of Alva in the Low Countries, the Scottish revolt against Mary Stuart and her execution in England. Nevertheless, in all of the war-torn countries (and beyond them, in so far as these polemics were read throughout Europe wherever the same problems had been experienced, as in the Empire, or were still to be feared), the same debates took place, focused essentially upon two closely related themes.

First, there was the assertion of a patriotic interest which transcended that of religious unity, which for so long had been considered of prime importance. This advance by a patriotic-monarchical ideology certainly cannot be separated from the conditions in which the struggles were being waged. In the Northern Netherlands the Calvinism of a vigorous minority was the cement of the unity of those provinces around the leadership of William the Silent in 1566, and of the secession decided on by Holland and Zeeland in 1576. In Scotland, when Queen Mary took a Catholic husband in the person of Darnley, in 1565, she aroused the indignation of Knox and the ministers of the Kirk, who preached against her and forced her, three years later, to flee to England and surrender to Elizabeth. But at the same time, these struggles caused a growth in the sense of national unity in face of the threats that might arise from conflicts in which the fortune of war was often capricious. When Catholic lords took up arms against their queen at Durham at the end of 1569, Elizabeth was able to suppress the rebellion without much difficulty, and struck hard at those responsible, so as firmly to establish her throne; eight hundred persons were executed, and punishment meted out to all the communities which had helped the rebels. Religious dissent, which enjoyed no very great support, mattered less in this instance than the attack on

monarchical authority. In the same way, the tergiversations of
Philip II and the Regent Margaret on the eve of the intervention by the *tercios*, the promises made in 1566 (amnesty,
abolition of the Inquisition), showed what sacrifices the King
of Spain, the champion of Catholicism, was prepared to agree
to in order to maintain his authority over that small part of
his immense domains, the distant Netherlands. Gradually,
everyone was bowing to the ruling notion that fatherland and
monarchy were one, and constituted a vital political fact which
it was of paramount importance to safeguard.

In this discussion the reflections of the French polemists
played a preponderant part. Having behind them the old
Gallican tradition which had counterposed, since the fourteenth century at least, the sovereignty of the King of France
to the power of the Papacy, those French magistrates and
statesmen who challenged the ultramontanist Catholics
found no difficulty in supporting their views with solid
references. Neither Michel de l'Hospital nor Gaspard de
Coligny, neither Etienne Pasquier, that persistent adversary
of the Jesuits, nor the lawyer Pierre de l'Estoile, had any
intention of letting the royal authority be subordinated to an
external power, even a religious one. Since the well-being of
the kingdom took precedence over the maintenance of
religious unity, the French Catholics thus found themselves
divided, in a way that gave men in other countries furiously to
think – in Italy, Spain and the Empire. The 'third party' of the
Politiques, always provided with excellent writers, well-
informed and eloquent, was able to support its positions with
substantial books such as the treatise on the *Libertés de l'église
gallicane* published by Pierre Pithou in 1594. Their arguments
proved all the more effective because the intransigent Catholic
party, already looked on as half-foreign because its leaders, the
Guises, were from Lorraine, did not hesitate, during the
crucial period 1589–98 to make use of Spanish funds and
Spanish soldiers, encamped in Paris itself, in order to promote

the triumph of their cause. The *Politiques*, among whom were both Protestants and good Catholics, had the chance to proclaim their loyalty to the Crown, to the King, and to the independence of their country. Fatherland and monarchy were one, and for the sake of maintaining the integrity of the kingdom some accommodation on the religious plane might well be agreed to: this consideration had already justified the zeal shown by these same *Politiques* in working for truces and agreements, such as the Colloquy at Poissy at the beginning of the civil wars.

The political debates that developed at the height of these wars also defined another problem, not perceivable in the same form in different countries, and which, in particular, was not perceived in the same way by all contemporaries as it was to be later. This was the idea of a contract, implicit rather than explicit, binding a sovereign to his subjects, as a function of his way of assuming the government of the realm. In this matter, too, the polemics in France did much to clarify the question, because the two contending parties each in turn utilized the body of theory according to which subjects are released from their duty of obedience when the king fails to respect the norms of equity or the fundamental laws of the given country: this was the theory of the tyrant king, invoked by the Reformed after the Massacre of St Bartholomew's Eve.

The first of these pamphlets (*Le Réveil-matin des Français, De furoribus gallicis*) denounced the tyrannical violence of the Valois, attacking the King as well as the Queen-Mother. Soon the jurists and theologians of the Protestant camp were arguing along the same lines – Théodore de Bèze in his *Droit des magistrats sur leurs sujets*, François Hotman in his *Franco-Gallia*. And the whole of Protestant Europe, as angry as Rome and Madrid were overjoyed, approved these well-based arguments, in which the King's perjury in relation to loyal subjects was presented as an act cancelling loyalty and allegiance and authorizing the Protestants to seek a different king, or even a different form of government. But when, after 1584, Henry of Navarre having become the legitimate heir to the throne in accordance with the Salic Law, the uncompromising Catholics wanted to prevent his accession to the throne, and came out against King Henri III himself when he favoured this succession, they took over that same theory of tyranny, and carried it even to the point of tyrannicide, with the murder of the King in 1589. In April of that year the Sorbonne had solemnly released the French from their oath of allegiance to their sovereign, and the Leaguer priest Jean Boucher called for 'the just abdication of Henri III', basing himself on the authority of Cardinal Bellarmine, who in previous polemics since 1584 had upheld against the Protestants the concepts of Rome's primacy and religious unity in Christendom. Outside France, the Dutch and Scots rebels went even further: putting into effect the same idea of a contract between a prince and his subjects, they claimed to exercise the subjects' right to choose another sovereign when the reigning one had become a tyrant, incapable of ruling justly. The Scots, inflamed by Knox's preaching, refused to obey their murderess Queen and proclaimed their intention to choose a new ruler, finding in George Buchanan, James VI's tutor, a defender of the choice they made – a choice soon regretted, so refractory did the pupil show himself to the lessons of his learned and pious *magister*. In Holland and Zeeland the line of development is still clearer. There, the fishermen and merchants of these little maritime provinces, resisting the tyranny of Spain, entrusted themselves to William of Orange, elected Stadtholder by their Estates, and founder of their independence: and they fought until 1648 to secure the recognition of their rights by Spain, the Empire and all Europe. Thus, the political setting in which the intellectuals had to express themselves and make their way became transformed: and this transformation was not a process external to them, since many among them took up positions for or against an evolution which dictated the conditions of their existence.

The changes brought about in these conditions were, as a whole, not necessarily beneficial to them, for the religious wars and the ideological confrontations they promoted had the ultimate consequence of strengthening monarchical power, to the detriment of freedom of expression, which had long been under threat. The predominant features of intellectual life in this period testify that that was so, along with the hardening of institutions which took place.

2. THE PREDOMINANT FEATURES OF INTELLECTUAL LIFE

To a certain extent the intellectual activities characteristic of the second half of the sixteenth century present no great originality. They continued the movement of the previous period, giving an impression of a petering-out of the impetus provided by earlier generations. This continuity calls for no learned explanation, in view of the conditions in which the disciples and descendants of those humanists and scholars who died in mid-century now had to work. Furthermore, when examining the course followed by publications during these troubled years, the historian is compelled to acknowledge that the directions marked out previously continued to attract writers and researchers. Translations and editions of the Greek and Latin authors of Antiquity had certainly become infrequent, apart from reprintings, but authors who still wrote in Latin were fairly numerous in every country. In the year of the St Bartholomew's Eve Massacre Henri Estienne published his Plutarch with a Latin translation; in 1574 Justus Lipsius brought out his edition of Tacitus, which was reissued many times thereafter; and in 1596 Pierre Pithou produced the first edition of Plato's *Phaedrus*. Besides these works in the established style there were Scaliger's *Poemata*, the writings of

Louis de Masures, the *Colloquia moralia* of the Dane Erasmus Michaelius Laetus, and the works of the astronomers Tycho Brahe and Kepler, *De admirabili proportione orbium caelestium*. The inspiration of Antiquity continued to be apparent, even when writers set themselves to translate into, or to write in, their own language. All this stock of big, fine books which had been built up during the century now ended was the common intellectual property of all who contributed to this scholarly culture. The impression of something permanently won is strengthened by the fact that the new education, especially in the colleges run by the Jesuits, utilized a great deal of this material for the upbringing of the young generation.

For researchers who were aged twenty or thirty in 1570 or 1580 assimilation of the culture of Antiquity no longer presented the exciting aspect of continuous discovery, renewed year by year as fresh publications revealed some hitherto little-known side of the civilizations of Greece and Rome. Even if not everything had yet been translated into the principal European languages, the main task had been accomplished with the establishment of a text and the publication of a critical edition of it in the original language, to which everyone could refer. Montaigne tells us of his disgust with college life and the methods used to teach the classical languages: he was able thereafter to spend ten years of his life closeted in his library, reading and annotating all those good authors whose works he had to hand, the companions of his solitude that was not really solitude. Nourished at the same sources as their predecessors, if not inspired by the same spirit of linguistic criticism, since philological endeavour was no longer so urgently needed, the humanists of the new generation readily engaged in commentary and transposition. One of them published his own *De rerum natura*, which was not a translation of Lucretius, but made use of all his arguments, together with some of the author's own. Another (Jan Zamoyski, in Cracow) emulated the method of which Budé was so fond, and published a study of the Roman Senate, *De senatu romano*, which needed to be read with reference to the political problems of Poland. Yet another published a new translation into German of Epictetus's *Encheiridion*, while in Antwerp a playwright composed a mythological drama, *Apollo en Pan*, which drew upon the rich resources of the Greco-Roman pantheon.

Thus, curiosity continued regarding the civilizations of Antiquity and the examples they offered: the interest taken in *opera moralia* – those by Plutarch, and others as well – was typical, even though this was not the predominant genre. Each humanist gathered honey in the garden that pleased him best. The Danes, of whom there was a prolific group in the 1560s, published pedagogic and moral poems, versions of the Psalms and learned studies like the *Idea medicinae philosophicae* by Sorensen (1571). Everywhere we find the same variety of inspiration, respecting neither our present-day classification of the sciences nor the need for specialization which was to be so often expressed later on. In the Italy where Tasso discoursed on the art of poetry and Palladio published his four books on architecture there also appeared the tales of Granucci and Erizzo, the discussions of Aristotle's philosophy by Patrizzi, the *novelle* of Bandello, and the translations of the *Odyssey* and the *Aeneid* into *ottava rima* made by Lodovico Dolce.

This modified continuity shown in the circles devoted to literature is observable also in the specially religious domain, which is occupied by marginal elements, the *Schwärmer* and other 'enthusiastic' sectaries, whom persecution and excommunication had not succeeded in eliminating, thanks to their perseverance and their ability to melt away in the depths of the cities and then re-emerge after a period of silence. Basically, their thinking was the same as before, being derived from the works left behind by the first masters in this field. Valentin Weigel, whom I have already mentioned, does not conceal his debt to Sebastian Franck and, especially, to Paracelsus: that physician-alchemist retained a great reputation, well beyond the circles of mystics who constituted the source of recruitment for the sects. Petrus Ramus had praised his empiricism, and his complete works were reissued several times towards the end of the century, in both Latin and German. A scholar in occult lore and for that reason respected even more in his capacity as a spiritual guide, Theophrastus Paracelsus continued to dominate those circles which were still seeking their own religious truth.

The little groups which came together and then broke up as their members moved around had one other point in common, namely, their hostility to the established theologians who claimed the right to impose *their* orthodox truth and did not shrink from ordering that the 'spirituals' be hunted down. Weigel thunders against them in his *Studium universale*: 'In the universities one fool teaches another, but whoever has not studied in the house of those people is called by them "self-taught",' and he adds, vindictively, in Latin: '*Frustra quaeritur extra cum magno labore quod in nobismet ipsis possidemus abundanter.*' In this continuing struggle the sects were not the losers. They learnt from the example of the Churches which had long known persecution, like the Bohemian Brethren, to trick the authorities, taking advantage of thinly populated areas and of the lack of funds available to those responsible for the costly business of repression. Their story is for this reason all the harder, and even impossible, to reconstruct. Their records (apart from those of the judicial proceedings taken against them) are confined to the packets of manuscript which the most powerful thinkers left behind when they died and which are now to be found scattered about in various libraries, many of them still awaiting identification, decipherment and critical study. And yet there can be no doubt as to the continuity preserved, for which there is evidence right on into the seventeenth century (down to Jakob Boehme and Johann

Valentin Andreae, in particular), the trends easiest to identify being those that at one time or another gave rise to a *political* problem, though they were not necessarily the most active or important.

Two movements of this nature can be briefly described here. In Western Europe, in the Northern Netherlands, which were exposed to all the variant forms of heterodoxy, Anabaptism of the peaceful sort made progress in the period following the fall of Münster. The Anabaptists of the Netherlands formed themselves in the middle years of the sixteenth century into two small Churches, one much like the other, but each with its own prophet. Under the leadership of Menno Simons, who died in 1559, the Mennonites followed a strictly 'spiritualist' line of conduct, refusing to subject themselves to any Church, but accepted the authority of the state, and this saved them from taking the dangerous path followed by their predecessors at Münster. In Menno Simons's sect discipline was somewhat severe, but they did not engage much in proselytism. Close to the Mennonites, geographically and as regards dogma, was the Church of David, founded by David Joris (who died in 1556), which also practised adult baptism, refused to accept any interference by political rulers in religious questions, and preached tolerance between Christians. Considering that the only true Church is the one that is persecuted, Joris denounced Calvin when he executed Michael Servetus. He was a fervent proselytizer and had to flee up the Rhine to escape arrest, ending his career in Basle, under an assumed name. The followers of David Joris nevertheless became numerous in Westphalia and, even more so in the Northern Netherlands (after 1581 the United Provinces), where the sects were welcomed and tolerated with a generosity that had no equivalent anywhere else in Europe. These two little Churches thus succeeded in continuing their existence far into the seventeenth century.

In the east of Europe the Socinian sect had a more eventful

fate. Its founders, Lelio and Fausto Sozzini, were Italians from Siena, who had to flee their country when persecution of unorthodox thinkers became intense. Lelio Sozzini (the name was latinized as Socinus) went to the great centres of the Reformation, meeting Calvin and Melanchthon, and also Castellio. When he died, at Zürich in 1562, he left his manuscripts to his nephew Fausto, who, after living for a time at Basle, went to Poland, where he joined the Anabaptist communities of that country, soon becoming their leader. In 1594 he published his *De Jesu Christo servatore*, containing the essence of a simple doctrine that denied the divinity of Christ, the Trinity, and the intervention of Providence in human affairs. The Passion was for him only an historical narrative, and the significance of religious ceremonies only symbolic. When he died, in 1604, Fausto Sozzini had recruited many disciples to his 'Church free from mysteries', and his influence transcended the frontiers of Poland – which had now, with the country's return to Catholicism, ceased to welcome his presence. But Socinianism, which enjoyed in the seventeenth century much greater prestige than in its founders' lifetime, survived without difficulty, especially in the United Provinces, where it coexisted with the Anabaptist sects. During his stay in Poland Fausto Sozzini appears to have played a far from negligible part also in the organization of the Polish Brethren, a sect categorized as Arian, anti-Trinitarian and pacifist, who founded the town of Raków and kept their place in Poland's popular religious life down to the middle of the seventeenth century.

The final manifestation of the fecundity in sects shown by the second half of the sixteenth century was the enigmatic Rosicrucian movement. We have proof of its existence in Germany, France and England at the beginning of the seventeenth century, but the origins of this sect of physicians who practised a sincere mysticism and made use of chemical therapy are utterly obscure. The writings of the well-known

Rosicrucian Johann Valentin Andreae sought to prove that these origins were remote, referring to a researcher in the fourteenth century who, he alleged, had travelled widely around the Mediterranean and brought back many medical secrets. As a branch grafted on to the tradition begun by Paracelsus this group devoted itself to medical practice, for the benefit of mankind, and became surrounded by an aura of mystery, an important element in its great reputation, which impressed Descartes himself.

On the other hand, we need to see as a new aspect of Europe's intellectual life the interest shown in witch-hunting, and the theoretical elaborations on this theme which appeared in great numbers in the last third of the century. Pamphlets and works written by lawyers and theologians accumulated at such a pace that the phenomenon commands attention, all the more so because it reveals the existence of a different view of the world, a complex of popular beliefs and practices in which Satanistic magic had its roots. The behaviour of the people and that of the magistracy is important for an overall study of the phenomenon. For our present purpose what demand examination are the theories which had the widest influence. There is no need to recall the well-known fact that prosecutions of rural witches multiplied in this period throughout Europe, from Southern Poland to the Basque country and from England to Tyrol and Friuli. Contemporaries themselves were aware of this, and chose to place the epicentre of the phenomenon in Germany – something which in the present state of documentation it is difficult either to confirm or to disprove. Some contemporaries gave facile explanations of this alleged fact, in which polemical passion played a part: thus, for Jean Boucher, a doctor of the Sorbonne and a famous Leaguer parish priest in Paris, it was 'that same Germany which produced the heresy of our times' that, naturally, also produced 'monstrosities of magic'. All who wrote about the matter regarded the hunting down of committed witches as the direct duty of every magistrate.

The treatises on demonology that appeared were not so evenly distributed as the prosecutions of witches seem to have been. Sprenger's large manual, written in fluid Latin, provided for all aspects of a thorough investigation, and so it is clear that the magistrates had no need of any other guide; while the theologians, though inevitably interested in the doctrinal aspect of the matter, had other preoccupations as well in this period of many-sided struggle against heretics of every sort. Pamphlets and substantial books on witchcraft and witches were not very numerous in several countries: for England MacFarlane mentions only three books in this period, two by George Gifford and one by Reginald Scot, apart from the treatise written by James VI of Scotland, published at the end of the century in Edinburgh, and reissued in London after its author had become James I of England. In the Low Countries only one work appeared, in 1599, but this was signed by a Grand Inquisitor, the Jesuit Delrio, who combined the equipment of a theologian and that of a magistrate: his *Disquisitiones magicae*, published at Louvain, caused far more sensation than many another work, if we are to judge by reprintings. In Italy, too, not many works of this nature saw the light. A translation of Bodin's treatise on witchcraft, which was published in Venice, went through three editions, in 1587, 1589 and 1592: *La Demonomania de gli stregoni cioè furori et malie de'demoni, col mezo de gl'huomini*, the translator being Ercole Cato. Of course, the magistrates had at their disposal manuals produced for use by the Inquisition (*Sacro arsenale, overa prattica dell'officio della santa inquisitione*), which gave much attention to the measures to be taken against magicians, witches and other criminals of the same sort.

On the whole, only two countries possess a large body of literature on this subject, namely, Germany and France, where magistrates and theologians, Catholic and Protestant alike, were united in denouncing witchcraft and expounding with zeal the many reasons they saw as justifying witch-hunts. In these two countries a dozen works, respectable by virtue both of their signatories and of their weight, set out the authors' experiences and their dogmatic conceptions with regard to the witch question. True, they were not all equally important. In Germany, Erastus (1581), Ewich (1584) and Binsfeld (1589) were undoubtedly the writers who were read the most, often even outside their own cultural area. In France, alongside soon-forgotten *minores* like Benoist, Crespet and Massé, two theologians and an advocate who were not among the most convincing of their kind, some talented writers came to prominence, and their works were soon translated into several languages. The first of these, who made his mark with a vehement attack on the Rhenish physician Johann Wier, was Jean Bodin, a well-known jurist, author of a substantial treatise on political science, the *Six Livres de la république* (in which theories of climatic influence in history and of national sovereignty were set forth); he was regarded as an eminent magistrate whose learning was limitless: economics, the occult, astronomy, theology (Jewish, Reformed and Catholic) . . . He frequented the library of M. de Mesmes, and wrote well and clearly when he chose, though he also knew how to dissimulate, as is shown by the story of his secret treatise *Heptaplomeres*, more remote from Christianity in any form than *Cymbalum mundi*, which did not become known (in manuscript) until after his death. But this Angevin magistrate, who had over a long period carried out investigations in cases of witchcraft, devoted a big book to discussing his experience and the lessons he derived from it. His treatise, published in 1580, *La Démonomanie des sorciers*, enjoyed a reputation as flattering as that of Sprenger's *Malleus*. His refutation of the arguments adduced by Wier to bring illness into the explanation of the phenomena attributed to witches made an impression on officiating magistrates, who sometimes quoted it in their judgements.

The Protestant pastor Lambert Daneau, author of two treatises on witches, spells, poisons and charms, was no less highly esteemed in this sphere than the Dominican Michaelis, prior of Saint-Maximin in Provence, author of *Pneumologie, discours des esprits en tant qu'il est de besoin pour entendre et resoudre la matière difficile des sorciers*, published in Paris in 1587. Michaelis was long regarded as a specialist to be consulted in cases of demonic possession, even twenty-five years after his book appeared. This abundance of works seeking to demonstrate to the educated public the large extent of Satan's power in the world and the need to take action to remedy it deserves to be placed in a wider setting. In a period in which theological polemic around heresies was pursued unremittingly, the provision of legal and doctrinal justification for the hunting down of witches constituted a minor phase of debates which had been going on for half a century. The fact that these demonstrations were undertaken by men who belonged to the world of scholarship and culture, but were also members of institutions, is not without bearing on our present theme. As defenders of orthodoxy in the law-courts, universities and monasteries they saw themselves as playing a fine role, with a good conscience, in the fight against Satan, the arch-enemy, and against poor defenceless women who were dragged unmercifully to the stake.

This flourishing of repressive thought has to be considered on two planes. On the one hand we have the dull discourses of demonologists saturated in theological and legal knowledge, heaping up justifications for the witch-hunt. Jean Bodin quoted largely from Aristotle and Apuleius, as well as from the Old and New Testaments and from St Paul and St Augustine. But the most weighty of these quotations are less significant than the specific knowledge of Satanism to which they refer, in relation either to the material furnished by Sprenger or to the cases they have personally conducted. Bodin, Delrio and Godelmann base themselves on accounts which are similar, if not identical, of the rites of Satanism (the witches' sabbath, evil spells, pacts with the Devil) and of the powers ascribed to the Supreme Tempter, capable of going beyond the bounds of nature to gratify his ambitions. All of them argue by way of the duplication of evidence, showing jubilant satisfaction when they can note a concordance between the terms defined by the first theoreticians of the subject and the observations made during interrogations and while the accused were being tortured. All these demonstrations make play with the same arsenal of spells and supernatural powers, recurring again and again in the disorder of arguments that are often confused: the spell that inflicts impotence, the werewolf phenomenon, the ride to the witches' sabbath and the Devil-worshipping ceremony, the gift of tongues, the use of powders, ointments and fats, charms and curses. The very strangeness of these practices, as denounced and confessed, commented on and repeated, is proof, in the eyes of the demonologists, of the 'great knowledge and experience possessed by the demons', and irrefutable proof of the validity of the fight being waged against them.

On the other hand, these lengthy justifications of the witch-hunt tell us about the position the victims were in and the way they behaved. Subjected to abrupt questioning which was conducted according to well-established patterns, it was impossible for them to escape condemnation. Their interrogations reflected, to a large extent, the convictions held by the judge, but they also echoed a whole complex of beliefs and practices which, though far from being all Satanic, were condemned *in toto* by the magistrates and theologians, defenders of an order in which a recognized place had always been accorded to Satanic forces of subversion that must be crushed. In line with good, orthodox belief, in which God and the Devil confront one another, the peasant women accused of witchcraft found themselves treated as criminals for having a conception of creatures and things which their judges reprobated as a whole. They cured people with herbs and decoctions of which they knew the secret, though they had no right to treat the sick. They respected, and caused others to respect, immemorial rites concerning the sowing of kitchen-gardens, the pruning of trees and vines, the reaping of harvests, but they could not explain these rules, the significance of which Paracelsus had sought to discover while observing them. They acted to bring relief when an animal was sick, or in times of storm or drought, without any other accounting for their powers than that they possessed certain secrets of nature. The condemnation, handed down from on high, made no subtle distinctions, since participation in the witches' sabbath, and even the pact with Satan, were either quickly confessed or else proved by the ordeals of water or of the finding of the 'witch's mark'.

Apart from the revealing reports of witch-trials, the demonological theories that were current argue in a way that conceals a cultural reality which it is hard for the historian to grasp, namely, the distance between the behaviour and conceptions characteristic of the lower orders of the countryside and those of the townsfolk, and even the difference in mental structures between one social milieu and another. The major demonstrations undertaken by the demonologists do at least enable us to glimpse the existence of this gap, and to divine, by careful deduction, by abstraction rather than direct apprehension, what may have been the cultural forms of the lives led by these countryfolk. It was a different world, repressed and held in leading-strings all the more vigorously, perhaps, because the 'little people' of town and country alike had been speaking up for themselves for the previous fifty years. This correlation has never been proved with rigour, but the hypothesis may well be put forward, since it would make clearer the obsession with demonological theories in the two countries where religious dissensions had turned most quickly into armed conflicts.

There remain to be considered, in this continuity which implies constant renewals, the scientific work that was carried on in the spheres which proved the most fruitful in this period, namely, mathematics and astronomy. The matter of the reform of the calendar by Pope Gregory XIII deserves mention first, in so far as it illustrates the ideological antagonisms that obtained in a sphere where calculation seems to us nowadays to enjoy a general consensus. The errors made in the fixing of the date of Easter each year in accordance with the so-called Julian calendar had long been known to calculators as well as to theologians. When after six years' work, a papal commission proposed, in 1576, a reform by which the ten days' gap the mathematicians had shown to exist could be made up, at least one university, that of Paris, protested against the adoption of a reform which would mean admitting that the Church had been mistaken. However, the suppression of the ten days, provided for in a Bull of February 1582, was accepted by the Catholic states, without too much difficulty, in December of that year. But the Eastern Churches refused to come into line. and so did the Protestant states: Denmark, the United Provinces, England, Sweden. In the divided Empire the Lutheran theologians fulminated against Rome's devilish work and rejected the decision taken by Rudolf II to apply the reform to the German states as a whole. (The disparity in chronology that resulted continued until the eighteenth century.) A fine example of the subordination of scientific work to the dogmatic requirements of institutional systems, the protracted dispute over the calendar (in which it was the Papacy that was in the right) also illustrates the tensions that could arise between the secular power and the Churches: at the height of the dispute in Germany the theologians of Tübingen accused the Emperor of idolatry, a crime that would release his subjects from their duty of allegiance – as would, elsewhere, the disruption of religious unity.

Two mathematicians, two figures symmetrical with each

other, played an important role in scientific activity. One, Girolamo Cardan, a pupil of his father, a lawyer and mathematician, and of Pomponazzi at Padua, became known in 1545 through his publication at Nuremberg of a treatise on algebra, *Ars magna*. After travelling around Northern Europe for a long time, in England, the Netherlands and Germany, and teaching in Italy, at Milan, Pavia and Bologna, Cardan eventually settled in Rome, where he lived by practising as a physician and a mathematician until his death in 1576. Cardan aimed at achieving universal knowledge through mathematics. He eagerly studied the occult sciences, the 'hidden' properties of numbers. His passion for algebra came direct from the speculations of Golden Numbers which are to be found especially in his big book published at Basle in 1570: *Opus novum de proportionibus numerorum, motuum, ponderum, sonorum aliarumque rerum mensurandarum*. A writer who is hard to read and to follow in his researches, which embrace all branches of knowledge and freely mingle politics, morality, the interpretation of miracles and calculations, Cardan founded no school of thought. His books such as *De subtilitate*, published at Basle in 1560, which Ronsard read, became known throughout Europe, but this physician-cum-mathematician of great renown had no immediate successors.

In this respect he was unlike Ramus, whose pleas and proofs in favour of the restoration of mathematics bore fruit for a long time after his passing – an influence all the more remarkable in that Ramus, unlike Cardan, made no discoveries and has no place in the traditional history of the sciences. Ramus sought to show the importance of mathematics by way of empirical observation of the activity of merchants and of everyday life, in the same period in which Bernard Palissy, a craftsman 'having no Latin' or any university education, was preparing to develop a dialogue between theory and practice, in opposition to sciences created in the study 'by the imagination of persons who have never practised anything'. Ramus observed

the work of the Paris bankers and travelled to Nuremberg –
a city whose mathematical fame went back to Albrecht
Dürer (*Treatise on the Circle*, 1525), Johann Schöner and
Willibald Pirckheimer – to pursue his studies among the makers
of optical apparatus. His refutations of Aristotle in the
Scholae physicae were based, page by page, upon concrete
observation. In his travels, fleeing from persecution, Ramus
compared the teaching of mathematics in different universities,
and gave the palm to the Germans (who accorded special
attention to calculation, he thought, on account of their
mines) and to the Italians (where the reasons were less
obvious). 'Ramist' doctrine spread, after 1572, in a very uneven way from country to country, all across Europe. In
France itself 'Ramism' was badly received by the universities
and the Jesuit colleges owing to the mathematician's religious
convictions. It found its Promised Land, to an even greater
degree than in Germany or Sweden, in England, where
Cambridge University went 'Ramist' with William Kempe
and Mark Ridley, and the spirit of research in applied mathematics was expressed at the end of the century in the teaching
of Gabriel Harvey, who declared: 'He that remembereth
Humfrey Cole, a mathematical mechanician, Matthew Baker,
a shipwright, John Shute, an architect, Robert Norman, a
navigator, William Bourne, a gunner, John Hester, a chemist,
or any like cunning and subtle empiric... is a proud man if he
contemn expert artisans, or any sensible industrious prac-
titioner, howsoever unlectured in schools or unlettered in
books.' The same spirit presided over the foundation of
Gresham College in 1597, entrusted by the will of Sir Thomas
Gresham to the Mercers' Company and the Corporation of
the City of London.

The two astronomers, Tycho Brahe and Kepler, who, at the
very end of the century, in the Imperial castle of Benatky in
Bohemia (lent by Rudolf II to the Dane after he had been
driven from his Uraniborg), found themselves opposed in

their conceptions and in their methods of work, did much to carry further the working out of the Copernican system. Tycho Brahe accumulated the observations made during long years of observatory work, while Kepler, more of a mathematician, 'inherited' this treasure which had been gathered by his host in Bohemia and was able, after the latter's death, to exploit it in his own way.

Three features can be distinguished in this itinerary of research, which serve to bring out the complexity of the scientific work involved. Kepler, trained at the University of Tübingen by the astronomer Maestlin, began his career as teacher and researcher at Graz, in Styria, where, for lack of students, he busied himself with casting horoscopes and making 'prognostications'. His reputation as an astrologer was consecrated by the accuracy of his first predictions – a cold winter, war with the Turks, and peasant revolts – and throughout his life Kepler was importuned to continue this activity. Convinced as he was that the stars do exercise an influence on human destinies, together with Divine Providence, Kepler spent some time casting horoscopes, including Wallenstein's.

Yet this same Kepler was, unlike Tycho Brahe, a fervent partisan of Copernicus. At the beginning of his *Mysterium cosmographicum*, published in 1597 (which he sent to the Dane and also to Galileo), he placed a eulogy of *De revolutionibus* refuting the interpretation of that work as merely hypothetical – an interpretation given after the Pole's death by those who presented it to the public – and showed clearly that Copernicus had revealed the actual order of the astral system, whereas the school of Ptolemy described only appearances. 'The principles established by Copernicus reveal the constant cause, unknown to the Ancients, of a great many phenomena.' Not only did these principles make it possible to demonstrate earlier movements which had been reported since ancient times, and to predict future phenomena, with much more accuracy than

Ptolemy, but Copernicus alone provides 'the reason for things which in other astronomers provoke amazement, and thereby removes the source of this amazement, which lies in our ignorance of causes.' This profession of Copernican faith was not appreciated by the teachers who had educated Kepler – Maestlin and, especially, the Rector of Tübingen University, Matthias Hafenreffer – who enjoined him to delete the passages extolling the truth of the Copernican system and to go back, where this matter was concerned, to the 'hypothesis' formula, which was alone acceptable to the Lutheran theologians.

Finally, the collaboration between Tycho Brahe and Kepler itself calls for examination. The former, essentially an observer, contributed many measurements and bare facts, whereas the latter, in the introduction to his *Mysterium*, announced his desire, and ability, to rediscover Copernicus's system through calculation, in order to grasp Copernican reality instead of mere appearances: 'I do not hesitate to affirm that everything which Copernicus demonstrated *a posteriori*, on the basis of observations interpreted by means of geometry, can be proved *a priori*, without any logical subtleties.' The contrast between the two approaches is absolute, and the first contacts between the two men, by letter and in person, were not easy. Tycho Brahe replied to the sending of the *Mysterium* with fervent thanks in which were wrapped thorns of advice to this ambitious youngster to proceed to undertake verifications, to find exactly observed proofs of the supposed relations between the distances of the planets and their orbits. A year later, however, he generously invited Kepler to join him, not now in his out-of-the-way retreat at Wandsbeck, but in the castle of Benatky, and eventually he kept the Swabian beside him until his death in 1601. And so the Copernican revolution made its way in the world, all the more tortuously because the maledictions of the theologians still threatened anyone who compared the new system with the letter of Scripture. At the same time, the practical astronomy of the navigators and merchants was progressing, the work which interested Thomas Gresham, Philip II and the States-General of the United Provinces alike – under the sign of contradictions which expressed the hardening of institutions characteristic of this period.

3. AFTER TRENT: THE STRENGTHENING OF INSTITUTIONS

By way of the wars and the confrontations between religious groups which were so frequent in France and Germany, and even in England, Europe's divided Christendom moved, as the sixteenth century ended, towards a tightening of the antagonisms which had been established earlier. This development was not so pronounced on the Protestant side, where, though Geneva's path had been firmly defined by Calvin and Theodore de Bèze, the Lutheran Churches were not quite broken in to their new orthodoxy; among them the work of the sects continued to cause waverings which began to fall off only in the seventeenth century, and then not very markedly. In the Catholic Church, however, a process of reorganization and reinforcement of discipline went forward, with a systematic effort to recover lost ground. In a way, part of the reform which had been advocated for so long by the Erasmians was now put into effect, and the Church sought to define afresh its relation to the mass of the laity. These concerns were all connected, of course, with the aim of redressing a difficult situation, with the Catholic Church pursuing one task and one alone from 1563 to 1598, when it accepted France's way of putting an end to forty years of civil war. The implications of this policy for Europe's intellectual life, sector by sector, are not easy to estimate, and in the last third of the century some of the dispositions adopted are to be seen as projects rather than achievements.

The Council of Trent, which concluded after twenty years of work (with some intervals) in December 1563, in division and amid the tumult provoked by the Gallicanist ambassadors of the King of France, made no innovations in matters of dogma. The canons adopted, which were published in March 1564, reaffirmed in their entirety the validity of the traditional beliefs that the Protestants had been challenging for the previous half-century. Giving a wider dimension to this defence of doctrine, the Curia took a number of complementary steps: provision for periodical revision of the *Index librorum prohibitorum* and publication in 1566 of the catechism composed for the Council by St Charles Borromeo, of the breviary in 1568 and of the missal in 1570, defined, negatively and positively, the limits of orthodoxy. The most important work of the Council related, however, to Church discipline, that is, to the training and functioning of the clergy. In this vital field, where criticism by reformers of all schools had been so virulent for so long, the Council drew up an ambitious programme which aimed to overhaul the Catholic Church completely – insofar as it succeeded in fully applying the measures proposed, which were sometimes in contradiction to concessions previously agreed to, as in the case of those granted to the King of France at Bologna in 1516.

The three essential points concerned the age at which men might enter into holy orders (the diaconate at twenty-one, the priesthood at twenty-five), together with the examination preceding ordination; the obligation of bishops and parish priests to reside in the places put in their care, and to take responsibility there for the religious instruction of the laity, this provision being completed by a ban on pluralism; finally, and most important, the establishment in every diocese of a seminary for the training of priests. All these changes were intended to put an end to lax practices which had become inveterate, and they were introduced very slowly: the diocesan seminaries were fully established only late in the seventeenth century, owing partly to lack of funds and of teaching staff, but also to a lack of sustained interest in these schools for parish priests among the well-to-do sections of society, which showed themselves so generous to other foundations, those of the religious orders, during the first third of the seventeenth century, especially in France. A long-term programme, typical of an institution which knows how to defy time, the disciplinary reform inaugurated by the Council of Trent bore fruit only much later, in a context that was quite different from the one in which it had been devised.

More rapid and spectacular was the action undertaken by the Society of Jesus, backed by the Curia, to wage a direct struggle against the heretics in all the areas which were under threat or which had already gone over to the other side. Firmly established in Rome, where Loyola set up in 1552 a *Collegium Germanicum* to train the Fathers who were to be despatched to the 'front', the Society did not bother with doctrinal subtleties, but taught, preached and defended in an intelligent way the canons of doctrine affirmed by the Council, proclaimed itself, even before the close of the Council, 'Roman and Tridentine', and prepared its members to refute the errors of the Reformed Churches. The Jesuits' preaching of justification by works and Divine Grace found its theoretician in 1588 in the person of Father Molina, who published in Lisbon his *De liberi arbitrii cum gratiae donis concordia*, a work which enjoyed increasing success well on into the seventeenth century, when the argument with the Jansenists took place.

What was most original in the work of the Jesuits did not lie there, however, but in the multiplication of their colleges, which proceeded vigorously from the middle of the sixteenth century onward, and did not lose momentum. Their main effort was concentrated in the Empire, where the Society was able to install itself in those principalities which had remained Catholic, and also in the Imperial cities, which were open to both religions, in accordance with the terms of the peace of 1555. The Jesuits had as their main bases in the West the ecclesiastical electorates of the Rhineland (Trier, Cologne, and Mainz), the Catholic states in the south, and the Emperor's hereditary possessions in the east: from these they closed in on Lutheran Germany, pressing into its interior through the enclaves of Münster, Fulda and Paderborn. The list of their foundations between 1544 and 1565 is impressive: Cologne, Vienna, Ingolstadt, Munich, Trier, Dillingen, Mainz, Braunsberg. To serve the British Isles the Society founded English colleges and seminaries at Douai, Rome, St Omer and Liège, Scottish ones at Rome, Douai and Madrid, and Irish ones at Rome, Poitiers, Seville and Lisbon. In Poland, which had been penetrated by Lutheranism on its north-west frontier, and where Calvinism was making gains in the middle of the century, the same method was followed, with the foundation of colleges in the threatened borderlands, at Vilna and Poznan. Even in France, where the Jesuits came up against the hostility of the Gallicans who surrounded Catherine de' Medici and staffed the Sorbonne, and who were all exasperated by the conclusions of the Council, they managed to secure footholds, by submitting to the special conditions, contrary to their own founder's statutes, that were imposed upon them. The Collège de Clermont, founded in 1564, under the jurisdiction of the Bishop of Paris, was the subject of a suit, carried on until 1578 before the Parlement, in which the Jesuits were attacked by Etienne Pasquier, the author of *Recherches de la France*. Nevertheless, the college had three thousand pupils by 1569. And the provincial cities followed the example of Paris: Toulouse, Nevers, Rodez, Lyon, Bordeaux. . .

This new scholastic institution, the same everywhere in

Europe, was a complete success. Provided with a carefully considered structure, which was codified in 1584-6 in Father Acquaviva's *Ratio atque institutio studiorum societatis Jesu*, the colleges were integrated into the life of the cities where they were established: their public contests between pupils and their theatrical performances, to which parents and notables were invited, became items in the calendar of city affairs, in a period when, too, the first buildings in the 'Jesuit' style began to be built. Families entrusted their sons to the Jesuits all the more readily because their teaching accorded a substantial place to the humanities and because this teaching was conducted more pleasantly than in the traditional type of school. The Jesuits' instruction of youth was wholly concentrated upon the ruling classes, the nobility and bourgeoisie, whom they strengthened in their Catholic faith or even gradually brought back to that faith, by a slow effort of persuasion, direct and indirect. The Jesuit college was, first and foremost, an instrument for reconquest. In the Imperial city of Augsburg, where 80 per cent of the inhabitants had been lost to Lutheranism for a generation at least, the Society opened one of their establishments in 1580, with the financial help of the Fuggers: forty years later, on the eve of the Thirty Years' War, the Lutheran proportion had been reduced to 75 per cent.

This method of reconquest, applied with extraordinary consistency, was extremely important for the development of European culture. The Jesuit network of establishments providing education for the youth of high society was improved and strengthened during two centuries, all over continental Europe. It created an educational model the influence of which proved all the greater because the old institutions, decayed and discredited, were in no state to resist it. The example of Paris is significant in this respect. Moreover, those rival schools which were able to develop later on shaped themselves in relation to the Jesuit model, either by giving a bigger place than the latter did to the new sciences, or else by reducing the share of attention accorded to the classics, so as to give a bigger share to the national humanities. The fundamental arrangement, however, remained everywhere the balance struck between a Catholic training regularly ensured, day by day; an education in the classics, based upon the best authors of Antiquity, both pagan and Christian; a scientific education embracing mathematics, geography and cosmography; and, finally, a training in good manners and *savoir-faire*, needed for life in good society. Similarly the pedagogical principles of the Jesuits, which made use of rhetoric, competition both between individuals and between groups, and public performances, were reproduced elsewhere and received with favour that is easily comprehensible, since parents found in them the basic social values of the society of the Ancien Régime. Finally, the influence won by the Jesuit pattern of education was facilitated by the tendency for every teaching institution to become petrified in routine. This happens whenever a certain formula has proved successful in a particular society in a particular epoch: eventually it happened to the Jesuit colleges just as it had happened to the universities of the Middle Ages. At the end of the sixteenth century, however, there was as yet no question of routine. The enthusiasm shown for the new colleges – which was such that in some German cities the Fathers even found the sons of nobles and bourgeois whose Lutheran faith was wavering being entered on their registers – provided the Society with a very strong and lasting basis in most of the countries of Europe.

By choosing this method the Society also indicated that it was renouncing – for this period of settling-in, at any rate – any other procedure for winning its battles but teaching and preaching (together with debating, when the Protestant pastors agreed to engage in public disputations). The mystical revival which had become manifest in the previous decades remained without effect on the Society. It had nothing to do with the foundation of the second Oratory, that of St Philip Neri, which began in a church in Rome soon after 1550, as simple gatherings of clergy and laymen to read, pray and sing with fervour the praises of God (from which developed a new musical form, the oratorio), gatherings recognized by the Papacy in 1575 as a Congregation of priests and secular clergy. Nor was there any connexion between the Society and the great Spanish mystics who exalted the inner dream and intimate relationship with God in ecstasy: St Teresa of Avila, a Carmelite for twenty-seven years, who reformed or founded seventeen convents before her death in 1582 and wrote a description of her ecstatic experiences and of her illnesses (*The Interior Castle, or the Mansions of the Soul*); and her disciple St John of the Cross, founder of the first convent of Discalced Carmelites, in 1568, who sang of *The Dark Night of the Soul* and *The Living Flame of Love*. Both St Teresa and St John were surrounded by pilgrims coming from afar, hermits and devout persons withdrawn from the world, concerned for the strict monastic way of life and inspired by this spiritual exaltation, which soon cast its beams beyond Spain, through books and through pilgrimages – but with no help from the Society, which did not venture upon these difficult paths accessible only to very small groups, enclosed and isolated in the perfectly regulated monasteries inspired by the piety of St Teresa.

However, the Roman Church's recovery was not entirely due to the rise of the Society of Jesus. Throughout the part of Europe that had remained Catholic, vigilance was reinforced in relation to deviations and temptations such as might eventually cause fresh losses. In Rome itself the Holy Office carried out the ultimate supervision of printed works, and put on the Index not only all the writings of Erasmus but also those of writers who do not seem to have been disposed to engage in any reforming ventures, such as Luis de Granada, whose *Guide for Sinners* was condemned in 1559. Again, the Holy Office directed the inquisitorial missions which the Dominicans undertook in various states, checking on any suspect signs of ritual innovation or doctrinal initiative, forbidding believers to read or even to have on their shelves any books suspected of heresy, and condemning the publication of any variants of or commentaries upon the sacred writings. Consequently, the little group of singers gathered around the Florentine Philip Neri was long regarded with suspicion, despite the protection given it by St Charles Borromeo. Recognition of the Oratory was delayed for ten years because their practice of readings followed by singing bore some resemblance to what was done at Lutheran gatherings. In Spain itself Teresa of Avila and John of the Cross had to defend themselves against the Inquisition, which hunted down relentlessly anyone who had anything in common with the *alumbrados*, the movement of *illuminati* which was held to open the gate to the Reformation. Teresa of Avila had taken from her the manuscript in which she told the story of her life, her hallucinations and her dreams: it was given back to her through the intervention of Philip II. John of the Cross was treated even worse, being thrown into prison for several months, and, towards the end of his life, persecuted by the prior of his monastery, although Teresa's reforms had been recognized by a papal brief ten years previously (in 1580).

The disciplinary rigour of the Holy Office was even more apparent in Italy, where it was exercised at the end of the century against two Dominicans who were in trouble with their order: Giordano Bruno and Campanella. The former, unfrocked in 1576, moved away from orthodoxy as a result of reading and of scientific work: he denied that Aristotle's world-system possessed any validity. Lucretius, Ramón Lull and Copernicus were the milestones of an intellectual journey which brought him to embrace, in the main intuitively, the discoveries of Copernicus, with bold modifications of his own – for Bruno, the stars were all so many suns, each surrounded by its own planetary system. This way of representing the world soon caused him to be accused of pantheism, and obliged him to lead a life of protracted journeying, which ended in a Roman prison. From Genoa, where he taught astronomy for a short time, he went to Geneva, where the Council jailed him (1579). Then he stayed for a while in France and in England, but had to flee from the conservative university of Oxford, which denounced his impiety. Germany proved no more hospitable: he moved from Wittenberg to Prague and from there to Helmstedt, where the Lutheran pastors excommunicated him. In this tour of Europe, Giordano Bruno thus suffered rejection and expulsion by all the different orthodoxies. Lured into a trap in Venice, he was handed over to the Holy Office, and, after a trial that lasted six years, condemned to the stake and burnt in the Campo dei Fiori in 1600.

At that time Campanella, too, was in prison. This Dominican from Calabria remained within his order, and stayed in Italy, where he preached a liberating deism, hostile to all tyranny, and announced the coming of a revolution which was to take place at the turn of the century, through the hidden power of numbers and through the action of three hundred persons – monks, priests and laymen. During his twenty-seven years' imprisonment, in the charge of the Jesuits whom he had abused in speech and writing, Campanella stood up to the long ordeal and wrote in his gaol in Rome *The City of the Sun*, a new Utopia, placed under the sign of Philosophy, divided into a trinity to which he gave the names Power, Wisdom and Love: written in 1602, the book was published in Frankfurt in 1623.

These striking expressions of Catholic disciplinary severity must not, however, cause to be forgotten a wider purpose which it is not hard to observe in the deliberations of the Council of Trent, and which was to constitute an important concern of the upper clergy for the next two centuries. This was the purgation of those popular beliefs and practices which reformers both within and without the church had long denounced – an operation which Erasmus himself had pressingly urged on several occasions, and which was undertaken by the Curia at the very moment when Paul IV decided to put on the Index even those of Erasmus's writings that did not deal with religion. The publishing in 1566 of the new catechism clearly showed the will of Rome to define precisely and at once what the people's beliefs should be: this would then be followed up by a slower struggle to separate acceptable practices from those that were dubious, and on which Reformed criticism had furnished plentiful comment. Between the beliefs of the laity, littered with traditions, as various as they were disconcerting for a strict theologian, which had been inherited from a distant past and were constantly being re-created in accordance with seasons and needs, and this will to classify, identify and authenticate, there was, of course, a great gulf fixed. The cult of saints and their relics; pilgrimages made for the sake of cures or other special reasons; confraternities of trades and local venerations; specially holy places, springs or hills, which had been Christianized for centuries: all this motley fabric of religious practice in country and town, all this piety which, though lively, came easily under suspicion as soon as the hierarchy applied itself to purifying Catholicism's own image of itself, was called in question. Similarly, when . the post-Tridentine Church decided to suppress or to reduce in number the festivals of mockery and abreaction – the Festival of Fools, the Carnival, the *Fête des Sots* – it was certainly cutting into the quick, even while depriving the Reformed of some of their excuse for irony. But this slow work of mutilating purgation was not accomplished in a decade: at the end of the sixteenth century it was still more of a project, a programme, than an achievement.

We can, however, see at least a prefiguring of what was

intended – caricatural in some respects – in the regime imposed on Bavaria by the Wittelsbachs, who were wholly devoted to the cause of a pugnacious Catholic reform capable of launching a counter-offensive against the Lutherans; especially Albrecht V, who ruled over the duchy between 1550 and 1579. Under his impulsion, supported by Canisius, the Jesuit Provincial of Upper Germany, and by the Cardinal Bishop of Augsburg, Otto Truchsess von Waldburg, Bavaria was subjected to a methodical 'reform from within'. After the Imperial Diet held at Augsburg in 1566, where Albrecht V appeared as 'the leader of the Counter-Reformation among the Catholic princes', measures were taken (in 1569–70) with a view to driving out of the country every trace of and every temptation toward dissent, whether Lutheran or other. An edict of censorship reproduced the lists of Rome's Index, a general educational ordinance strengthened Catholic teaching in schools and colleges, and a general visitation of parishes was instituted forthwith. There followed a thorough 'moralization' of private life (which was especially severe as far as the executive agents and officers of the duchy were concerned), affecting costume, bathing, and so on: checking on the practice of religion in all its forms – Sunday Mass, communion at Easter, pilgrimages and processions, and, especially, strict supervision of popular festivals and celebrations: banning of peasant dances, regulation of the ceremonies, libations and other practices which had grown up around baptisms, weddings and funerals. The Bavaria of Albrecht V presented the image of an Anti-Geneva, similar to the capital of Calvinism in the exigencies imposed on the conduct of the laity. This model of Catholic reform in the German lands did not, to be sure, retain for long its aspect of austerity: nevertheless, the undertaking attempted by the duke and his ecclesiastical advisers deserves to be mentioned in connexion with the Catholic reorganization, as a preliminary sketch for that religion of rites purified and made aseptic by an effort of

trationality which was to assume form and colour in the nex
century.

There remain to be described the politico-religious forms
of the struggle between the Roman Church and the new
Churches which, as we have seen, dictated the course taken
by political thinking throughout this period, and which took a
new direction, in 1598, with the signing of the Edict of
Nantes in France. Down to that time, leaving aside reconquest
by the edge of the sword or by slow persuasion, the only
recognized form of coexistence had been the Peace of
Augsburg, signed in 1555, in which Catholics and Lutherans
divided the Empire between them. With the passage of time,
the formula *cujus regio, ejus religio* showed that it was pre-
carious for both sides. The enterprises of Canisius and his
Jesuits, who aimed at methodically recovering the cities and
principalities which had gone over to the Reformation, were
balanced by the steps taken by the Lutheran princes who were
unwilling to honour the *reservatum ecclesiasticum*, by which
holders of Catholic benefices who crossed over to the
Reformed camp after 1552 were obliged to abandon the
property that went with their Church functions. These
princes had obtained from the Emperor, moreover, after the
signing of the Augsburg agreement, the right to practise their
religion freely when in the Catholic ecclesiastical territories.
These contrary strivings gave rise very soon to a sense of
instability which lasted until the Thirty Years' War, and was
sustained by a whole pamphlet literature commenting
vehemently on all encroachments and threats.

Polemics were intensified, in the western part of the Empire
at least, by the contributions of the Calvinists, who were
gradually increasing their numbers by recruiting among the
'enthusiasts' and by the adhesion of the dissenters belonging to
the municipal Churches of the Upper Rhine, which discreetly
merged with the Calvinist Church. Ignored by the Treaty of
Augsburg, powerful in such Imperial cities as Strasbourg, and

present in quasi-clandestine fashion even in episcopal cities like Trier and Mainz, the Calvinists demanded to enjoy the benefits of the Treaty, and so kept up an atmosphere of contestation which was both doctrinal and political, directed simultaneously against Rome and against Wittenberg. By the end of the century this poorly respected agreement – which, nevertheless, had secured for Germany a truce from fighting for half a century – looked like a misconceived solution to the problem of coexistence.

It was then that the 'French solution', adopted not without difficulty by Henri IV, gave a fresh stimulus to the general polemic and a new dimension to this institutional problem. Instead of *cujus regio, ejus religio*, here was an accord which implied the existence of a national state that was dualistic on the religious plane, in a partly 'extraterritorial' way, in a kind of federalism guaranteed by the monarch, who was both head of the Gallican Church and at the same time protector of the Calvinist Church. The details of the clauses adopted at Nantes, or amended in subsequent years under the twofold pressure of the Catholics (of the Jesuits specifically, after their return in 1603) and of the Protestants, are significant in this respect: bi-partite arbitration boards and access to public appointments, on the one hand; on the other, granting of 150 'places of refuge', including fifty strongholds, to safeguard the security of the Protestants; limited recognition of places of worship and authorization for schools and academies of the 'religion alleged to be reformed'. All these were elements contributing to the originality of this solution, which was consecrated by a document that had been discussed line by line, and completed with secret clauses and codicils. The Reformed religion was not placed on a footing of equality with the official Catholic Church, but its legal existence had been recognized, just as in Poland and Hungary: with its strongholds, its political assemblies and its representatives in the King's Council, it formed a state within the state, under the supreme authority of the King.

Having established these points, it must be said that the 'French solution', seen as a whole, had two features which constituted its real originality and account for the reverberations it produced all over Europe. On the one hand, it proclaimed, more clearly than the Peace of Augsburg had done, the *provisional* character of the situation. Where the text adopted in 1555 had spoken of the need for the German nation to establish peace between the different religions, and proclaimed that religious disputes must thenceforth be carried on only by Christian, friendly and peaceful means, so as to arrive at Christian understanding and conciliation (*soll die strittig Religion nicht anderst den durch christlichen, freundliche, friedtliche Mittel und Wege zu einhelligem christlichen verstandt und vergleichung gepracht werden*), the preamble of the Edict of Nantes states, without beating about the bush, that religious unity of the kingdom remains an ideal which the monarchy cannot renounce, and expresses the King's hope of a reunification in the near future (though forty years of conflict had shown this to be impossible of attainment, whether by colloquy or by force).

This passage, authorizing royal interventions and validating the ceaseless demands of the assemblies of the Catholic clergy, was undoubtedly an important point in the pacification undertaken by Henri IV in relation to his former co-religionists. And yet it had less weight, seemingly, even in the eyes of contemporaries, than the extension of royal tutelage to include religious affairs which emerges from the totality of the measures taken by the King – and accepted, for better or worse, by Rome as well as by the Protestant Assembly at Saumur. It was the monarch who had himself decided, in full sovereignty, what should be the extent of the concessions made to the Protestants, and in so doing, had determined, *ipso facto*, what could be tolerated by the Catholics: bishops, priests and laity alike. Henri IV made this well understood to the Parlements who sought to oppose the registration of the Edict. The lawyers, who had suffered in the time of the League and refused to accept the decisions of the Council of Trent, now tried to stand up to the King. He had to go and hold a *lit de justice* on more than one occasion, at Rouen and at Toulouse, to bring the recalcitrants to heel. Before the Parlement of Languedoc, grumbling at the admission of Protestants to public appointments, he recalled the still fresh memories of the League, when many Catholics had played Spain's game, and defined the essential criterion of his decision: 'I wish that *ceux de la Religion* may live in peace in my kingdom and be capable of filling public appointments, not because they are *de la Religion*, but in so far as they have been very loyal servitors to me and to the Crown of France.' Here was a fine definition, in a single phrase, of the primacy of the state: a man's loyalty to the kingdom, that is, to the higher interests of the monarchy, counts for more than his belonging to one or other of the two religions which are allowed to exist in France. The Edict of Nantes, as a solution to the religious divisions which still endangered the state as a whole at the end of the sixteenth century, was a formula restricting the initiative of Rome, and constituted, in the concrete originality of its provisions organizing the co-existence of the two religions, a setback for Ultramontane Catholicism to the advantage of royal Gallicanism.

More effectively than the Treaty of Augsburg, the peace-making function of which could be called in question with every succession of one ruler by another (as happened at Aachen and in many Rhineland towns during the last decade of the century), the Edict of Nantes ensured religious peace by consolidating political sovereignty, a factor which came into play even while the Catholic Church was recovering its strength, and the effects of this twofold process rapidly made themselves felt in the seventeenth century. In the short run, however, the reverberations of the French Edict can easily be estimated from the publications that were devoted to it and the commentaries referring to it, first and foremost in the Empire, where politico-religious agitation went on unceasingly, and secondly, just as logically, in Italy, where the grip of Spain and of the Papacy was becoming harsher. It was in Venice, the first state to recognize Henri IV in 1589, that the liveliest interest in French policy was shown, thanks to Fra Paolo Sarpi, author of a celebrated *History of the Council of Trent* and adviser to the Signoria in a complicated conflict with Rome. Sarpi, a notable writer and jurist, and the friend and correspondent of prominent French Gallicans, Leschassier, Servin, Villiers-Hotman and J.-A. de Thou, was plainly inspired by the precedent France had provided, in his long struggle against the Curia, which ended in 1607 by a compromise which Henri IV helped to bring about. A new epoch was opening for political thought, as for intellectual life in general, with the entry into the new century.

Chapter 4

MYSTICS AND
FREETHINKERS

(1600–1640)

THE new climate cannot be considered as constituting a
major discontinuity. Reformation and Counter-Reformation,
enthusiasts and scholars were still grappling with the same
problems, though under conditions that time had made
different; and, most important, the established institutions
exerted all their weight, sociologically and intellectually, to
ensure that the oldest disputes were resumed. In 1618 the
Prague Defenestration expressed the vitality of a Czech
national tradition, hostile to Roman Catholicism and to
Germanization, which neither the Battle of the White
Mountain, two years later, nor the policy pursued with
tenacity for decades by the Habsburgs succeeded in destroying.
In that same year there was held at Dordrecht, in the heart of
the United Provinces, the most important of the synods at
which religious uniformity of the Calvinist communities
throughout Europe was sought. Here are a few examples,
from among many equally striking cases: James I regulating
entry into the English universities; Henri IV authorizing the
return of the Jesuits to France after some years of exile;
Philip III expelling from Spain the Moriscos who had been
settled there for so long; Gustavus Adolphus intervening in
the German war as a Lutheran prince protecting sister-
Churches threatened with reconquest by Rome. There is no
point in adding to the list. And yet, in the intellectual and
spiritual life of Europe during the first half of the seventeenth
century, two movements persisted in a particularly significant

way: on the one hand the movement tending to reinforce orthodoxy inside the different ideological frameworks, and, on the other, the movement which continued, along more complicated paths, the learned researches of the previous century. This was a century of saints, say the general histories, with justification, recalling, after the Spanish mystics, the French wave of these first decades: but it was also a century of scholars, of learned 'freethought', without frontiers if not without prudence, which counted for no less, in the quantitatively limited circles in which information circulated and where new departures could find the economic support needed if they were to come to fruition.

I. REFORMED ORTHODOXIES AND CATHOLIC PIETIES

The two principal new religions, with firm roots across Europe, Lutheranism and Calvinism, faced at the beginning of the seventeenth century those problems of doctrinal unity which the Catholic Church had found so hard to settle at the Council of Trent; but they faced them in much more difficult circumstances, because of their youth, because of their basic principles, which even allowed every layman to be his own theologian, and also because of reasons specific to each religion.

For the Lutherans, the subjection of each Church to the temporal power had created all the conditions for dispersion. Every State Church had set up a university of its own, whose originality and fecundity was vigorously affirmed by the theologians. The 'formula of concord' which had been adopted in the previous century had soon been covered with glosses, often of an original kind, which, though certainly not departing from the fundamental Lutheran doctrine (the Bible and Christ as Saviour), nevertheless opened the way to ingenious exegeses of the symbols and even of the nature of Christ, and of many other matters that were non-essential.

Moreover, the misfortunes of war, after 1618, with plague and epidemics, gave rise, where men's emotions were concerned, to a crisis of confidence which found expression in the life of the universities in a drying-up of recruitment and a lukewarmness in study which was felt even at Wittenberg. This disaffection coincided with the installation of certain families in the most important positions in the new hierarchy of Church and university in the Lutheran countries. Veritable dynasties came into being in this way in Germany, the most illustrious being the Carpzovs (jurists and theologians) and, especially, the Osianders, who included, around 1640, dozens of theologians, professors of law, physicians and princes' stewards, beginning with the first of their name, Andreas Osiander, the well-known reformer who died in the middle of the sixteenth century.

Finally, the Lutheran Churches were shaken by the constant progress of Calvinism, especially when certain princes decided, interpreting the Peace of Augsburg in a new way, to convert their subjects to the Calvinist faith once they had embraced it themselves. Among these were Maurice of Hesse-Marburg, who drove out the Lutherans in 1604 and installed Calvinism in the University of Marburg, and the Elector John Sigismund of Brandenburg, who became a Calvinist in 1613 and tried to bring the population of his electorate along with him into his new Church. This situation accounts for a two-fold movement characteristic of Lutheranism in Germany. On the one hand, sharp conflicts, which it is not easy to reconstitute, in principalities whose heads had gone over to Calvinism but where the population, attached to Lutheran ways for a century now, resisted Calvinist regimentation and saw the Genevan Reformation as the most redoubtable foe of the 'holy doctrine'. On the other hand, the interminable disputes and discussions which were carried on between the Lutheran theologians of different universities ended by interesting nobody other than these specialists themselves, as they emulated each other in bad temper and hair splitting. From this superabundance of debates that were often specious in character there stands out, uniquely, the most peaceful of the contenders, Johann Gerhard, professor at the University of Jena. A smiling defender of orthodoxy, he published, long after Melanchthon, his own *Loci communes theologiae* (1621), which were to be regarded for many years as the oracle of Lutheran orthodoxy. But the effort to achieve unity got no further than that.

For the Calvinists the difficulties were of a different order. Calvin and his successor, Théodore de Bèze, had set up the organizational model of a Church dominating closely the magistracy of Geneva, that is, the political authority; but this type of organization was not directly transferable to other countries where Calvinism was not in power, countries such as France. Even in places where the balance of forces was more favourable than in France, such as the United Provinces or Hungary, it was not found possible to adopt the Genevan organization of the Consistory in pure and simple form. The attempts made by some pastors (such as Lambert Daneau at Leyden) to introduce the strict Genevan system into the Dutch cities came up against lively resistance on the part of the political institutions, and the strict Calvinists had to draw back and accept a relative degree of autonomy for the civil authority. Finally, and above all, Calvin had been more concerned to train pastors, to provide himself with human means of spreading the Gospel, than to regulate relations between the different Calvinist communities, under the aegis of the mother-Church of Geneva. The phenomenon of the Lutheran universities was therefore reproduced, on a smaller scale, among the Calvinists. Heidelberg, which became Calvinist at the end of the sixteenth century, attracted as many students as Geneva, and ranked higher than the 'academies' established in France, at Saumur, Angers and Sedan. Moreover, since disputes over the interpretation of doctrine could not be submitted to organized arbitration, they quickly took a turn that was dangerous for the whole Calvinist community. The great debate in the Netherlands between the Arminians and the Gomarists was an example of this: it led to the convening of the Synod of Dordrecht, at which all the provinces of the Calvinist world were entitled to representation, with Geneva having only two delegates.

The opposition between Arminius and Gomar, both professors at the University of Leyden, was doctrinal in character, with Gomar propounding a theory of predestination that was stricter and more complete than that of Arminius. When the latter died, in 1609, the Gomarists, who wanted to drive their adversaries out of the universities and Churches, met with resistance from the 'Arminians', the liberal tendency who were called Remonstrants because of their protests against the intolerance of the Gomarists. The dispute quickly assumed a political and social dimension, as the Arminians were backed by the bourgeoisie of the big trading cities, headed by Rotterdam, with its Pensionary, Oldenbarnevelt, whereas the Gomarists had the support of the popular elements and of Maurice of Nassau: these combinations were to constitute one of the principal cleavages in the political and social life of the United Provinces in the seventeenth century. Dragged through the States of all the provinces, each of which possessed complete independence in religious matters, the quarrel might have gone on indefinitely, had there not been found Arminians like Hugo Grotius, Oldenbarnevelt's successor as Pensionary of Rotterdam, who considered, like the Gomarists, that since theological conflicts ought to be settled by the civil power, it was for the States-General to intervene.

The Synod of Dordrecht, which met in November 1618 on the initiative of the States-General, brought together commissioners who represented the different states, professors of theology, pastors and elders nominated by the provincial synods, and twenty-eight foreign delegates, coming from

England, Switzerland, Geneva, Hesse, the Palatinate, Bremen, Emden and Nassau: the French delegates had not been allowed to leave France, by order of the King. The Gomarist majority in the Synod, after six months' work, produced a blanket condemnation of the Arminians. Oldenbarnevelt was executed immediately after the closure of the Synod, and two hundred ministers were deposed and eighty banished (to England and Schleswig). This Synod, which in theory had no responsibility for defining doctrine for the entire Calvinist community, had assumed this responsibility and had carried it out with a severity that impressed the delegates from abroad. Ten years later, the Arminians, regrouped and organized with their own confession, constitution and discipline, present in all the provinces and recognized abroad, had kept their place in the Calvinist world. Calvinist orthodoxy had not found definition, either at Geneva or at Dordrecht, and the debate around it went on indecisively for a long time afterwards.

The woes of the age and the vehement severities of the theologians caused a revival of sectarian movements, especially in Germany. We cannot now reconstruct very much of the secret life of associations in which alchemists, Anabaptists and pantheists rubbed shoulders, and often struggled with each other, despite the numerous pieces of jetsam left here and there, in the form of erudite, hermetic treatises and letters in great quantity, as in the case of Johann Valentin Andreae, the Stuttgart preacher and founder of the Rosicrucians. Two witnesses to this revival of the 'enthusiasts' stand out in Germany: Johann Arndt, chaplain to the Duke of Zell and writer of works which extolled the inner life of believers, while respecting Lutheran doctrine (*Vier Bücher vom wahren Christentum*, 1609); and, especially, the celebrated Jakob Boehme, a disciple of Paracelsus, a cobbler by trade, who, despite condemnations and prohibitions, wrote a great deal which was highly appreciated by politically minded sectaries and defended even by orthodox theologians like Johann

Gerhard. Boehme, a Lutheran to the end of his days, was a mystic who described his visions and also an encyclopaedic thinker, one who had read the cabbalists and meditated upon ancient philosophy: his reputation spread far beyond the German-speaking lands, into England especially, for he revived, in a highly personal way, the liberating inspiration of the Lutheranism of 1517–20. His immediate disciples, such as Johann von Werdenhagen, professor at Helmstedt, were soon accused of illuminism and harried by the Lutheran pastors whom they had abused in their writings.

This same twofold movement – the attempt to give definition to orthodoxy, and the mystical and 'sectarian' reaction – occurred in England, amplified by the tensions inherited from the preceding century. On the one hand, there was the established Church, under the protection of the King of England as an institution of state, and directed by vigilant bishops. James I, despite his theological pretensions, and even his *Demonology*, and Charles I as well, counted for less than these Anglican bishops determined to maintain the orthodoxy of their Church against both the Romanists' attempts to recover control of the Church of England (even at the price of confirming the Thirty-Nine Articles) and the demands being pressed by the Puritans and Independents of Scotland and England. The arch-upholder of Anglican orthodoxy was Laud, Archbishop of Canterbury, Charles I's adviser, a fierce persecutor of dissenters until the revolt of 1640.

But this crypto-Romanist Church, jealous of its prerogatives and its creed, was continually being challenged, either from within or on its fringes, by opponents who called for a more thorough Reformation. These included disciples of Ramus and Calvin, Scottish Presbyterians attached to their national and religious liberties (and in open revolt in 1637), and Puritans of every sort who urged freedom for the individual Christian more than anything else. These dissenters (a better term than Puritans, if the latter be taken to connote a

moral asceticism which did not necessarily apply) were against
the established Church in so far as it presented an obstacle to
that return to the Scriptures which was for them the essential
thing: in this respect they were hardly Calvinist (in England
at any rate) since they cared little for Geneva or any link with
the Genevan Church. More demanding still, and more
sharply at odds with the official Church, were those Independents and sectaries who called for absolute freedom of conscience
and denied the right of the political ruler to interfere in
religious questions. Among them were the Ramists to whom
Milton had taught logic in accordance with Ramus's dialectics
and the Baptists who maintained the teachings of their
sixteenth-century predecessors. They included also some who
went into exile to escape harassment and persecution by the
Anglicans, in Laud's time, taking their congregations over to
Holland and to North America – the voyage of the *Mayflower*
in 1620 was undertaken by dissenters who carried with them
the works of Ramus as well as the Bible. Above all, an intense
work of 'unauthorized preaching' was carried out all over
England, which the established religious authorities proved
unable to check, the activists being 'lecturers' without
appointments, clergymen of dissenting opinions, and this
ensured recruitment to the sects and a ceaseless challenge to
the religious organization, rites and dogmas of the Church of
England, which retained many 'Roman' features and continued to make use of the harshest methods to uphold its
power. The Baptists who followed Smyth and Helwys (the
General Baptists) had five communities in England in 1626:
by 1644 they had forty-seven. Even more than on the
Continent, owing to the wide gap between Anglicanism and
the most vigorous spirit of the Reformation, doctrinal rigours
gave rise to movements of protest, 'sectarian' formations
which demanded toleration, at the very least, the freedom of
the believer, and fought against the tyranny of the Anglican
bishops. Smyth, Milton, Robinson, Murton and their like

were the general staff of a numerous vanguard who made their weight felt in England's religious and political life after 1640.

In the Catholic world, on the frontiers of Reformed Europe as in Rome, this was a time for reconquest through multiplying pious endeavours. New orders were created, old ones put forth new branches, Rome and the episcopate encouraged every step that might contribute to give Catholicism a new image: such was the tendency everywhere. In Europe as a whole two general features can easily be distinguished. First, there was the adoption of the Jesuit pattern in education: their colleges were opened everywhere, with substantial local endowments, and provided by the Society with good masters who knew both how to teach and how to become persons of consequence in the towns where their establishments were among the institutions held in highest honour. Pious humanism found in this network of schools, the like of which Europe had never seen before, the channel for its diffusion among the dominant classes of society: other, rival colleges not having yet succeeded in making their mark, those of the Jesuits exerted their power of attraction in every country where they sprang up. When a nobleman of Cahors wished, in 1640, to praise his town to a correspondent living far away, after employing the traditional hyperboles ('it is a town which in Guienne is, so far as good letters are concerned, what Athens was in ancient Greece'), he can find nothing better to add than this very plain statement: 'There is here, moreover, a good college of the Jesuit Fathers.' The time was not distant when Antoine Arnauld, together with some other worthies of the capital, would express regret that to have attended the Collège de Clermont had become a necessity for anyone who wanted to make a career in Paris, at court or in offices of state.

The second feature, perhaps less universal than the first, was the role played by women in this Catholic revival. There were foundresses of orders, like Jeanne de Chantal, Madame

Acarie, Elisabeth de Ranfaing; ordinary nuns who flocked to fill the convents that were established here, there and everywhere, even in the New World; zealous reformers of old communities vegetating in conformism and laxity of discipline; inspirers of charitable foundations created to deal with the miserable consequences of war. They operated at various levels, but the importance of their contribution must not be underestimated, for this phenomenon contrasts so strongly (in the Catholic context, at any rate) with preceding periods, and especially with the period of the wars, when women had to watch, rather than participate in, the disputes and battles of the time. Laywomen who aspired to a more positive and more exalting religious activity, or nuns withdrawn from the world and devoted to education or to contemplation, these women helped to give a tone that was at once mystical and efficient to this process of renewal going on within the Catholic Church, in forms which the Council of Trent had not been able to foresee. During a period of forty years this hectic activity resulting in pious foundations developed especially in France – the country *par excellence* of Catholic reconquest.

The flowering of French piety in this period found, half a century ago, its historian, copious and erudite, in the person of the Abbé Brémond. His *Histoire littéraire du sentiment religieux en France depuis la fin des guerres de religion* presented all the different aspects of this movement with such precision and skill that for a long time it discouraged any further writing on the subject. Brémond arranged and categorized everything in accordance with chronology and with the filiations which it is permissible to perceive in order to give coherence to the movement. The author's prejudices, for and against, are, of course, irritating and a hindrance, and so is his classification of those who participated in the 'mystical conquest' into a number of schools. Nevertheless, following this guiding thread brings out the most important trends showing how

French piety at the beginning of the seventeenth century continued, in a minor mode, the Spanish mysticism of Philip II's time.

Two personages dominate the movement from a great height. First, François de Sales, Bishop of Geneva, resident at Annecy, who, in writings that had an extraordinary success, depicted piety in a smiling, optimistic manner. His *Introduction à la vie dévote* (1609) and *Traité de l'amour de Dieu* (1616) are easily read works (especially the former) which are addressed to all believers and which do not seek after the terrifying trances or ecstatic states of the Spanish mystics. The life of piety, which it is open to anyone to lead, in accordance with his station, lay or ecclesiastical, is free from polemical or metaphysical agonies. The *Introduction à la vie dévote* illustrates most clearly the carefully marked-out path which is to lead the soul to piety: preliminary purgation (of sins mortal and venial, vain attachments, bad inclinations), elevation through meditation, prayer and the sacraments, exercise of the virtues and remedies for the usual temptations, and, finally, confirmation in piety. Philotheus, to whom this protracted advice is being given, is taken by the hand and led with gentleness: he is shown the obstacles that will be encountered – 'dryness' in meditation, and spiritual sterility – and told of the recreations that are praiseworthy, those that are forbidden, and those which, though 'permissible', are dangerous to the soul. Cases are specified: the married and the single, those who practise a trade and the others. Here we see the pious life offered to every Catholic who submits himself to his director of conscience and loves God. Furthermore, in his capacity as an awakener of vocations, François de Sales founded with the help of Jeanne Fremyot, Rabutin-Chantal's widow, an order for women, the first houses of which were established at his own residence at Annecy and in Dijon, home of Jeanne de Chantal. The order of the Visitation of St Mary, a contemplative one according to the accepted terminology, welcomed women who wished to devote themselves to pious practices away from the miseries of the world. When the bishop died, in 1622, the Visitation had twelve houses; when Jeanne de Chantal died, in 1641, it had eighty, spread over France, Lorraine and Piedmont. The tomb of François de Sales became a place of pilgrimage and Annecy was regarded as a mystical centre, attracting to itself great numbers of Catholics from all parts of France.

The second great founder of institutions in France was Pierre de Bérulle, who wrote nothing, but devoted himself to installing and acclimatizing in France two foreign orders. One of these was that of the Spanish Carmelites. They were able to establish themselves first in Paris, in the Faubourg Saint-Jacques, in 1603–5, thanks to Barbe Acarie, the wife of an official of the Paris Chambre des Comptes, who gave them hospitality and later initiated a number of foundations for them outside the capital: by 1640 there were about fifty of these houses, testifying to the attraction inspired by the severe piety and rigorous discipline of the Carmelites of France. Bérulle also installed in Paris the Italian Oratory of Philip Neri, whose role in France developed differently from the way it had in Italy. Its principal object became the training of priests, through founding colleges: these soon opened their doors to young persons who had no vocation for the priesthood, and offered an education in which a big place was given to the scientific subjects then developing fast: mathematics, astronomy, geography. Whereas the Congrégation de St Sulpice, founded by Jean-Jacques Olier, and the Lazarists of Vincent de Paul restricted their ambitions to fulfilling the function of seminaries, as required by the Council of Trent, the general concern with education shown by the Oratorians gives them a place at the heart of the intellectual transformations of their time, from the middle of the seventeenth century onward.

These great figures of the Catholic Church in France were,

however, only the vanguard, and there were many more initiatives of various kinds undertaken in those years. Brémond rightly included in his study personages as strange as Marie de l'Incarnation, an Ursuline who went to Quebec to found a convent of her order and who was tortured by visions of hell, an austere mystic and able organizer of an especially difficult day-to-day existence in the little town clinging to its rock and constantly threatened by the most frightful calamities of war and famine; or Jeanne des Anges, another Ursuline who became celebrated for a decade at Loudun, where, possessed by a devil, she caused Urbain Grandier to be burnt in 1634, and then experienced until 1638, under the spiritual direction of Jean-Joseph Surin, four years of mystical exaltation of such fervour that eventually the Provincial of the Society of Jesus recalled and isolated this Jesuit. He ought, however, to have mentioned also the strange personality of Elisabeth de Ranfaing, at Nancy in French Lorraine: on the borders of obsessions and mysticism, this other sufferer from demonic possession also claimed several victims before she emerged to become known as the founder of the Order of Penitent Fallen Women, which by the time of her death had about fifteen houses, between Nancy and Avignon.

In order to have a better notion of this atmosphere of piety, one should also take note of the Compagnie du Saint-Sacrement, a society of priests and laymen founded by the Duc de Ventadour in 1627, which set out to practise a particular form of devotion, the adoration of the Blessed Sacrament, and soon came to dedicate itself to keeping watch over and censuring moral behaviour. This confraternity spread to all the big cities of the kingdom, to Marseilles, Dijon, and Toulouse, and acquired representation at court and among the high officers of state. The Compagnie du Saint-Sacrement and its various branches was bold in denunciation and condemnation, combating blasphemy and prostitution, supervising hospitals as well as prisons. This form of pious police-work is also to be included among the features of the period and of the revival of religious life in France, and perhaps had something to do with the sudden slowing-down of the movement which became apparent in the middle of the seventeenth century. The Compagnie du Saint-Sacrement – which was later to be denounced as the Cabale des Dévots (the 'Bigots' Caucus') – by seeking to establish a rigorous moral order through devious methods caused irritation to the civil and judicial authorities as well as disquiet among many pious Catholics. For whatever reason, this revival of Catholic piety, in a time of war and misery, soon ran out of steam. After about 1640 the vitality of Catholicism found expression in other ways. But even earlier such developments as these were far from constituting the whole of the intellectual life of war-torn Europe. Other innovations were making their appearance elsewhere.

2. THE LEARNED FREETHINKERS

Scholarship was given a fresh impetus in the early seventeenth century through the coming of new participants, as we can see at every stage from those who played the leading roles: the lists of regular correspondents of Mersenne or of Peiresc, together with travel diaries and letters from Italy, provide many examples. Around the brothers Du Puy, in the library of the De Thou family, as in the academies of Florence and Rome, there gathered dozens of men who were both researchers (with, among them, some merely curious persons, attracted by fashion) and professional men who employed their leisure in extending their own erudition and in advancing the frontiers of knowledge. They present, on the whole, a strange kaleidoscope, if we lose sight of the essential fact of the continuity of research and the prestige long since associated with all these activities: around Mersenne and in the Du Puy brothers' library, motley constellations formed, difficult to define exactly, but working together in pursuit of common interests. The Republic of Letters, continuing to exist regardless of frontiers, all over Europe, in the form of little open groups, was still recruiting extensively.

There were many clergy among its citizens, both bishops and mere abbés, Jesuits of great learning like Sirmond and Petau, teachers of theology, keen-minded canons like Pierre Gassendi, Canon of Digne, who were proud of the knowledge they possessed outside the limits of theology – not to mention those holders of benefices, in France and Italy especially, who did not burden themselves with pastoral duties, but pocketed comfortable incomes and enjoyed the protection their clerical status gave them in carrying on their researches. Michel de Marolles, a worthy abbé with a lively pen, left memoirs which explain very well how agreeable such situations were. What efforts Jean-Jacques Bouchard, a well-known freethinker, had to expend, in vain, trying to persuade the cardinals of the Curia, Bagni and others, to give him the cosy little benefice in Rome or Florence, or even the bishopric, that would enable him to pursue his career under the skies of Italy – more clement, in his view, than those of Paris. Then, almost as numerous as the clerics, came the lawyers, members of the sovereign courts (La Mothe le Vayer, Fermat, Etienne Pascal) and advocates or mere *lieutenants criminels*, who doubtless devoted more time and interest to their scientific work than to their professional duties. This was probably the case with Nicolas-Claude Fabri de Peiresc, the famous Provençal scholar who kept open house at Aix and at his country seat for any man of learning, and invited his friends to join him in the astronomical observations he was able to make by using the first telescopes; or, still more discreetly, the *lieutenant criminel* of Moulins, in the Bourbonnais, Gilbert Gaulmin, well known all over Europe as an Orientalist, who spent a few months in the Bastille for speaking too freely. Another group of assiduous participants in these gatherings were the men engaged in scientific occupations who came to learn more about their own art and that of their neighbours, having no other means of information, as yet, than correspondence and the direct exchanges and mutual lending of books that were current practice in these assemblies of the learned. There were physicians there, split between rival schools: Guy Patin and Riolan against Eusèbe Renaudot and Claude Quillet, Paris against Montpellier and Padua, over the question of antimony, or over Harvey's theory of the circulation of the blood. With them were astronomers and mathematicians, who had no practices to support them and, for lack of benefices, taught in this or that college. Mersenne, Boulliau and Gassendi had correspondents everywhere in Europe, with whom they discussed eclipses, longitudes and the length of the meridian. This list still does not exhaust the variety of professions represented in the scholars' meetings. There were librarians and collectors of books on many subjects, like Gabriel Naudé; philologists who were carrying onward the first traditions of humanism, like Ménage and Du Cange; scholars who made compilations of charters for use by their governments; and even men who were merely wits, moved by interest in new things and fine language, more 'men of letters' than scholars, who played a part in these discussions, turning to account what the scholars contributed. Someone like La Mothe le Vayer, who wrote, on all fashionable topics, brief little essays which when collected, make up several volumes, would have been not much more than that had he not also touched on certain great themes, like the virtue of the pagans, and had he not been tutor to a prince and to a king, which helped to promote the understanding of politics among the learned freethinkers. Nor must it be forgotten that among this crowd of 'men of letters' without any clearly defined speciality there were persons of quality, courtiers and provincial nobles, who neglected the traditional amusements of their order to take part in scholarly discussions, men such as Roannez and Méré, dear to the young Pascal.

This enumeration, like a numerical breakdown (however approximate) of the participants in the world of learning, would be fallacious, though, if it suggested that *belles lettres* and the humanities were predominant among their concerns. Between the *sodalitates* of Erasmus's time and the learned gatherings of the seventeenth century a threshold had been crossed, which we appreciate explicitly when we read the correspondence of these men: the Republic of Letters had become a Republic of Savants, who prided themselves more on their knowledge of mathematics, astronomy and music than on their knowledge of humanist philology, and who were more interested (publicly, at any rate) in the charters and memoirs of their country's history than in current theological controversy.

Proof of this is given by the activities of the assemblies, as yet informal and not institutionalized, which were formed in a number of centres. Unfortunately they did not often leave behind them the minutes of their proceedings or the papers read to them, which would have enabled us to follow their preferred interests. In Italy, where conflicts with the papal authorities were intensified – Campanella had to seek refuge in France, first with Peiresc at Aix, in 1629, then in Paris and subsequently in Holland, and Galileo's fate is well known – men of learning came together outside the framework of the universities. In Rome itself a periodical gathering was held in the first years of the century, which in 1609 took the name Accademia dei Lincei. Its ambition was to collect curiosities and establish laboratories in various cities of Italy. It supported Galileo when he included the essence of the discoveries he had made at Padua and Venice in his *Sidereus nuncius* ('Messenger of the Stars'), published in 1610; when he was denounced to the Holy Office for having, in the wake of Copernicus, defended the heliocentric theory, contrary to 'Catholic truth'; and again in 1632 when he published his final defence, the *Dialogues on the Two Principal World-systems, That of Ptolemy and That of Copernicus* (*Dialoghi dei massimi sistemi del mondo* . . .), which received the approval of learned Europe, from Grotius to Descartes, Gassendi and Peiresc – the work appeared a few months earlier than the trial before the Holy Office during which Galileo abjured his errors and heresies. The Accademia dei Lincei suffered as a result of the condemnation of Galileo, and went out of existence soon after its founder; but the baton was taken up by others, in Florence and Venice.

In England, where scientific studies were given at the beginning of the century the double stimulus of the foundation of Gresham College, in London, and the first publication of Francis Bacon's book on *The Advancement of Learning*, the first meetings of this kind were held within the framework of the new teaching establishment. Attended by professors and students, merchants and amateurs interested in new developments in science, these meetings were for a long time mere gatherings for receiving information about recently published books and letters which had arrived from the Continent. They started to be held at regular intervals, and their concerns came to be defined more precisely later on, during the Civil War, in the extraordinary effervescence of ideas and movements that marked the period 1645–53 in London.

Germany and the United Provinces presented a striking contrast to Italy and England. In the Empire, many of the petty capitals, where intellectual life was concentrated under the more or less generous protection of the princes, remained devoted to the theological disputes inherited from the sixteenth century, in the north and the south alike. For one Duke August of Wolfenbüttel, who caused books, pamphlets and learned papers to be sent to him from all over Europe, how many others there were who granted pensions and endowments exclusively to master-theologians of the right colour who perpetuated the disputes of former times. Continuing war fostered this tendency among the princes for a quarter of a century. In the United Provinces, however, which were rapidly developing demographically, economically and intellectually, every city, every reformed university and every school of distinction was (though not without interference by religious dogmatism) a centre of discussion and invention. The learned men of France, such as Sorbière and Saumaise, fully realized this, and turned their gaze towards Holland no less than towards Italy, praising what Sorbière was soon to describe to Patin as 'the new Attica' to which the sciences had been transferred – 'a strange fact', as he wrote, since the country had become 'a battlefield'.

It was in France, however, that the phenomenon of learned assemblies enjoyed its greatest development (or, at least, that which has left most traces for the historian to investigate). A number of provincial capitals created around a group of scholars that atmosphere of work and of information on curious matters which was characteristic of the whole world of learning in those days. The nucleus might be a canon, as, at Limoges, the celebrated collector De Cordes, who went to Paris from time to time to take the air of the capital. Or it might be a lawyer philologist with a love for controversy, such as, at Cahors, Marc-Antoine Dominici, correspondent and later friend of the Pascal family and author of polemical works on the history of law: together with the local bishop he inspired a little academy which brought together, on the premises of a charterhouse, chroniclers of the locality, lawyers and scholars, for a period of about ten years. At Dijon an important group was led by members of the Parlement of Burgundy: Jean-Baptiste Lantin, Jean Boulier, Philibert de la Mare, Jacques-Auguste de Chevanes. Similar assemblies of learned men were to be found in many other cities – in Bordeaux, Rouen, Lyon, Toulouse (at Fermat's house).

The most remarkable instance in the provinces, however, was that of Peiresc, an outstanding collector and scholar, who was interested both in astronomy and in the history of his country, and kept up a Europe-wide correspondence. In his house at Aix-en-Provence and on his country estate at Belgentier he brought together manuscripts and rare objects and set up telescopes on the roofs, and he encouraged all his visitors to join in discovering the wonders of earth and heaven. Jean-Jacques Bouchard, on his way to Italy in 1630, expressed better than anyone else the admiration aroused by the Provençal savant during the last years of his life: 'A man without parallel in Europe for courtesy and kindness as also for wisdom, curiosity in relation to all fine things, and knowledge of all that is happening in the world: there is no realm nor any famous city where he does not have a correspondent, and where he does not know or possess whatever they have that is remarkable and rare, either through the persons of merit and learning with whom he exchanges letters or through the men whom he maintains in those places for that very purpose. His study is thus the most interesting in Europe, with a library full of both printed books and manuscripts.' The catalogues of his correspondence preserved at Carpentras confirm this picture of widespread contacts. With some five hundred correspondents all over the world, from Aleppo and Damascus to Goa, Lübeck and Hamburg, and a hundred-odd close friends whom he recommended his brother to call upon, when he left for a journey in England, the Netherlands and France, there was no man of learning who enjoyed such fame in those days as Peiresc.

Yet Paris could show in those same decades an exceptional variety of assemblies, which were to a large extent complementary (though no thorough study of this complementarity has ever been made). The scholars of Paris had at their disposal in the 1620s and 1630s a range of opportunities to meet each other that made them the envy of their colleagues living, nostalgically, far from the capital. The most celebrated of these gatherings, known to us from the praise of it which we find in letters and from the lamentations uttered by those who frequented it when its inspirers, the brothers Du Puy, died in the 1650s, was the Académie Putéane. This was a meeting held daily in the library of the famous historian and member of the Parlement Jacques-Auguste de Thou, who at his death in 1617 had bequeathed it to his kinsmen, the Du Puys, 'for the benefit of good letters'. Having been formed over a period of forty years, 'with great care and expense', and including books, manuscripts, 'ancient works of art and medallions of gold, silver and bronze', this library, which the brothers Du Puy continually added to, was the richest and most important in Paris – more so even than the King's Library. The study of the Du Puy brothers was both a daily meeting-place, being opened to its habitués at the end of every afternoon, and also a workplace. Books and manuscripts were consulted in the course of discussions, compared with the revelations and news brought by letters lately received, and added to as new publications followed up the works published in the previous century. Philosophy, history and literature were certainly more often discussed than mathematics or astronomy, but the Académie Putéane was a daily rendezvous of universal interests, without any specialization, attended by savants of every kind and where questions of every kind were talked about. It was of all such places the most important in the scholarly life of Paris throughout the period.

The other assemblies, which came into being after 1630, were not only later in time but also more restricted in their scope. They included the philological gatherings of Nicolas Bourbon, Professor of Greek at the Collège de France, which Guy Patin frequented with assiduity; the meetings where doctors and natural philosophers compared notes which Pierre Bourdelot, physician to the Condé family, organized in the prince's town house; and the meetings of mathematicians that Habert de Montmor promoted at his residence in 1635–40, with the help of Etienne Pascal and Gassendi. Above all, better known and certainly more important, there were two weekly gatherings which had a wide influence. The Minim Father Marin Mersenne, an enthusiast for mathematics and astronomy, brought together in his cell in the Place Royale those friends of his who shared these interests, and during the 1630s these meetings became regular weekly occasions, held either at the home of the magistrate De Montholon or in the Place Royale, and soon acquired great renown, which was due both to the extensive Europe-wide correspondence which Mersenne kept up and to the quality of those who took part in the group's discussions: Etienne Pascal (and, soon, his son Blaise as well), Desargues, Roberval, Boulliau, Gassendi, and even Descartes, when he came to Paris. The group included about sixty ecclesiastics of various kinds, over twenty lawyers, nearly the same number of doctors, and a dozen noblemen. Often the cell in the Place Royale proved too small to hold all the participants, especially as instruments and books took up a lot of space in it. Though more exclusively scientific, not to say mathematical, than the other assemblies, Mersenne's 'academy' did not eschew philosophical discussion directly related to mathematical reasoning. As his correspondence amply shows, the Minim, who was no less a teacher than a savant, stimulated research and arranged encounters as a result of which the most difficult problems were defined and acutely antagonistic positions were brought into confrontation: Descartes *versus* Gassendi. Always on the lookout for new developments, this pious man who had once dismissively condemned Campanella and Galileo and inveighed against Parisian atheism gave many proofs of independent judgement and of that capacity, which is so rare, for correcting one's own mistakes. Even after 1633 he continued to work on the propositions of Copernicus and to read and re-read Galileo. Later he was to express loud approval of Hobbes's *De cive*, but soon retracted that rash opinion. Thanks to his personal approach and to the freedom that prevailed in his 'academy' Mersenne brought into being a centre of scientific activity which exercised for a long time an influence that extended far beyond the cultural area of Paris and France.

The other outstanding important assembly, one of a very different sort, which had a great influence through its publications, was that which gathered at the office of the address-finding service founded by Théophraste Renaudot and his brother Eusèbe. Soon after they launched the *Gazette de France*, the brothers began holding in their office, every Monday, an assembly at which men of learning exchanged views on topical matters which were related, indirectly at least, to the problems of philosophy and science being discussed elsewhere (but not to politics, a subject forbidden by the royal authority, nor to theology, the business of the Sorbonne). At every meeting one or two subjects were dealt with, participants taking turns in expounding their point of view, after which (under conditions about which we know nothing) a summary of the proceedings was composed, in which the different attitudes were set forth in the same way, without any names being given or conclusions drawn. These summaries were published in five stout volumes, the *Centuries* published by Renaudot's address-finding service: they constitute an amazing repertory of the problems that were submitted to the wisdom of the participants: classic questions of medicine, like the contrariety of humours, and general questions, such as the frivolity of the French, or 'imagination', or 'custom'; but displaying, as a whole, a clear predilection for the occult sciences (the philosopher's stone, the sympathetic powder), for medical matters (scrofula, madness, fevers), moral problems considered in a general way (anger, feminine caprice, compliments), and universal logic (the chicken and the egg, the virtue of numbers, the atom).

Despite the anonymity of the contributions, attentive reading of these debates allows us to recognize the major schools of thought into which these savants and 'men of the world' were divided – mechanists, naturalists, scholastics, humoralist doctors and chemists. This identification of the different attitudes represented is the easier to carry out because the subjects of debate tackled in the Renaudots' office correspond to the preoccupations of the freethinkers of the time, as these are found set out in their writings. It is therefore not surprising to find here 'Jansenists' *avant la lettre*, affected by Saint-Cyran and Port-Royal, and 'Cartesians' arguing about the soul's passions. The success of this enterprise is proved by the length of time that it continued (about twenty years after 1633) and by the testimony of those who took part. In May 1633 Gassendi, who was staying at Aix, thanks Boulliau for having informed him in some detail of 'the assembly which meets every week at the office of the address-finding service'.

We still need to find out how these Parisian scholars (and foreign ones passing through Paris) came to be able to take part in the various assemblies. Letters and the hints given in some memoirs provide no more than a glimpse. This numerically small world conveys an impression of great mobility, stimulated by its inhabitants' insatiable curiosity. The same mathematicians who regularly visit Mersenne also turn up at M. de Montmor's; a doctor like Guy Patin goes now to this meeting, now to that, depending on how he feels and on the leisure his practice allows him; and all these men are at home to their colleagues, displaying proudly their libraries and their collections of medallions – there were many numismatists in this aristocratic circle, in which large sums might be spent in order to acquire rare specimens, brought from the Levant or from neighbouring Italy. The multiplicity of these assemblies certainly enables us to perceive the pre-eminence occupied by a few of the participants, whose position or whose facility in

writing and discussion easily put them in the forefront.
Pierre and Jacques Du Puy are among those whose position
gave them this status along with Eusèbe Renaudot; F. la
Mothe le Vayer, Gassendi, Sorbière and Saumaise were
among those whose readiness of speech and pen so elevated
them; others, such as Gabriel Naudé, possessed both advantages. Yet others stood more to one side and cannot be enrolled
under any banner – persons who were 'outsiders' by vocation
or conviction, and also in their careers, such as Cyrano de
Bergerac, or, even better examples, Descartes and Pascal, who,
though they regularly frequented this circle, nevertheless did
not belong to it.

Mobility was the rule. For one *Tétrade*, identified by
R. Pintard (La Mothe le Vayer, Elie Diodati, Gassendi,
Naudé), and even that did not last long, there were ten more
transient constellations, and a hundred relationships lasting
for a few months and then breaking up as the partners'
interests fluctuated. Mobility was, in a sense, a normal condition in this world of scholars, manifesting itself on three
planes. All these men were great readers who visited each
other all the more eagerly because they regularly lent one
another books. Borrowing and returning of books were
commonplace in a period when these were always expensive
and often scarce, because the limited printings were soon sold
out. Even manuscripts, those precious items to which collectors were so devoted, might be lent. Jacques-Auguste de
Thou, in his will of 1616, made the provision, where his own
treasures were concerned, that his heirs should 'share my
manuscripts with those who shall have need of them, taking
good care that they be returned'. Thirty years later, Duke
August of Wolfenbüttel, who took such a great interest in
scientific life in Paris, spent a small fortune, through the agency
of his representative at the French court, the Dutchman
Abraham Wicquefort, on obtaining copies of manuscripts
preserved in Mazarin's library. Purchases, borrowings,

reproductions, all were means that contributed to widening the range of these men's knowledge, increasing their stock of information and developing their thought about the world. La Mothe le Vayer never went to China, about which he wrote in twenty different works, discussing music, housing and political organization. Nor did he ever go to America, though he discusses in his work *La Vertu des païens* the destiny awaiting the Indians of the New World: 'How, then, can it be supposed that a poor Indian, who, two hundred years ago, had never heard tell of the true religion, can therefore in no way avoid eternal punishment, even though he lived a moral life . . .'

All of them were, in the second place, avid for news of the world as it wagged: their curiosity was political in so far as information about war and peace, concerning the successions of princes, and on new books and discoveries in other countries was what they sought from their correspondents as an essential element of their daily lives. Observations of the heavens, eclipses, the geography of the moon, the spots on the sun (once astronomical telescopes had made it possible to describe them) were subjects of copious and unceasing exchanges, as also were the great, well-known experiments of Torricelli, communicated by Mersenne to young Pascal, who set about his own measuring experiments on the Puy de Dôme. They also sought every kind of information regarding both the new worlds and also the most ancient worlds of the Eastern Mediterranean – accounts of voyages, descriptions of rare animals, or of human inventions. The postal service, which had progressed in organization very greatly during the previous hundred years, helped considerably in the development of these exchanges, and scholars also took advantage of the travels of merchants who repeated the same journeys month after month.

Finally, and above all, it was the rule in this domain for one scholar to help another, for services of this order were always

performed on a basis of reciprocity. Guy Patin is without
contacts in Germany through which he can procure a certain
book that interests him, so he asks his friend Spon to help:
'If ever you are writing to Augsburg, do me the favour of
trying to obtain a little quarto which was printed there in
1607, entitled *Vita Joannis Vincenti Pinelli*, who was an
excellent man and who is often mentioned in the life of
M. Peiresc written by M. Gassendi.' Each scholar was in more
or less regular correspondence with a substantial number of
others, with Peiresc and Mersenne outdoing all the rest, a
hundred cubits higher than the average in this respect. A
minor provincial scholar like the Dijonnais Philibert de la
Mare possessed at the very least (as we know from the last
inventory made of his papers) thirty correspondents, the
most important being Samuel Petit, Nicolas Heinsius,
Gassendi, Spanheim, Johann von Petersdorf, De Court and
Joseph Suaverius. Their range of correspondents provides a
good way of defining the geographical and intellectual horizon
of these promoters of clubs of learned men.

Furthermore, their mobility was associated with their
taste for travel. Even more, perhaps, than their predecessors
of a century earlier, these savants made a practice of travelling,
and often stayed away for a long time, far from their home
bases. When young they had attended foreign universities –
Saumaise, like a good Protestant, had been to Heidelberg,
Peiresc to Padua, Spon to Ulm. Later, once established and
connected with a whole circle, they had no hesitation in
setting out – one in the train of a cardinal returning to Rome;
another entrusted with the task of finding some rare books for
a highly placed personage (like Naudé, on behalf of Mazarin);
yet another, without any particular destination, teaching here
and there, as employment proved available and as interesting
encounters came his way. The directions in which these
scholars tended to travel are not easy to account for. Few went,

as Peiresc did, to England, even though they all paid attention
to what was being published in that country, and Mersenne
had his most faithful correspondents there, in the persons of
Hartlib and Hubner. Rare, too, were visitors to the cities of
Germany, though the valley of the Rhine and Upper
Germany remained attractive. The United Provinces were
more frequented, especially as Protestants and enemies of the
Jesuits could breathe freely there. But the centre of attraction
was Italy – Venice, Padua, Florence, Rome. Bouchard and
Naudé stayed a long time there. Claude Quillet, the doctor
from Chinon who dared to challenge Laubardemont during
the exorcisms of Jeanne des Anges at Loudun in 1634, settled
in Rome and spent most of his life there. Others who went to
Italy included Sirmond, Bourdelot and Mersenne and they
met there both wits like Scarron and Saint-Amant and artists
like Nicolas Poussin. In this enthusiasm we must see, on the
whole, a journey of love which took these men to a country
whose intellectual traditions still had a certain fascination for
every scholar. Of the Italy of Galileo and of the treasures of
Antiquity that was certainly true. For Quillet, though, travel
was undertaken to escape, as it was for Saumaise, installed at
Leyden, or Descartes himself, who roamed about for a long
time, keeping at a distance from likely arrest in France. Others
travelled systematically in pursuit of their investigations, like
(a little later, to be sure) the Lyonnais De Monconys, whose
interest lay in machines and all sorts of human inventions.
Nevertheless, all of them were susceptible to the original
features they found in countries other than their own, and
amassed observations as they amassed books, always seeking
to enrich their knowledge. This very mobility of theirs was
related to the aims of their quest, the nature of their way of
thought, in the continuity of an endeavour which stretched
beyond 1640, into the decade 1650–60. When, suddenly,
within a few years, a number of their leading members died –

the Du Puy brothers in 1651 and 1656, Mersenne in 1648, Naudé in 1653, Gassendi in 1655 – a phase of Europe's intellectual life came to an end.

3. SAVANTS IN QUEST OF METHODS

It is not an easy task to define the intellectual procedures of the Republic of Science. Among its members no rule had been laid down that one should set everything out under three headings: premises, sequence of argument, conclusions. What could be more incoherent than Naudé's *Mascurat*? It is certainly easy to read, but littered with a thousand digressions which cause one to lose sight of the book's purpose. Reason was indeed frequently invoked by these writers, but that did not mean very much in a period when scientific (and even non-scientific) language made such free use of that word, counterposing it to the foolishness and credulity of the ordinary person, and when it was current practice, almost a school exercise, to argue successively for and against a given proposition, and we find examples of this in everyone's writings. It was a way of concealing one's own attitude, from politic prudence, no doubt, but it was also, and even more, an expression of concern to find thesis and antithesis. The learned men of the early seventeenth century wrote a great deal, on all subjects, and did not always draw, from protracted demonstrations which we read today with a certain boredom, any very clear conclusions, on which one could base oneself in order to determine the lines of force. Everyone described, recalled and quoted from certain well-known ancient sources, and everyone experimented or observed, often with shrewdness, but sometimes with no less credulity than that which had been repudiated two pages earlier. But all these quotations and observations remained unmarshalled; and sometimes were contradicted by the same writer a few years later.

These scholars of the early seventeenth century had remained, in part, humanists, in the sixteenth-century sense of the word, at once overwhelmed and delighted by the mass of knowledge provided by the writers of Antiquity, whose resources seemed to them not to be exhausted. They continued, or rather resumed, at second or third reading, the collation of manuscripts, the translations which had been made before their time and the interpretations that had followed these. For they were fully persuaded that they had to assimilate this ancient learning. It formed part of the language they needed in order to combine it with what they had learnt about their own time, about the new worlds and peoples of which neither the Bible nor the Elder Pliny nor Herodotus had been in a position to say anything. The papers left by Peiresc, as preserved in Bishop Inguimbert's library at Carpentras, are significant in this regard. Under all sorts of headings – Joan of Arc, for example – we find a mass of quotations and references, with a few remarks of his own, in the margin, so to speak. Saumaise, the most learned Protestant of his time, was similarly well known for being able to assemble all possible references on any subject. He carried them in his head, and when he left for Holland his friends rejoiced at the thought that he would find the time, thanks to this extraordinary capacity to file information away in his memory, to write while there the good books that he alone was capable of producing. Guy Patin wrote this to Spon in 1643 in so many words: 'The good M. Saumaise left for Holland on the fourth of this month: *utinam felici cursu naviget*. It is a very good thing for the Republic of Letters that he has gone there, so that he can get printed for us the many fine books that he has ready.' And there can be no doubt that this lively erudition, nourished by friendly exchanges and contributions, and presupposing perpetual vigilance for new books and belatedly discovered manuscripts, was regarded by them all as the very sign of their success. Some of them, such as Sorbière, write

letters which are veritable consultations, in which, on the
subject in hand, they make a complete 'review of the
question', first quoting all the writers who have ever said
anything on the matter, whatever their divergences, and
eventually give the most recently expressed opinions, chosen
not in accordance with the authority necessarily ascribed to the
classical writers but with the fame possessed by these modern
authors. After that come their own views, which are not, as
we would expect, presented as deductions or conclusions, but
merely added, eclectically, to all that has gone before. Only
astronomical and medical observations and mathematical
proofs are free from this long-drawn-out demonstration by
means of piling reference upon reference.

The galloping erudition of these insatiable and omnivorous
scholars showed itself very severely critical, however, where
popular notions and sentiments were concerned. Long before
the Catholic theologians applied themselves to denouncing
the superstitions and parasitical cults which had grown up
around religious practices, many of these learned persons had
proclaimed their disdain for such errors of the common man.
'Sophisticates' (déniaisés) as the members of the Paris Tétrade
called themselves, unbelievers as Cyrano or the physician
Bourdelot hinted, violently and constantly opposed to the
regular clergy and the Jesuits as Guy Patin persisted in
affirming (he was the only one of them who was unwilling
to go to Italy – the homeland of the monks), all the scholars
of Paris professed thorough contempt for everything that was
accepted as true by the lower orders. Michel de Marolles
gloated mockingly in his memoirs over the cult of relics as
he had seen it celebrated in the cities of Northern France. The
correspondents of Mersenne and Peiresc who lived outside
France expressed the same sentiments when they had occasion
to report a miracle or some popular enthusiasm. The public
exorcisms at Loudun and Louviers gave scope for much
sarcasm. A good deal earlier, when a poster announcing the

arrival of the Rosicrucians in Paris set the capital agog, Gabriel Naudé wrote, in 1623, a little book, *Instruction à la France sur la vérité de l'histoire des frères de la Rose-Croix*, to show that the popular success obtained by this sect was due not to the visionary insight which it flattered itself that it possessed, but to the light-mindedness of the masses, who flung themselves eagerly upon any picturesque novelty and believed anything they were told. These aristocrats of the mind were well above such old wives' tales and all vain beliefs of that sort. There was nothing here of Paracelsus's approach, seeking, contrariwise, to discover what was valid in empirical traditions and popular wisdom, which might preserve the lost secrets of ancestral knowledge. Learning was considered scholarly to the precise extent that it kept itself remote from these vulgar notions.

Hence the impression of critical scepticism conveyed by so many of the writings of these scholars. And yet their reasoning went further than that would imply, even where minor problems, dealt with in a few pages, were concerned. Here we have La Mothe le Vayer comparing the French and the Spaniards, whom he tries to present as being as much unlike each other as possible, in their way of life, dress, religious conceptions, and so on. In order to account for this contrast he has recourse to the classical medical theory of individual humours connected with the elements (earth, air, water, fire), that is, to soils and climates, winds and water-supplies. Many another scholar applied the same method, defining the characters of different nations by using this theory of the effects of environment. However, the argument stumbled over some embarrassing contradictions. Why, for instance, were Spaniards, Italians and Turks so different from each other, although the natural factors moulding them were (in the view of these writers) exactly the same? The explanation given was that the effects of political administration also played a part, which was capable of modifying profoundly what nature had created. This dualistic approach signified a great deal more than an orator's trick for resolving an incongruity between the theory being applied and what was actually observed: it testified to a search in which all these men were engaged, with uneven success – the search for a method that would enable them to coordinate the knowledge, accumulated during centuries, of which they were the possessors, struggling to master this vast inheritance.

The scholars of the early seventeenth century had already been urged to undertake this task of setting their knowledge in order at the very beginning of the century, by Francis Bacon. This not particularly distinguished Lord Chancellor of England described the path to be followed in order to master information of disparate kinds, in two works which found a great echo in learned circles: in 1604 *The Advancement of Learning* and in 1620 the *Novum organum scientiarum*. Bacon rejected all arguments based on authority (Aristotle's, in particular) and advised savants to proceed by way of observation and experiment, without bothering about the theological *impedimenta* their investigations might encounter as they did so. With his dream of laboratories and observatories where experiments could be carried out and learned men could do their work, Bacon sketched the path along which Galileo and Kepler were advancing at the very time that he wrote. He pointed out the path to be taken rather than preaching by example. The stimulus given by his works left open to those who were inspired by them a choice between several different approaches. Many men referred to Bacon as their inspiration in following lines of work that were very dissimilar, since observation and experiment can themselves lead to quite contradictory interpretations. At the time of Galileo's trial, how many were there who were able to accept the correct view, that the earth revolves around the sun and the sun only *seems* to revolve around the earth? Bacon himself, before his death, condemned the boldness of *The Messenger of the Stars*.

Observing and experimenting was not easy, since evidence was hard to corroborate in a period when bloody rain, storms and tornadoes were habitually interpreted as signs of Fate and interventions by God or the Devil. Making observations presupposes a rigorous definition of what constitutes Nature, otherwise everything is regarded as Nature, and physics loses itself in a confused mass of uncoordinated notes. The savants of the early seventeenth century were struggling amid such incoherences: and yet some of them succeeded in achieving remarkable things.

First and foremost was the incomparable savant, tormented both by his fate and by his ambitions, the Czech Jan Amos Komensky (Comenius) – a great admirer of Bacon, to the point of travelling to England, at Hartlib's invitation, shortly before the Civil War – who represents the encyclopaedic, 'pansophic' approach. Comenius, a minister of the Church of the Bohemian Brethren (the Utraquists), in 1616, when he was aged twenty-four, fell victim to the persecutions launched after the Battle of the White Mountain, left Bohemia in 1628 and settled at Leszno, in Poland. There he served for thirteen years as a schoolteacher in a transplanted community of Czechs, and at the same time acted as an elder uniting the Bohemian Brethren in exile, and wrote his first books, which soon became known even in the West. No less a mystic than a scholar, Comenius maintained relations for some time with the founder of the Rosicrucians, Johann Valentin Andreae. After 1641 he set out on his travels, visiting scholars in other parts of Europe, those men whom he greeted grandiloquently as 'you who are the light of Europe, you who are learned, pious and illustrious'. For seven years he travelled in Germany and in Holland, in England, where he decided not to settle, in Sweden, where Queen Christina invited him to organize a new system of schools, in Northern Poland (Torun) and in Hungary. Then he returned to Leszno, where he spent eight years writing his *Pansophia*. Forced to leave Leszno by the fire which destroyed the town in 1656, he spent the last years of his life in Holland, where he was his publisher's guest for a dozen years, dying, almost eighty years old, in 1670.

Despite these tribulations and the miseries of a nomadic life far from his homeland, Comenius succeeded in publishing a great deal, about a hundred works in his lifetime (not including the many re-editions), and, in addition, he left behind him twenty-odd manuscripts which have not been published even now. Comenius's work is better known in our time for its educational than for its scientific aspect. Yet this tireless and indomitable man, who corresponded with all the learned of Europe, was read by Mersenne, Hartlib and Descartes, and his innovations in pedagogy were discussed in the schools of Port-Royal and the colleges of the Oratory. His works provide a good idea of what, in the world of learning of those days, the aspiration to encyclopaedic knowledge could mean. His *Pansophiae Prodromus* presents a method of assembling all the information contained in books, classifying and ordering it so as to constitute that higher knowledge at which true savants should aim. This cumulative and regulated acquisition of knowledge involved undoubtedly a gigantic effort, but one which did not seem to the indefatigable pastor to be beyond men's power.

The biggest obstacle lay, for certain, in the fact that in order to read works written by modern savants in their respective national languages, instead of in Latin, one had first to learn these languages. In order to overcome this obstacle, Comenius wrote a manual of method, *Janua linguarum reserata* (*The Gate of Tongues*) which proceeds by way of the listing of words, without repetition or recapitulation – a hard method calling for an exceptional effort of memory (for which reason the teachers of Port-Royal declined to adopt it for their own schools). However, Comenius supplemented his *Pansophia* with a *Didactica magna* – along with a work on 'universal education' (*Panpaedia*) and one on the Pansophic School, written during his stay in Hungary – which was intended to establish, in accordance with his own experience, a comprehensive art of imparting all forms of knowledge, in town and country alike, 'with pleasure and thoroughness'. Here too Comenius was not afraid to take a broad view, and his teaching method was presented as applicable to literary subjects, to the sciences and to religion. The Pansophic School was to be a 'general workshop of wisdom' in which young people might learn 'to know things, to understand them, and to put them to use'. In the introduction to his *Didactica magna* he describes it as 'the universal art of teaching everything to everyone, so that the youth of both sexes, without any exception anywhere, may be educated in letters and science, moulded in good manners, filled with piety, and instructed from their earliest years in all that may be of service to them, in their lives both present and to come'.

Comenius set out his teaching programme in a timetable of years, days and hours, with the meticulous detail of an educational planner, taking for granted that pupils were endowed with exceptional powers of endurance, both physical and mental. He constructed his educational programme, like his scientific method, with the loftiest of ambitions – inspired by his religious ethics and by his actual experience as a man persecuted and driven from his country, and one disappointed from his early years by stultifying schools and universities. The *Pansophia* and the *Didactica* were to make it possible to change the world in the way dreamt of by a pastor for whom 'all men on earth are brothers', and who wanted to remedy the miseries of his time, being convinced that a wider dissemination of knowledge was the road to salvation, since, as he wrote, 'what are rich men without wisdom but swine stuffing themselves with husks? And what are poor men living in ignorance but pitiful little donkeys loaded with burdens?'

This preacher who maintained in exile the faith of his

fellow-Czechs and their allegiance to their lost homeland (in 1632, moved by vague hopes of a Czech restoration, he hastened to compose a project for re-establishing schools in the kingdom of Bohemia), this educational reformer from whom plans were requested in Sweden and Hungary, did not accomplish any scientific work of his own, any more than the Englishman who was his model. But his books – the *Orbis pictus*, the *Physicae synopsis*, the *Pansophia* – were read and commented on, throughout Europe, for a long time to come. *The Gate of Tongues* was translated into a dozen European languages and also into Persian, Turkish, Arabic and Mongolian (if Bayle is to be believed). Even minor works like his *Fortunae faber* were sought by scholars in the book-markets of Europe. Whatever his limitations, he represents one of the major tendencies in the research of his time, and others determined their line of thought either as his continuators or as his opponents, taking up positions and deciding on their paths accordingly. In this sense he has his place in the discordant concert of the European world of learning to which he felt he belonged, despite the isolation that was his lot for such a long time, in his modest home in exile.

A different attitude was that of Mersenne's group. They aimed to build a new science through mathematics and experiment. The savants who attended Mersenne's receptions were attracted, like his correspondents, by the clarity and force with which this Father of the Minim Order was able to frame questions and indicate the lines leading to answers. The weekly meetings in the Place Royale were certainly first and foremost meetings for the discussion of problems, at which everyone profited by the definitions and propositions put forward by the leader of the group: whether what was involved was observations recently made with telescopes, theories about music or knotty problems of mathematics, what Mersenne had to say was always useful. Pascal puts it excellently in his *Histoire de la roulette, autrement appelée cycloïde*: 'He possessed a special talent for framing good questions, and in this had perhaps no peer; and although he was not so successful in answering them – and it is in that, strictly speaking, that all the honour lies – it is nevertheless true that we are indebted to him, and he occasioned many notable discoveries which would perhaps never have been made if he had not stirred up the interest of savants.' Pascal's formulation is even somewhat harsh, since we know that when a question has been rightly framed it is to some extent already answered; but his last point expresses well the feeling of gratitude that the Republic of Savants entertained towards this incomparable 'instigator'.

Mersenne was certainly something more than a stimulus to his colleagues, in so far as his theory of method, as set forth in juxtaposed fragments in his *Questions théologiques, physiques, morales et mathématiques* and *Questions curieuses utiles aux prédicateurs, aux théologiens, aux astrologues, aux médecins et aux philosophes*, both published in 1634, offered an alternative to that of Comenius. The way in which every question put before these gatherings of savants was subjected to discussion signified, implicitly at least (in so far as Father Mersenne did not care to bring down the thunderbolts of the theologians by rejecting categorically and clearly the orthodoxy taught at the Sorbonne), a rejection of all pre-established authority, no matter what prestige or institutionalized approval this might possess, and so a complete rejection of the scholastic tradition. Where strictly mathematical problems were concerned, such as Archimedes' spiral, the risk was obviously less serious than with astronomical matters, yet the Mersenne group does not seem to have proceeded differently in its discussions of the two types of subject. Moreover, Mersenne's comrades in study advocated, as he did, resort to experiment wherever this was practicable. In the musical sphere, the studies of sounds and their harmonies which were proposed were connected with the construction and playing of instruments. In astronomy, all argument regarding longitude and latitude was based upon observation and measurement, which Mersenne himself practised assiduously. The famous question of the vacuum (or, rather, of Nature's alleged 'abhorrence' of a vacuum, that excellent example of qualitative physics) was dealt with by way of experiment and measurement, from the top of the Tour St Jacques. Finally, and especially, they all saw mathematics as the essential means of understanding natural phenomena. It was this characteristic, stressed by Mersenne in 1623–5, that explains both the effectiveness of their procedure, and also the tentativeness: the former because this translation of everything into mathematical terms eliminated *ipso facto*, in every problem, the uncertainties and confusions always present in the 'qualitative physics' of natural philosophers like Campanella and Pomponazzi; and the latter because the mathematical instruments at the disposal of these investigators, who were particularly fond of geometry, were not always adequate to enable them to make much progress, with a procedure that dealt with questions one after the other, in rapid succession, as it were.

This primacy accorded to mathematics, which they saw as 'the truth of the sciences' (this was the title that Mersenne gave in 1625 to his book 'against the Sceptics or Pyrrhonists'), this mathematicizing of natural phenomena, justified the term mechanism which the historians of science have applied to the method of Mersenne and his friends. It did indeed amount to a reduction of connexions in nature to the mechanical relationship aimed at in this procedure, and which was affirmed in those 'notable discoveries' mentioned by Pascal, whose own scientific work can be quoted as illustrating what he says. And yet Mersenne's mechanism, even though stoutly supported by great thinkers like Gassendi, did not seem at all to contemporaries to be a universal method which could make possible a continuous advance in scientific knowledge. This was partly because Mersenne concerned himself with describing and commenting on particular cases, neglecting general theory, and partly because this theory was contributed from elsewhere, and was given to the world at the very moment when the mathematical academy of the Place Royale had just developed its full scope: this was the *Discours de la méthode* of René Descartes, published in 1637.

Although Descartes did not belong to the circle of 'learned freethinkers' nor even to Mersenne's group, he has to be seen in relation to them. This great traveller participated in the activities of the Place Royale only very incidentally, while he was in Paris, that is to say, not for very long in a life of protracted wandering which took him from his native Touraine and the Jesuit college of La Flèche to Upper Germany, where he fought in the army led by Maurice of Nassau, then later to the United Provinces, to Amsterdam, Franeker, Leyden and Utrecht, where he was very happy until the persecuting mood of some Calvinist theologians caused him to flee, and finally to Stockholm, where he died in the middle of the century, at the height of a glory acquired over a period of twenty years.

A correspondent of Mersenne's in the 1620s, he soon became known for his early work, which attracted attention well beyond Paris circles. In 1626 an inhabitant of Rouen, who was interested in telescopes and refraction, asked Mersenne for help: 'I shall be greatly obliged to you and to M. Descartes if you will inform me of his excellent method and inventions.' Descartes kept assiduously in touch with all his acquaintances, in Paris and elsewhere, as his abundant correspondence is enough to prove, and he did not conceal his debt to these exchanges of letters and the discussions and debates about which he learnt. More than some others, who bitterly disputed over priority in the discoveries made in this period, René Descartes was able to appreciate the extent to which research is, in all sciences, a collective task. He wrote in 1631: 'So that many people's experience may help to discover the finest things in Nature, and to build a science of physics which would be clear, and certain, and based on proof and more useful than that commonly taught.' But he placed himself outside this joint effort, aimed at replacing the outworn physics of Aristotle, precisely because he was able to set forth and define the method, valid for all sciences, which he offered to everyone 'for rightly conducting one's reason and seeking for truth in the sciences', according to the phrase he took over from Bacon.

The little book which appeared in 1637 presented the extraordinary merit of setting forth in simple language the precepts to which the other mechanist savants referred confusedly and implicitly, and giving them a plain and clear expression so that they sound like proverbs: 'To accept as true nothing that I did not know to be evidently so', 'to conduct my thoughts in an orderly fashion, starting with what was simplest and easiest to know, and rising little by little to the knowledge of the most complex'. Written and published in French, 'because I hope for a better judgement of my opinions from those who use only their natural reason in its purity than from those who only trust old books' (written in Latin), the *Discours de la méthode* provided its contemporaries with a sure guide – or, rather, with a set of themes on which they might reflect at length with advantage, so as the better to grasp the articulation of scientific reasoning and thereby construct a science that should be solid, with foundations all the more resistant because everything in them would have been subjected to the test of systematic doubt. The truth of science was thenceforth not to be arrived at by mere mathematicizing of whatever was measurable, but by the logical test that the savant could apply to his entire procedure, broken down into its separate elements and their interconnexions. 'Those long chains of reasons, all quite simple and quite easy, which geometers are wont to employ in reaching their most difficult demonstrations, had given me occasion to imagine that all the possible objects of human knowledge were linked together in the same way . . .'

Science is constituted through testing, selecting and setting in order, and is therefore quite the contrary of the cumulative encyclopaedism advocated by Comenius and the confused naturalism of Campanella and Giordano Bruno. When Campanella, fleeing from the Holy Office, came to Holland while Descartes was living there, the latter was not even at home to him. As for Comenius, one of whose works he read with attention, Descartes indicated to a correspondent the respect that so great an aspiration could arouse and acknowledged the justification of the criticism made in the book: 'The author is clearly an intelligent and learned man, of great integrity and public spirit. All his criticisms of the accepted sciences and teaching methods are only too true, and his complaints are only too justified.' Then, however, he condemns, with the sharp clarity that goes with the self-assurance given him by his own method: 'It is often very difficult to judge accurately what others have written, and to draw the good out of them without taking the bad too. Moreover, the particular truths which are scattered in books are so detached and so independent of each other, that I think one would need more talent and energy to assemble them into a well-ordered collection, as your author plans to do, than to make up such a collection of one's own discoveries.' Which amounts to saying that the Cartesian method is superior to that of Comenius, and that the savant will progress faster if he builds his knowledge on the basis of his own discoveries, patiently formed into a coherent whole, than if he applies himself to collecting the wheat from the mass of already published books, separating this, for better or worse, from the tares.

But Descartes also marked himself off, in a way that it is more difficult to define, from those savants who, following Mersenne, employed the mathematical method and were no less mechanistic than he was. In Part Three of the *Discours* he

sets forth the bases for 'a provisional morality' which is not
subject to methodical doubt, and which furnishes him with his
rules of conduct: 'to obey the laws and customs of my
country' and 'always to attempt the mastery over myself
rather than over fortune, to try to alter my desires rather than
the course of the world'. These are rules which in some
respects resemble those guiding the conduct of the freethinkers of the time. But these maxims are set apart, like the
truths of faith, and this is where we observe the essential
divergence, which concerns metaphysics: whereas Mersenne's
friends tried (even if they did not always say this very clearly
in their writing) to exclude all metaphysics from their
speculations, and refused to allow it scientific status, Descartes
gave a place, in his *Discours* and his *Méditations*, to a realm of
faith which is independent of doubt and scientific method – a
realm of revealed truths which impose themselves by argument alone and are not subject to that critical examination and
systematic reconstruction that other branches of knowledge
must undergo. In Part Four of the *Discours*, which gives 'the
reasons by which he proves the existence of God and of the
human soul, which are the foundation of his metaphysics',
after having affirmed: *Cogito, ergo sum*, Descartes – 'here, by
your leave, I will freely use scholastic terms' – proves that
God exists, by analysing the idea of perfection, and declares:
'it follows that it is as certain as any geometrical proof can
be that God, who is this perfect being, is or exists.'

This Cartesian metaphysics worried and alarmed the other
mechanists. In 1641 Gassendi published his *Dubitationes*,
devoted to this part of Descartes's philosophy: the very title
shows what his own attitude was. Again, in 1644, he produced
a *Disquisitio metaphysica* which recapitulated all the criticisms
he had levelled previously against this 'deviation' in
Cartesianism. This duality in the thought of Descartes, which
caused so much ink to flow, even later on, and which does not
impair the liberating virtues of his method, in relation to the

uncertainties and muddles of the previous period in science, is also of interest in connexion with Descartes's existential situation. It reminds us of the caution dictated by the insecurity of innovating intellectuals in a European society where the reigning orthodoxies were intensifying their inquisitorial vigilance.

4. THE GEOGRAPHY OF EUROPE'S INTELLECTUAL LIFE

No European country can be presented as having been in this epoch a land of liberty where the savant could work and publish just as he liked. Holland, so highly appreciated by the French, from Sorbière to Descartes, was not really an exception to the rule, since the Gomarists were able brutally to impose their will there, for a while; but the position of men of learning was, on the whole, more tolerable there than elsewhere. Taking Europe in its entirety, however, the essential factor to be kept in mind is the diffidence and caution which everyone who wanted to write had to impose upon himself. Even where an Inquisition in the Spanish style had no power, there was a censorship that functioned with more or less redoubtable efficiency. Some advances in this respect were made in France during this period. In 1604 a royal ordinance required that a copy of every new book be deposited in the Royal Library, to be examined by an official reader. In 1623 a state censorship was organized (without superseding the censorship which had already been exercised for a century by the theological faculty of the Sorbonne): every new book had to be submitted to an office for control of the book-trade, and this office gave the publisher, on application, the sole right to publish the book in question, for a certain period. In 1629 this office came under the authority of the Chancellor, who improved its services, providing specialist readers – some for theology (whose opinions might differ from those of the doctors of the Sorbonne), others for politics, literature and the sciences. When Descartes wanted to have his *Discourse on Method* printed, in 1637, Chancellor Séguier asked to examine this work personally. In other countries, where the services for the supervision of the printed word were less highly developed, it was the religious authorities who undertook to exercise a measure of control *a posteriori* which was no less severe: in one place the Consistory performed this task, in another the Lutheran bishops, and everywhere the most expert theologians took a hand. When the monarch in person fancied himself as a theologian, as in the case of King James I of England, the interests of scholars were in even graver jeopardy.

Finally, mention must be made of the virulent animosities created by the persistent debates provoked by certain events. Was the murder of Henri IV to be attributed to the Jesuits, like that of his predecessor? Then there was the Prague defenestration, the Diet of Regensburg, the death of Gustavus Adolphus ... Polemic flourished in every sphere in which both sides had good writers at their command to indict the adversary. Father Garasse, and Mersenne himself in his early days, wrote pamphlets to denounce, to the authorities who were empowered to punish them, the proliferating atheistic freethinkers of Paris in the 1620s: they were said to number, broadly, fifty thousand (out of a total population of 400,000 ...). For one Pascal who, twenty years later, took the trouble patiently to compose a compendium of arguments aimed at convincing the freethinkers of their errors, there were ten Garasses who preferred to point their fingers at the criminals and demand the harshest punishments for them. Pierre Du Puy found this to be so in 1638, when he wished to publish a *Traité des droits et libertés de l'Eglise gallicane* in which he put together nineteen small works already published, all having been approved for copyright when they first appeared: worthy preachers were distressed at the project, the Nuncio himself intervened, and eventually a decision by the King's Council banned the new *Traité* – without withdrawing the approvals already granted. Denunciations, oratorical exaggerations, false imputations ... The intelligentsia did not wait until the twentieth century to invent this kind of terrorism, and the time of troubles and of fanatical conflicts of which Jacques Callot furnished the most realistic picture gave wide scope for such base practices. No doubt these verbal excesses were not all followed by the desired effects, any more than the measures of supervision in the realm of publication were always effective, since the police were not sufficiently numerous or well enough equipped to prevent either the pirating of publications or the circulation of prohibited works. Nevertheless, that there was a tightening up of supervising and suspicion is clear.

This explains to a large extent the equivocal behaviour of the men of learning, who wanted to spare themselves the indignities of prosecution and police inquiries. The most obvious example is that of the Parisian scholar-freethinkers to whom R. Pintard has devoted a lengthy study. Respecting the laws of the kingdom and the rules of their world, they were firmly conformist, went to Mass, and to communion at Easter, *more majorum*. In the discreet privacy of their gatherings of friends, however, far from the curious and from informers, they showed themselves resolutely impious, in words, and not very virtuous, either. At church they were outwardly pious, as required, but in an arbour where white wine loosened tongues, in a remote retreat at Choisy-sur-Seine, they were bold fellows, indifferent to their positions in the Church and their responsibilities of state. We will say nothing about the moral libertinism which was freely ascribed to them by envious contemporaries, and by historians fascinated by the scabrous memoirs of Jean-Jacques Bouchard. But their two-faced attitude where intellectual and spiritual matters

were concerned seems beyond doubt: other memoirs, those
of Michel de Marolles, are there to prove it, not to mention
many a hint in their correspondence.

This ambiguity is also to be found in their works, in which
there are so many dialogues, enabling the *pro* and the *contra*
to be argued, the orthodox position and also the blasphemous
one, and so many references solemnly given which enable the
writer to take cover behind the authority of some classical
author and slyly put forward his own opinion without
formally accepting responsibility for it. This was an art that
they all practised, and, because of it, exegetists were to wear
themselves out trying to ascertain what these writers *really*
thought. On more than one point, to be sure, it is possible to
see clearly. Cyrano, for example, was indeed against witch-
trials. But what did Naudé think on that subject, judging by
his *Apologie pour les grands hommes accusés de magie*? What was
the actual philosophy of Gassendi, who wrote an apologia for
Epicurus and opposed Descartes, and left a large part of his
work in manuscript, as Jean Bodin had done formerly with
his *Heptaplomeres*? On any and every theme they were always
as slippery as eels. If they wrote about men's attitude to their
mother-country, after duly quoting the best authors of
Antiquity, they are to be observed advancing in extended
order, one praising parish-pump patriotism and evoking the
mother-country that one inherits at birth, while another
repudiates this allegiance and will allow no 'mother-country'
but that which a man chooses for himself, the place where he
finds it is good to live: one says he is a Frenchman first and
foremost, while another prefers London to Paris. Who was
being deceived by this game and who was getting the point?
It is not surprising, in the circumstances, that their contemporaries pulled them this way and that, some praising
their bottomless knowledge and rigorous judgement while
others were hostile and contemptuous towards these impious
men who dared not come out openly: nor that, in this

connexion, some saw in Descartes's metaphysics only something spatchcocked in, serving merely as a pretence intended to
let the rest of the work get by – a view long accepted by
lovers of coherent philosophical systems, denouncing the
'philosopher in the mask'.

We should certainly not confine ourselves to these men's
writings, but consider them also in the way they behaved in a
society where nothing favoured the new ideas they were
advancing. Throughout Europe, men of letters and learning
were, unless they had suffered some calamity, included in the
entourages of the great, or in some social situation that *ipso
facto* guaranteed them a degree of protection against the
repressive institutions. They were councillors in the sovereign
courts of France, stewards in the courts of petty German
princes, incumbents of ecclesiastical benefices – all positions of
some comfort. Some of them had done even better, acquiring
places in the immediate service of the rulers: librarians to
Mazarin or to Richelieu, like Naudé and La Mothe le Vayer,
tutors to kings and princes, like La Mothe le Vayer, again, and
Gassendi. Such functions of intellectual service could be
perilous – Naudé had experience of that during the Fronde –
and confining, but they constituted a reliable form of protection. An even grander case was that of Francis Bacon, who
became Lord Chancellor of England, like Thomas More
before him: no doubt his career was not a very successful one,
and brought him some disappointment, but that did not
happen on account of his scientific work. Giving good
measure, some of these learned men who placed themselves
so haughtily above the common level acted as apologists for
the absolutism preached by their masters, the cardinal-
ministers: against the turbulence of the nobles, the dissidence
of the Protestants and the endemic popular revolts, they
recommended taking the most despotic measures. Naudé said
in his political writings that the Massacre of St Bartholomew's
Eve was a failure because not all the Protestants were extermi-

nated, and later he was angry with Mazarin for not imprison-
ing and silencing the pamphleteers who attacked him in
1648–9. They preached the doctrine of 'reason of state' –
provided that its severities did not affect the sovereign's
councillors.

Such language and such conduct on the part of savants who
had to work on the fringe of orthodoxy and against the stream
indicate the general atmosphere of a society in which they
had not managed to find a place: they were led, so to speak,
to put themselves under the direct and personal protection of
those whose task it would be, if they were to expose themselves completely, to hunt down and destroy them. Theirs
was a double duplicity, or ambiguity, which shows us the
degree of oppression that was felt and experienced by these
men. As Descartes, constantly on the run, happy to be free,
'with one foot in one country, and one in another', expressed
it so well in 1648, returning from a stay in France shortly
before his death: 'I was not sorry to have been there, but much
happier to have left, for those who make the most brilliant
show there seemed to me to be the ones most to be pitied.'
In a more subtle way this was expressed in the enigmatic
pictures of the painter Georges de la Tour, from Lorraine,
those pictures in which the source of light, always hidden,
seems to express the occultation of the eternal Church after
the Council of Trent; in which Saint Jerome, the smiling
patron of the humanists of the sixteenth century, has become
a victim of flogging, crushed and bloodstained beneath his
purple robe; and in which the wretchedness and poverty of
the humble folk, and the vice and cheating of the great, have
become objects for visual contemplation and expressions of a
baroque society wherein the flickering light of hope has sought
refuge in some place where the powers of this world do not
take it to be. The society of the early seventeenth century was
indeed baroque, throughout Europe, and baroque in the
sense that J. Rousset and Ortega y Gasset defined, for the men

of learning as for everyone else. For the men of learning, migration, moving about from one country to another, was certainly a safeguard. Nomadism was a remedy for insecurity, and perhaps the most reliable one: Campanella, Descartes, Quillet, Comenius, Saumaise, Sorbiere exemplify this existential truth. It is not possible to draw up a complete list of these migrations: nearly all the learned men of the early seventeenth century would appear in it.

What this meant was that conditions for work and publication were not equally favourable in every country, not only as regards the repressive intentions of governments and Churches but also with respect to the support, mutual aid and shelter that were available. When we read these men's complaints and eulogies and follow the itineraries that they liked best, we become aware of an intellectual geography which must not be overlooked if we want to understand how collective work developed in the middle of the seventeenth century. In one group were the states in which surveillance of savants and of their works was at its most severe, namely, Spain and France. In picaresque Spain the Inquisition, restored half a century earlier, revealed remarkable efficiency in dealing with whatever might, even remotely, endanger Roman orthodoxy. Suspicion of illuminism, more to be feared even than suspicion of Protestantism, enabled anyone to be prosecuted who had not succeeded in securing the protection of a bishop: *alumbrados*, like witches, were harassed all the more energetically because poverty was forcing so many beggars, knights errant, hermits and clerics to take to the road, and the state's police combined with the Catholic Church to maintain a strict subordination which lasted all through the century.

In France, where institutional harmony between the judiciary and the ecclesiastical authorities was less complete, oppression was nevertheless equally heavy. The disputes over Gallicanism, in which theologians and magistrates took opposing sides, did not, on the whole, bring any benefit to those who were developing and expressing ideas that were remote from orthodoxy. The exaltation of royal sovereignty, for which the sovereign courts of justice had been working for decades contributed to stimulate the repression undertaken by the Parlements of Paris and the provinces. Two trials which received a measure of publicity offer illustrations of this rigour: that of Giulio-Cesare Vanini before the Parlement of Toulouse in 1618 and that of Théophile de Viau in Paris. The former, a physician from Padua and an unfrocked Carmelite, had written blasphemies on the subject of miracles and advocated a natural morality. Imprisoned and sentenced to be burnt, he made when before the executioner a profession of his atheist beliefs which would doubtless not have attracted much attention if the *Mercure français* had not published a lengthy report of the case and of the scandalous words uttered by the physician, and moralized about his impious end. A few years later, Théophile de Viau, a licentious poet who had been received at court, being denounced by Father Garasse and some other censor, found himself in trouble with the Parlement of Paris: sentenced to death, then saved through the intervention of a highly placed personage, he succeeded, by recantation after recantation, in avoiding the worst. But his trial and experiences served as a warning to the freethinkers of the age. France's courts of law, which were pitiless towards men who uttered blasphemies in taverns, or humble folk who forgot some saint's day, in this way caused a louring threat to hover over all who openly attacked authority and made themselves liable to the charge of lese-majesty, whether human or divine. When the administration of justice was under Cardinal Richelieu's supreme control, and creatures of his like Martin de Laubardemont were its ruthless executants, the full significance of this threat became apparent. In 1638 the Abbé de Saint-Cyran was thrown into prison for having shown a critical attitude towards Richelieu's policy, and there he stayed despite the scandal involved, until the cardinal's death. During the Fronde, in the few months when the Parlement set itself against the new cardinal-minister, forgetting its duty to the state, this constraint was certainly relaxed, and pamphleteers could publish whatever they liked, but that was only an interlude which prepared the way for regulations that were even stricter than before. In the period as a whole, France proved to be a country of firm police control, where the savants, the learned men, no less than the politicians, were hard put to it to gain expression for their ideas: Saumaise, though a pensioner of Mazarin's, said this more than once, as also did Sorbière and Naudé, like Descartes.

Eastward from France, in Italy and the Empire, and even in Poland and Hungary, conditions were not the same, and, on the whole, they were less difficult. In a Germany fragmented both politically and in respect of religion, and tormented by war for over a quarter-century, there could be no question of establishing a single-minded censorship and system of repression. The Swedish invasions, the changes of sovereignty, the distrust shown by all the princes, even the Catholics among them, towards the Emperor's ambitions – all this told in favour of a fragmentation which allowed of freedom of expression far greater than in a highly centralized country. So long as he could find a good protector, or could manage to run away in time, the German savant could always get by unharmed, and even voice his ideas.

This was the case especially because princes who were keenly interested in literature and the sciences were not lacking, and were generous patrons within the limits of their resources and their enthusiasms. At the court of Württemberg, in Stuttgart, the office of Court Chaplain (*Hofprediger*) was held for a long time by Johann Valentin Andreae, Grand Master of the Rosicrucians, whose reputation transcended the frontiers of the Empire. In North Germany, Duke August of Brunswick-Wolfenbüttel, ruler of his little duchy since 1635, was the greatest collector of books in all Germany: a man

whose curiosity extended to all the sciences, but especially to
the occult ones, and a great builder, who maintained in his
household two painters and a dozen other artists, he had
representatives in all the cities that were important intellectually – in Rome, Augsburg, Strasbourg, Vienna, Paris,
Hamburg – and these bought books for him in trunks-full at a
time. His correspondence, and his largesse to savants both
German and otherwise (Mézeray, for instance), prove his
goodwill towards the world of learning. The Elector of
Brandenburg, though he did not show such great interest in
scientific affairs, likewise had a representative in Paris in the
1640s who kept him informed about intellectual (and political)
life in France.

Thus, the climate differed from principality to principality,
and conditions varied in degree of difficulty. In Bohemia,
subject since 1620 to a Catholic Germanization that was
extremely oppressive, an entire tradition was crushed: elsewhere, through the will of a prince who was interested in the
arts and sciences, savants were encouraged; elsewhere again,
in the free cities, which were often divided in religion, a
quarrelsome and stimulating coexistence was the rule. In
Italy, equally fragmented and in part under Spanish rule, and
where the Holy Office closely supervised everything published,
repressive severity was mitigated by Rome's administrative
slackness at the police level, by the rivalries between the
different religious orders, and by the pretensions of the great
princely and Roman families. Venice, Florence and Rome
continued to be international meeting-places, owing to the
monuments of Antiquity and to the reputation retained by
Padua and kept alive by savants like Torricelli, but also owing
to the relative impunity that a good protector ensured, something that was appreciated by De Monconys and Naudé,
Bouchard and Quillet. To be sure, everyone knew the fate of
Campanella and Galileo. But while this made men shudder,
it did not seem irremediable: a few months before he died,

Peiresc wrote a touching letter to a Roman cardinal, asking him to put an end to the imprisonment of an old man whose fame was assured for centuries to come. Whether it was listened to or not, this appeal was sent, and that showed not so much Peiresc's naïveté as his exact knowledge of Roman society and of the resources available to those who knew how to make use of them.

In Poland and Hungary, where the nobles possessed a *de facto* independence which was at least as great as that enjoyed by the princes of the Empire, the situation of the savants would have been comparable to that which prevailed in Germany, had not important changes been under way in both countries, resulting from the thrust of the Catholic campaign of reconquest. In Poland, where Protestant sects had flourished in the sixteenth century and the Socinians had won serious influence for several decades, the tide was running in favour of Catholicism: the Polish 'sectaries' then sought refuge in the United Provinces, where their coming caused a stir, and in some of the small German states. In Hungary the magnates, who were mostly Calvinist, maintained their religious positions firmly against the Jesuits, who were protected by the Habsburgs and established in the towns. In both countries the intellectual and religious debate was reserved to the great noble families, who were not well equipped to offer effective resistance to the Catholic offensive.

To the same style belonged, finally, the court of Queen Christina of Sweden, that amazing figure of the middle years of the century, protectress of the freethinkers who came confidently to seek refuge with her, suffered under her overwhelming erudition, and went away again. A hospitable host to Frenchmen, she welcomed in Stockholm, after 1650, some scholars nearing the end of their careers – Bourdelot, Naudé and Du Fresne – who gave a good account of themselves in argument with her. Naudé, whom she appointed her librarian, wrote a fine eulogy of her (which gives a good description of a

learned person's study in those days, apart from the mathematical instruments) in a letter to Gassendi: 'As for her
library, of which I have the management *cum absoluto imperio*,
it is very rich in manuscripts, including those of M. Petau,
M. Gaulmin, Monseigneur le Cardinal Mazarin, a certain
Stephanides, Ravius and others. But in respect of printed
books it must be said that it will be possible to make it much
better than it is now, only as a result of the negligence of
those who had charge of the library before me. In addition,
she has a gallery of statues, both in bronze and in marble,
medallions made of gold, silver and bronze, pieces of ivory,
amber, coral and cut glass, mirrors of steel, clocks, tables, bas-
reliefs and other objects, both man-made and natural, as rich
as ever I saw in Italy. There are also pictures, of which she
possesses a marvellous number; and so you see that *habet
animum apertum ad omnia*.' So open was her mind, indeed, that
the Queen abandoned both her freethinker friends and her
faithful subjects, indefectibly attached to Lutheranism, to
become a convert to the Catholic faith, far from her Swedish
homeland, which had been so briefly an asylum for innovating
intellectual activity.

There remain to be discussed two countries which enjoy
the reputation of having favoured savants and dissidents of
every kind, the two rising maritime powers of the seventeenth
century: England and the United Provinces. In both cases the
reputation is to some extent undeserved, since the regime of
Laud and Strafford, under Charles I, and the reign of the
Gomarists cannot be classed as liberal. Nevertheless, scholars
who came to England or Holland from elsewhere appreciated
in both countries a freedom of demeanour and of speech that
was rare in that period. Sorbière, describing his first visit to
England, waxes ecstatic, as De Monconys also was to do, later.
Saumaise wrote, after the execution of Charles I, a long treatise
in defence of this good Protestant king whose death could
not be treated as tyrannicide, as it could if he had been a

Catholic (*Apologie royale pour Charles Ier, roi d'Angleterre*, published in 1650). Yet what most impressed visitors to London, Oxford and Cambridge was not the institutional regime but the liberties actually taken by 'lecturers', those Anglican preachers on the verge of dissent, and also the important amount of work that was published in England: savants like William Harvey and Hartlib and political thinkers like Hobbes were leading figures in an intellectual activity which seemed all the richer for being largely concentrated in London. To this was added the abundance of political publications, that frenzy of pamphleteering that broke out during crises – in 1628 and, especially, after 1640. For whoever discovered England after the latter date there could be no doubt: such truly complete freedom of expression had no equivalent on the Continent.

The only possible exception to that statement was the tiny, newly established state of the United Provinces. The provinces which had wrested independence from their Spanish rulers after thirty years of struggle did indeed offer a place of welcome to the dissenters of all Europe, whatever their colour might be – except for Catholics, of course. When the Anabaptists were being hunted down, at the end of the sixteenth century, throughout Germany, in Lutheran and Catholic states alike, they came to Holland. The Polish Socinians, ill-treated by the Catholics, did the same. Comenius and Descartes both chose the Holland of merchants, painters and preachers, where everyone followed his own course without troubling too much about his neighbour, provided he did not disturb public order. Descartes noted one day the long period during which he had been able to live quietly, without disturbing or being disturbed by anyone, in the towns where he was received.

These various influxes certainly gave rise to a problem, one that constantly divided the mass of the Dutch population: whereas the business bourgeoisie accepted *de facto* a state of religious pluralism, the 'integrist' Calvinists who dominated the Consistories, and leant for support on the House of Orange and on the lower orders, wanted to fight against this. However, despite a series of conflicts and compromises, the United Provinces succeeded in upholding their principles of hospitality. Whenever a persecution of Protestants occurred in Europe, Holland offered them refuge: when Richelieu began his struggle against the Protestants of La Rochelle, Holland proved as hospitable to them as England. Soon the Dutch made provision in their distinguished schools and universities for the pastors and theologians who had been driven from their own countries. Dutch students went to Heidelberg, while German students, and French ones too (until the King forbade this), went to study in these schools in the United Provinces. All those who knew themselves to be regarded as 'of unsound faith' in their own countries turned towards Holland. All forms of Protestantism, including the tiniest sects, heirs of the little groups of enthusiasts of the preceding century, found homes there, established in the great commercial and manufacturing cities then in constant expansion, and practised a more or less discreet proselytism. It is not easy to reconstitute the details of this vitality of the sects on Dutch territory: however, along with other unmistakable signs, the boom enjoyed by the book trade offers especially convincing evidence. Whoever wanted to obtain new publications needed to have a correspondent in Amsterdam, and the Dutch booksellers showed themselves capable of profiting by this situation: their confidential agents travelled all over Europe, to Bohemia, Italy and France.

But the clearest sign of this opening of their gates practised by the States General of the United Provinces is certainly the welcome they gave to the Jews who arrived from Central Europe and from the Iberian Peninsula, allowing them to establish synagogues and seminaries for their rabbis, on the sole condition that they must be loyal to the state, a condition that the Jewish communities never wavered in observing. In mid-century Amsterdam had two synagogues: one for the Sephardim, who, originating in Portugal and Spain, had swarmed from Bayonne to Nantes and as far as Hamburg, but had settled in especially large numbers in Holland, and the other for the Ashkenazim, originating in Central Europe, who, having encountered ill-treatment in Prague and Cracow, found a kindly welcome in Holland. There, Hebrew studies and Jewish religious life were soon flourishing, carrying on the torch from Prague and Venice. The most famous of the 'doctors' of the new synagogue, Menasseh ben Israel, enjoyed in the 1640s a reputation that extended far beyond Jewish circles: his books *De termino vitae*, *De resurrectione mortuorum*, *De fragilitate humana*, were to be found in numerous learned libraries, sought for and appreciated on a par with many a Christian theological dissertation of the time. It was in this milieu that, in 1632, was born Baruch Spinoza, son of the head of the Sephardic community in Amsterdam. The equilibrium, under Calvinist domination, which had been achieved in the intellectual and spiritual life of the United Provinces was given full symbolic expression by an artist, who, without turning his back on the civic and everyday-life subjects dear to his predecessors, Vermeer and Frans Hals in particular, found inspiration in the Scriptures, without troubling himself with the theologians, and painted no longer set portraits but scenes from life, like *The Syndics of the Cloth Hall* and *The Night Watch*, and, above all, evoked the great religious themes which also constituted the daily bread of his countrymen: *Saul, The Pilgrims at Emmaus, Lazarus, The Holy Family* – Rembrandt, the painter of Holland triumphant on the morrow of the Peace of Westphalia.

Chapter 5

THE SCIENTIFIC SPIRIT
(1640–1700)

FROM 1640 until the last decades of the seventeenth century the scientific movement gained speed, despite ups and downs which might seem extremely unfavourable to intellectual activity and exchanges. This half-century laden with wars, civil and international, in France and in England, in the United Provinces and all across the Empire, was the moment when the main lines of scientific work, as Descartes's contemporaries had traced them, became definitely established, and very quickly made clear, to the minority of Europeans who followed all these discussions, what the basic answers were to certain questions which until then had been asked without any hope of a solution. This many-sided advance which took place, and became polarized eventually around three great names – Newton, Spinzoa and Leibniz – cannot easily be grasped, so complex were the interactions, especially if one is trying to single out only the most important movements. The years between 1640 and 1660–70 are particularly hard to define, because the threads criss-cross in a thousand ways, in certain parts of Europe at any rate. Even before France and England were shaken by disturbances and civil war, Paris was the scene of a religious creation of exceptional richness, the Jansenism of Port-Royal, which for a quarter of a century stirred the consciences of the élite in France and gave to the French Counter-Reformation an unexpected tone. Around Port-Royal were debated, thanks to Pascal, Antoine Arnauld, Nicole and others, all the great problems of the age, and not merely those of Jesuit theology. The phenomenon was indeed essentially French at the outset, and only later reached the Spanish Netherlands and Italy in a serious way. But its significance transcended the frontiers of the kingdom, in that the debate about Jansenism concerned the Roman Curia very closely, while at the same time helping to endow French Catholicism with new features.

The same period saw an intensification of the struggle of the authorities, both lay and religious, against movements that called for unorthodox interpretations of the faith. This happened in England especially, because the twenty years of the Civil War and Interregnum and the first ten years of the Restoration witnessed the affirmation and then the crushing by ferocious repression, first Cromwellian and then Stuart, of the boldest political and religious claims that Europe had yet known – but also elsewhere, in the Empire, obsessed with demons during the Thirty Years' War, and in France, brought to heel after the Fronde, and with some rigour, in Colbert's time. The restoration of order, with supervision of book-sellers and subjection of writers, acquires its full significance in the most general perspective, in which we perceive not only the sovereign's will to power but also the consent accorded by a high society which rejects any calling in question of the social and spiritual order.

Finally, the last complication: it was in this same period, after 1660, that scientific activity found the forms of organ-ization it had hitherto lacked. Regularly constituted societies were set up, and worked assiduously to help savants in their mutual information and emulation. Learned journals began appearing, containing reviews of new works, and these took their place, which was soon a highly important one, in intellectual life alongside the mainly political journals published until that time. The fact that these divergent movements were all happening at the same time, to the point of counteracting each other in some countries, shows how far was intellectual life in this period from obeying a linear tendency by which all the savants defined their investigations in terms of faith and in which fluctuations in the ecclesiastical disciplines were already dictated by scientific progress. In this respect Pascal and Leibniz are just as significant as Spinoza and Malebranche.

I. THE BEGINNINGS OF JANSENISM IN FRANCE

Although it struck root in France, Jansenism originated in the Walloon country, in the person of its founder Cornelius Jansenius, who gave to it his name and his breviary, the *Augustinus*, and left to his disciples the responsibility for a movement which bore the appearance of a sectarian enterprise within the Catholic Church, and even of a heresy, as the Jesuits never tired of repeating, down to the nineteenth century at any rate. And yet the enigmatic figure of this Bishop of Ypres, whose big book, the *Augustinus*, was published only after his death, mattered less in the formation of the movement than that of his comrade, the Abbé de Saint-Cyran, who in a dozen years founded what historians of the Church call 'the school of Port-Royal'.

A few biographical details are important if we are to understand this dichotomy. By their education and their approach, both men belonged to that reforming Catholicism which came to flower too soon in the first half of the century. The first-named, a Catholic born in Holland who had moved to the Southern Netherlands and become a doctor of divinity at Louvain in a period when the old university was defending its privileges and traditions against the Jesuit invaders, was a contemplative who meditated on the problems of Grace in a Pauline framework of thought, taking up afresh, in a Catholic context, the theme which had been that of the first reformers, a hundred years earlier. The second, whose family name was Du Vergier de Hauranne, also studied at Louvain, and the two men went together, soon after the death of Henri IV, to South-western France, where they spent some years in meditation and in work on problems of doctrine which called in question both the most subtle interpretations of man's freedom of will and Grace and also the practices that were current in the Church in matters of the direction of consciences, the sacraments, and morality. Then the two separated. Jansenius published in 1635, when France entered the Thirty Years' War, *Mars gallicus*, a work that attracted attention in the courts of Europe. Between 1636 and his death in 1638 he was Bishop of Ypres. When he died, a large book from his pen, entitled *Augustinus*, was still with a local printer: this work developed, in a scholarly, theological way, a doctrine of Grace which was destined to be discussed and denounced for half a century with unprecedented fury – not so much on account of its heterodoxy, which was open to debate, as because of the wide interest ensured for this neo-Augustinian doctrine by the first 'Jansenist', the Abbé de Saint-Cyran. The latter, who was more often in Paris than at his abbey in the depths of Brenne, soon became well known in ecclesiastical circles in the capital through his eloquence as a preacher and his unusual knowledge of theology, which embraced all the Fathers of the Church (and enabled him to show up the mistakes of Father Garasse, the famous smiter of freethinkers, in 1626). For some years he was attached to Bérulle and thus became closely involved with the great reforming trend fostered by the cardinal. Most important, he found in the 1630s an ideal setting in which to exercise a direction of consciences which was as severe as that of the Jesuits was considered indulgent: the Convent of Port-Royal, a house of nuns of the Order of the Blessed Sacrament, under the protection of Saint Bernard, which soon became divided into a town house in the Faubourg St-Jacques, and Port-Royal des Champs, in the Chevreuse valley. Famed for the strictness with which the convent's rules were respected, Port-Royal gradually became a spiritual centre the reputation of which was all the greater because many other religious houses were at this time suffering from disorders and from spiritual mediocrity. When Richelieu had Saint-Cyran put in prison, in 1638, the Port-Royal group consisted not only of the nuns whose director of conscience he was but also included some gentlemen who had withdrawn from the world to lead a Christian life as hermits, near the convent, and the families, living in Paris, of these nuns and solitaries, who were indirectly subject to the influence of Jansenius's comrade: among the most notable of them were the Arnauld, Pascal and Périer families.

The history of the Jansenist movement shows the spread of this influence. When the *Augustinus* appeared, in the year when the Society of Jesus celebrated its first centenary, the Abbé de Saint-Cyran had been in prison for more than two years, and was in no position to promote the book. When Richelieu died, in December 1642, Saint-Cyran was soon released, but himself died only a few months later. Yet the movement had been firmly implanted, for it began its greatest advance at that very time. The year 1643 saw the publication, over the name of Antoine Arnauld, who was to become 'the Doctor of Jansenism' for some fifty years, of the book which opened the debate on sacramental practices in the Catholic Church, *De la fréquente communion*. This work furnished the basis for the severely austere way in which the Jansenists judged those acts of the laity and the clergy which constitute the essence of spiritual life. Thus, with the contrast between their attitude and the laxer attitude of the Jesuits, there began a struggle which went on, in the first place, for a quarter of a century, until the truce of 1668 ('the Peace of the Church').

What, in this first phase of Jansenism in Paris, is least studied nowadays and no longer stirs up strong feelings is its theological foundation, that is, the *Augustinus* itself. The lengthy dissertations on Efficient Grace have found no convinced exegetes, even among specialists: perhaps they were appreciated by contemporaries only when they had been put into

French, and embodied in concrete instances, in the *Lettres provinciales*, by the genius of Pascal. Although, on this plane, the Jansenists were soon convicted by their opponents of being just as much believers in predestination as the Calvinists were, the theological debate was overlaid, or transcended, by arguments about Catholic morality and about ideas connected with the various practices that were advocated for the élite of the laity. Essentially, *De la fréquente communion* does not rebuke the Catholic who communicates several times a week, but the one who approaches the altar without preparation, without that 'regret for and detestation of Sin' which is required for communion: it stresses the sacred character of religious acts and thereby rejects all laxity and indulgence in connexion with them. Fundamentally, Jansenism signified a call for the purification of the Church, and proceeded, like other, earlier movements of the kind, from a nostalgia for the 'primitive Church', as it was customary to imagine this to have been.

Thirteen years later, at the height of the litigious battle which the Jesuits waged against Port-Royal (with the condemnation of five heretical propositions in the *Augustinus*, by Rome and by the Sorbonne), a little work, *Lettres à un provincial*, written by Blaise Pascal (with advice, no doubt, from Antoine Arnauld on strictly theological points), brought before the public, with extraordinary success, all the problems of morality with which the Jesuits' casuistry confronted men's consciences. After the first letters there was no discussion of Grace, but rather of those 'differences between cases' which set all Paris laughing, those subtle distinctions which the pamphleteer turned against their authors. You claim to be right in absolving a thief in the case where he is without bread to sustain life, and in some other cases. But why, then, did the Fathers of the Collège de Clermont prosecute a servant of theirs who stole some pewter plates? All the maxims of the Jesuit confessors, all their indulgent practices were examined, from one letter to the next: permission to kill, for the sake of honour and for the sake of property; justification of usurers and bankrupts; dubious formulations regarding gluttony, women's dress, and girls' freedom; the mental reservation. The frankly aggressive tone of the *Provinciales* and their incisive style, without any of the circumlocution and restraint that were still normally observed, contributed greatly to their success. The enemies of the Jesuits exulted more and more as the months went by and more of the letters appeared: Guy Patin especially, who promised to send them all to his friend Spon. 'You will be receiving the letters of the theologian of Port-Royal: we are awaiting his Number Seventeen. Lord, how he deals with those smart fellows in Numbers Fifteen and Sixteen!'

With the *Provinciales*, published between March 1656 and January 1657, Pascal and the Jansenist 'party' laid the foundations of a morality which based its authenticity on the freedom of the individual Christian and on the universality of its principles. The strictly intellectual activities of the Port-Royal group did not as yet directly involve theology to any great extent. These men, who had left the world in order to live near the convent of Port-Royal des Champs, opened schools in which they taught their friends' children, claiming to use methods that were more effective than those of the Jesuits: they taught in French, gave a great deal of attention to the modern sciences, and omitted the 'social' activities and prestige performances that were cultivated so assiduously in the Jesuit colleges. The Little Schools of Port-Royal quickly achieved great success. They were particularly important in causing the improvised teachers who worked there to publish books on teaching method and on general philosophy which played a vital part in the development of French intellectual life. The *Logique* produced by Port-Royal – half-way between Descartes's *Discours* and Malebranche's *Recherche de la vérité* – provides the best example. *La Logique, ou l'art de penser*, which, according to its preamble, was an outcome of the teaching given in the Little Schools, was presented by its authors as a systematic treatise, and was revised several times between successive editions. The essential idea set forth at the beginning of the book – 'Logic is the art of rightly directing our reason in the knowledge of things ... This art consists in the reflections men have made upon the four principal operations of the mind: conceiving, judging, reasoning and disposing' – was applied with a rigour and a didactic clarity which inspired the admiration of contemporaries.

The development of Jansenism was thus marked by a series of publications which were among the outstanding best-sellers of their time and which throw light on complementary aspects of the movement at the height of its expansion. What is least clear about this expansion, however, is what its sociological basis was. The great Parisian lawyer families who wrote and who led the debates conceal from us what lay beneath. It is certain that Jansenism did not seek recruits among the lower orders: the very forms in which it spread show well enough that these schools, convents, and homes for solitaries were not open to the populace. But it was not only lawyers who took part in the movement. Nobles also figured in it, and several who had been active in the Fronde, when they were chagrined by defeat, hid themselves in, or sought the shade of, Port-Royal after 1652–3. Bourgeois of less renown than the magistrates also found places in the move-ment, it seems. When persecution struck the convents, after 1660, their allies whom the Archbishop of Paris encountered in the localities – especially in the Faubourg Saint-Jacques – were not members of lawyer families. Above all, the rigour of the Jansenists soon made its appeal to a large section of the lower clergy of Paris. The *Ecrits des curés de Paris*, which carried on where the *Provinciales* left off when Pascal fell silent, showed that Jansenism had become widespread well beyond the circles of the higher magistracy, and when, soon afterwards, the parish priests of Rouen rallied to the cause, proof was given of its extension into the provinces, through ecclesiastical channels. However, these landmarks in the movement's history are not adequate to establish precisely the actual social basis of the first phase of Jansenism in Paris.

It is possible, nevertheless, to measure the influence that Port-Royal had acquired within a few years, in particular from the comments on it that were made by contemporaries. We see becoming defined a group which was a sect rather than a party, a meeting-point for certain people, but which was above all a factor in a new mode of expression in French sensibility. When Antoine Arnauld confronted the Jesuits and their political allies in the polemic that was started up by the Pope's condemnation of five propositions taken from the *Augustinus*, he was supported by theologians who were not themselves in favour of the new variant of Augustinism. The theologian of Port-Royal had retained friends in the divided Sorbonne, and enjoyed a great reputation there deriving from his book of 1643: before they could obtain a condemnation in proper form, the Jesuits were compelled to drum up all the doctors with voting rights, so as to swell the numbers of those in favour of their proposal. Even then, their victory was won by only a few votes, and after much argument. Most of the Oratorians sided with Arnauld. Outside the bounds of the Faculty, clergy and laity declared themselves with vehemence in favour of the victim of persecution: even Monsieur Vincent, who had little liking for these theological and procedural debates, recalled how highly he had esteemed the late Saint-Cyran. And magistrates as balanced as Omer Talon and Lefèvre d'Ormesson made known how ridiculous they thought the attack launched against the inmates of Port-Royal on the basis of those five little phrases cunningly extracted from that big folio, the *Augustinus* – well before the *Provinciales* came on the scene to make every reader a judge of the debate which had till then been confined to square-capped clerics.

Thereafter, in the years that immediately followed the Fronde, theological discussion and Catholic intellectual life in France revolved mainly around the problems raised by the Jansenists. Historians favourable to the Jesuit case have often stressed the pettifogging spirit of the men of Port-Royal, so ready to argue about points of law and of fact, the presence of the formulations in the *Augustinus* and the condemnation of the propositions as such. However, apart from the fact that the other side was just as unrestrained in its pettifogging and intrigue, the important point clearly lies elsewhere – in the challenging, in these theological terms, of a certain kind of Catholic religious sensibility, in favour of a more rigorous and more comprehensive conception of the fundamental mysteries which had been reaffirmed at the Council of Trent.

On another level, Port-Royal stands out as one of the high places of literary and scientific life in Paris in the middle of the seventeenth century. 'Messieurs de Port-Royal' showed themselves to be talented and highly productive writers. Little attracted to the academic discussion which was being carried on in those years at the homes of the Du Puy brothers or of Montmor, they wrote more, and got themselves into print. Men like M. de Saci, who was in prison with Saint-Cyran, and translated the New and Old Testaments, the *Imitation*, and other works; Lancelot, grammarian and philologist, author (with Arnauld) of a *Grammaire générale et raisonnée* and (on his own) of a series of works intended to facilitate learning the languages of Antiquity – *Nouvelle Méthode pour apprendre facilement et en peu de temps la langue latine* (1644), and *La Langue grecque* (1657), and the well-known *Jardin des racines grecques*; Nicole, who published (in addition to *La Logique*) *Essais de morale* which were long regarded as among the great books of the age, and numerous polemical works directed against the Protestants (not to mention writings that were perhaps more in the nature of schoolbooks, like *Nouveaux Éléments de géometrie*, in which Antoine Arnauld also had a hand): all these contributed to ensure long-lasting fame for their group, through their publications, which were reissued regularly until the end of the century at least. These teachers of the young Racine and fellow-workers with Pascal were in the front ranks of the intellectual life of Paris, as is shown by the copiousness and the success of their works (demonstrated by H.-J. Martin in his *Livre, pouvoirs et société à Paris au XVIIe siècle*).

The most striking case, owing to its strangeness, is perhaps that of Lemaistre, an advocate before the Parlement, whose withdrawal to Port-Royal while at the height of his glory stupefied the magistracy and the literary world of Paris. After retiring to live near the convent, Lemaistre published nothing – apart from the collection of his speeches in court, which were preserved as models of forensic eloquence – and devoted himself to leading the life of study and devotion which was common to all the solitaries of Port-Royal. Nevertheless, when he died, in 1658, his death was noted as one of the greatest losses suffered by the intelligentsia of Paris. Guy Patin wrote to his friend Falconet in terms which give a good definition of the group to which Lemaistre belonged: 'The Republic of Letters has suffered a great loss in the death of M. Lemaistre, the famous advocate, whose fine speeches in court were published in quartos and folios. He is regretted by all worthy people, for he was a man beyond compare in virtue, learning, Christian piety and eloquence. He had deliberately withdrawn to Port-Royal in order to spend the rest of his life there practising the principles of Christianity, which it is so difficult to observe in the business of the world, in the way we live now.' Unlike the other groups of scholars which had been formed earlier in Paris (and which, moreover, were in the process of being renewed), the Port-Royal group showed its originality in the combination of concerns with learning, morality and Christianity that was characteristic of all in this retreat remote from the world, and which was expressed most outstandingly in the brief career and achievements of Blaise Pascal.

The young savant brought up by his mathematician father in the scientific circle around Mersenne, and who at the age of sixteen astonished Descartes and the habitués of the Place Royale with his essay on conic sections, was at one and the same time a scholar and researcher interested in the great problems being debated in his time, a mathematician preoccupied with practical calculation, the inventor of a calculating machine and promoter of a system of public coach transport in the city of Paris, a polemist who took up arms in his friends' defence at the height of the crisis over the five propositions, and a man of piety, capable of disputing with his freethinker friends in order to bring them back to 'true religion'. All this in a single movement of thought bringing together the scientific polemics and the most difficult problems raised by the Duc de Roannez or the Chevalier de Méré, or aroused by a close reading of Montaigne.

As a savant, Pascal opposed as plainly as possible (in the *Provinciales*) the condemnation of Galileo and declared for the 'Copernican revolution'. As an assiduous participant in Mersenne's discussions, Pascal took up the argument about Nature's alleged horror of a vacuum, and repeated Torricelli's experiments. He published in 1647 a treatise entitled *Expériences nouvelles touchant le vide*, and organized at Clermont in Auvergne the Puy-de-Dôme experiment which in 1648 furnished a decisive solution to the dispute about the vacuum and the weight of the air. In both of these matters he came up against the Jesuits (on the question of the vacuum, with Father Noël), and polemized against them on scientific as well as on religious questions. At the same time, finding himself among learned freethinkers for whom scientific method served as a way of casting doubt on revealed truth, Pascal sought to discover the elements of a refutation that would sweep all contradictions away. This unfinished inquiry of his was not published until 1670, and then only in an abridged and mangled form. Nevertheless, the elements collected by Pascal, when arranged in what may have been their proper order, enable us to appreciate the clash between science and faith as this was experienced, to one extent or another, by the most fervent of the Jansenists. From his learning, and from the potentialities that the many discoveries made in these fruitful years enabled him to glimpse, Pascal derived first and foremost a sense of the grandeur of God's creation: 'the eternal silence of these infinite spaces terrifies me'; 'the infinitely large and the infinitely small'. In his observation of contemporary societies, in which he partly followed Montaigne, he saw signs of the weakness of man in his thinking dignity: 'That is droll justice which is bounded by a stream'; 'what does an ermine-robed magistrate amount to when a soldier throws his cap out of the window?'; 'when force attacks humbug and a private soldier takes the square cap of a *premier président* and sends it flying out of the window'. Pascal accords to the grandeur of the state, to dukes and princes, the external respect which is their due, but, apart from that, it is a matter of opinion, for every person to judge for himself: 'the grandeurs of the powers that be, meaning certain external ceremonies which ought nevertheless to be accompanied, according to reason, by an inward acknowledgement of the justice of this order, but which do not cause us to conceive any real quality in those whom we honour in this way'. Besides, what is authority, if it be not delegated from God? Already in the *Provinciales* he had said that it is always permissible to appeal against a denial of justice: from one's bishop to the Pope, and from the Pope to God the Father: and in another place he gives his view of the matter in a single sentence: 'If my letters are condemned in Rome, what

I condemn in them is condemned in heaven.' This young savant who shrank from no speculative investigation during his short life reckoned nothing human higher than these activities: 'All the glamour of worldly greatness is without lustre for those who are engaged in intellectual researches. The greatness of these men of the mind is invisible to kings, to the rich, to captains, to all those great ones of the flesh.'

Against his freethinker friends Pascal brought up the arguments of a logician who knew how to link together, all the time, the extremes and the contrasts, divine grandeur and human wretchedness: 'The misery of Man without God', on the one hand, and, on the other, the impossibility that man should fail to seek God. Finally, on the supposition that those with whom he is disputing are unshakable in their scepticism, detached from all the vital truths, he offers in reserve, or as a last resort, his wager: what can you lose by supposing that God does exist? A procedure like this, in its profound coherence, was clearly quite the contrary of the methods employed normally in the intellectual debates in which the Jansenists' opponents were engaged. There was no question here of threats or repression against wrong-thinking persons, nor any subtle compromises, carefully calculated concessions aimed to safeguard external practices even if not faith. Pascal, like the men of Port-Royal, intended to assert his faith through his scientific work and through his attempt to interpret the universe. He did not separate, as did so many learned men of his time, scholarship, in which men may proceed in freedom, and faith, in which everything is defined and given by Scripture and the Tradition of the Church. In its highest expression, the Pensées, the Jansenism of Paris in the middle years of the seventeenth century was dialectical.

This aspect, like the bitterness of the struggle between Jesuits and Jansenists and the scope of the repressive measures taken by the French monarchy (solemn condemnation of the Provinciales to be burnt; establishment of a formulary repudiating the five propositions, to be signed by all the clergy of France; dispersal of the nuns of Port-Royal des Champs, the solitaries and the schools, and prohibition of recruitment) – these factors have long attracted the attention of researchers struck by this open conflict within the dominant classes of French society. Twice, with an interval of about twenty years, a 'Marxist' interpretation of the Jansenist movement has been put forward which deserves to be noted as an overall explanatory hypothesis, as it does not restrict the phenomenon of Jansenism to its spiritual aspects.

For Franz Borkenau, studying European philosophic thought in the age of manufacture (*Der Uebergang vom feudalen zum buergerlichen Weltbild: Studien zur Geschichte der Philosophie der Manufakturperiode*), the task is to comprehend and explain the entire movement leading from medieval thought to the modern world by way of the defining of a new theology and a new morality. His itinerary runs, therefore, via Calvin and Bodin, Luther, Copernicus and the Counter-Reformation, but when he reaches the middle of the seventeenth century he dwells at length upon Descartes, Hobbes and Gassendi, and concludes with Pascal his critique of the social life of the period and the ideas of the freethinkers. According to Borkenau, the Jansenist contradiction was centred in a section of the ruling groups which found itself in an unstable situation. Against the traditional social order based on the nobility, opposition could come neither from the business bourgeoisie, absorbed in non-political concerns, nor from the masses, subjected to authority, and as yet unorganized: it developed in the stratum of the lawyers, the so-called *noblesse de robe*, whose social position was half-way between the nobility and the bourgeoisie – social half-castes who were more sensitive than any other group to the situation with no way forward into which they were plunged by a social order that refused to change. The conflict took place on the only ideological plane on which this contradiction could effectively express itself, since it had been a field of discussion for the past century, namely, the religious plane, in which the Jansenists launched their attack against the group which was dominant in the Church. Borkenau thus takes the identity of the Jansenists with the *noblesse de robe* as a datum, and moves on to analyse the dialectical subtlety of Pascal, the internal contradictions of the higher ranks of French society, and the particularly equivocal position of the *noblesse de robe*, which the Fronde had made obvious on the strictly political plane. At the same time, Borkenau acknowledges that the Jansenist movement spread considerably beyond this world of legal dignitaries, writing, for example: 'The political significance of Jansenism lies in the influence it exercised over the majority of the outstanding personalities and over the French bourgeoisie as a whole, for three-quarters of a century.'

Lucien Goldmann, in *The Hidden God*, argues on three levels. The discovery of the letters of Martin Barcos, nephew and successor of Saint-Cyran in his abbey and as mentor of the nuns of Port-Royal, enables him to identify the various tendencies into which the Jansenists were divided, especially during the 'formulary' crisis, and to recognize thereby the outstanding differences in the way various individuals behaved. His analysis of Pascal's *Pensées*, more thorough than Borkenau's, arrives at similar conclusions so far as the definition of Pascal's dialectics is concerned. Finally Goldmann analyses Racine's plays, defining the conception of tragedy found in them as an absolute no-way-out situation, Berenice's *invitus invitam*, just as Pascal's thought imprisons his opponent in a choice between all or nothing. This amounts to affirming that Jansenist thought expressed, on three different levels, the same impossibility of accepting the world as it is; and Goldmann refers to those same lawyers who formed the majority group among the recruits to Jansenism. In this sense,

the approaches of Borkenau and Goldmann are indeed identical, based on the same assumptions and leading to the same
conclusions.

The Hidden God has been more widely discussed than
Borkenau's book (which was published in German, and not
long before the War). Specialists in religious history have
reproached Goldmann with dealing too lightly with strictly
Jansenist writings, like *De la fréquente communion* and *La
Logique*, and even of studying the behaviour of the sect merely
through the correspondence of a vehement and prolix abbé
who did not in fact play the important role which Goldmann
assigns to him. Neo-positivist historians have argued against
his thesis both the presence of others besides lawyers among
the supporters of Port-Royal and the large number of Paris
magistrates who supported the Jesuits, approved of the condemnation of the *Provinciales*, and even took part in the establishing of the 'formulary'. Much work needs to be done to
answer these objections, which are of unequal validity. We
also need, in order to undertake a more fully comprehensive
interpretation, a thorough reconstruction of the conduct of the
Jansenists in the crisis of 1657–68, and, especially, more reliable information about the social circles in which the Port-
Royal group recruited and wielded influence. The situation of
tragic impasse and contradiction applied, after all, no less to
the bourgeoisie as a whole, poorly armed economically and
politically held down in an inferior position, than to the
little group of lawyers who had recently been promoted to the
status of a second-rate nobility.

There would still remain the task of accounting, otherwise
than by the linear path of ideological influences, for the way
that a militant Jansenism spread, beyond France, among
social groups that were considerably different. In this first
period, even before Antoine Arnauld had taken refuge in the
Low Countries, after the breaking of the truce of 1668,
Jansenism found a receptive soil in that region, which the

memory of Jansenius may have prepared. The virulence of the Jesuits' activities stirred up a spirit of conflict there, and in Louvain and Brussels the writings of the Paris Jansenists brought much trade to the bookshops, whereas the heavy quartos of the Molinists remained on their shelves. Throughout the Southern Netherlands, where Catholic life had followed the same process of creative recovery as in France, the Jansenist sect made recruits, attracted by the severity of its demands, which could stand up to comparison with those of the Protestant neighbours to the north. In Holland itself, for the same reasons, Jansenism was well received in the circles which had remained loyal to the Roman Church. Jansenist piety had made encroachments in Italy too, even in Rome: already when the Jesuits were mounting their great campaign to secure condemnation of the five propositions, the Jansenists had without difficulty found protectors in the Curia who were impressed by the moral rigour and Augustinism of the Port-Royal group. Arnauld and his friend did not fail, moreover, to send emissary after emissary to expound their views, disseminate good books, and make known the outstanding events in the life of Port-Royal (such as the miracle of the Holy Thorn). And when, after the failure of the policy of the 'formulary', a path of compromise was sought in Rome itself, there was no lack of men of goodwill to prepare the truce of 1668, accomplished amid ambiguities and cross-purposes, with the help of the French Embassy and in defiance of the Jesuits, who were unable to prevent it. Jansenism also found an audience among the Italian clergy: bishops and parish priests in the big cities were won over and (discreetly, of course) gave their approval to the men of Port-Royal.

Catholic reform from within took shape, paradoxically, a century after the defeat of Erasmus, under the aegis of a sect accused of heresy, which preached a return to the greatness of the primitive Church and expounded a disinterested morality which was soon to become that of a section of modern society. Whatever the deviations and perversions of the later Jansenism, in the eighteenth century, when it became polemically Gallicanist, these cannot be imputed, on a basis of recurrent responsibility, to the founders of this movement. In its first phase, Jansenism was a mutation of ideas and feeling which was vital to Europe's intellectual life: a call for rigour and order in a period that seemed still doomed to the worst confusion.

2. THE INTERSECTION OF 'DISORDERS'

When the learned freethinkers, who lived in a period of incessant popular revolts, and of the Fronde, stigmatized popular errors, the 'foolishness' of certain forms of worship (relics, processions), denounced exorcisms of persons allegedly possessed by devils, and at the same time called on the royal authority to show greater firmness towards agitators of every kind, and especially those who stirred up the common people, they certainly defined a political attitude that was soon appreciated. But they also testified, first and foremost, to the disarray of a period in which riots and commotions kept the powerful in constant alarm, and revealed the strength of the people, 'fierce and untamable', who needed to be held down tightly, at a time when their strength was being expressed with such vigour, in London and in Bordeaux more than in Paris. When, a few years later, the worthy Burgundian scholar Jacques Chevanes, a Capuchin belonging to the Dijon group, devoted a book of 900 pages to denouncing the incredulity of the learned and the credulity of the ignorant, in connexion with witches and magicians, he provided another example pointing in the same direction. In his conscientious way he was arguing both against the freethinkers whose scepticism frightened him and against the very same popular errors that these freethinkers denounced at their gatherings and in their letters – the errors of 'the beast', to use the expression they frequently used in order to refer to, rather than to describe, that other culture, kept under and little known, which found expression vehemently and spontaneously, in 1649–50.

Two levels can be distinguished here, one of which was not so widespread and was not treated in the same way as the other by the clergy and the politicians. First, there is everything that belonged to the sphere of popular belief – superstition, as it was soon to be called by preachers deploring the defects in Christian education. In this sphere, the changes that occurred in connexion with the witch-trials held in various parts of Europe are quite remarkable. For twenty years already voices had been raised in protest against the harshness of the magistrates and the ease with which persons were sent to the stake on the basis of denunciations and groundless allegations. In 1631 the Rhineland Jesuit Friedrich Spee, who had attended the victims of these sentences for many years, set forth in his *Cautio criminalis* the reasons why he could not agree with the procedures followed; his book was widely read, even before it was translated into French in 1660 by a Besançon physician. During the 1630s the Parlement of Paris considered the reservations expressed by theologians and physicians regarding the major possession cases (in the first place, Loudun) and decided to put an end to a judicial procedure which had long been in use. But these expressions, which were harbingers of a more general challenge to come, did not win wide support – not immediately, at least. Denunciations and prosecutions continued for a long time yet. In Upper Burgundy in 1644–5 the village communities were disturbed when a young shepherd, regarded as a witch-finder, denounced dozens of people, one after another, but the Dijon Parlement forbade the judges under its jurisdiction to investigate these cases, and begin proceedings against the accused: the peasants decided to deal with the matter themselves, and subjected the suspects to the ordeal by drowning. In the same period witch-hunts continued in the Rhineland

and in South Germany, especially just after the end of the
Thirty Years' War, the princes having apparently failed to
listen to the Jesuits' appeal. Similarly, in England, during the
first phase of the Civil War, in Essex, witchcraft cases began
to become numerous in 1645, at much the same time as in
France.

For the magistrates who set themselves to fight against this
plague of Satan's which kept returning, such persistence was
not a matter for surprise – until some of them started to
question the method of proceeding and its automatic results.
Witch-hunts, sometimes halted by the higher judicial authorities and sometimes not, continued for a long time yet: in
Burgundy and Champagne there were still cases in 1660, and
in Guyenne, Béarn and Normandy around 1670, when the
King's Government at last intervened directly to stop investigations. Rural witchcraft, which was certainly more tenacious than the cases of diabolic possession in urban convents,
and of more serious significance, survived until long after
special judicial prosecution had been given up, doubtless
because it expressed one form of the cultural tensions of
which everyday life in the village communities was made
up. Historians have not yet succeeded in reconstructing the
social and cultural image of the witch – an old woman
whose stories were listened to at gatherings in the evening,
who was feared and yet regarded as a protectress, occupying a
large place in the imagination of the countryfolk, and who
could not but be rejected by the authorities, whether near
(the parish priest or the pastor) or far (the judicial apparatus
centred in the towns). However, the witch fitted into the
system of generally accepted religious notions, since her power
and prestige were bound up with the pact she had made with
Satan, that is, with an essential factor in Christian dogma. At
the same time, the witch's image and the knowledge she
possessed were related to the antagonism between the strong
and the weak, the village rich and the labourers, in some way

that the proceedings, denunciations and sworn statements fail to make clear. Indeed, these relations were far from being clear in the minds of contemporaries, who had been fed upon notions spread by the Churches. Those who discussed the witch-trials, basing themselves on the images accumulated by oral tradition and on the 'old wives' tales' that the free-thinkers ridiculed, particularly stressed what they saw as a defect in the Christian education that the 'credulous' layfolk had received: the witch-finder, whether he appeared in Béarn or in Burgundy, ought to be sent not before a court of fear-inspiring judges, but into a good monastery, or to a good priest, to be taught 'sound Christian doctrine'.

Indeed, when witchcraft was reduced to a case, even if a major one, of the 'superstitions' which had always pro-liferated around the dogmas and forms of worship of religion, as shown by Jean-Baptiste Thiers in his well-known treatise, the campaign against it formed an integral part of the drive for a purgation of Catholicism which had been undertaken at the Council of Trent, and corresponding drives in the Pro-testant countries, where the new orthodoxies required firmer definition. In the Catholic context, of course, this redefinition, eliminating practices and beliefs some of which had been consecrated by usage for several centuries, was especially spectacular: it revealed the extent of the fear that was aroused, during this period of persevering reorganization, by these deviations existing in many forms, infinitely varied from one region to another ('each kingdom, each province, each dio-cese, each town, each parish has its own'), which were being sifted by theologians on the basis of the authority of the Fathers of the Church. J.-B. Thiers observed very acutely in this connexion: 'I have sometimes marked down as super-stition certain practices which appear to be innocent and blameless because they are accompanied by things that are holy and worthy, phrases from Scripture, crosses, prayers, blessings, fasts, the giving of alms, mortification of the flesh, confession, communion, pilgrimages, masses . . .' And he adds, so that the reader may be well and truly warned: 'I am aware, moreover, that the more superstition is accompanied by things holy and worthy, the more criminal it is.'

Certainly not all those who drew up synodal statutes, which were frequently revised during the seventeenth century, and not all episcopal visitors of parishes were able to maintain as strict a vigilance as the theologian writing in the calm of his library, collecting references. But Thiers's list reveals very clearly the contamination that had gradually been suffered by the forms of worship, by the conduct of believers and by their notions of sacred matters. Thereby it indicates how difficult the clearing-up process was, and why it lasted for so long, all through the seventeenth and eighteenth centuries. It does not speak about, but it does enable us to divine, the resistance that the purgation may have encountered from the laity, who were gradually being deprived, on the initiative of the clergy, higher and lower alike (now better disciplined and better trained for their task), of a substantial part of their cultural habits and their ideas about the world they lived in. From the theologians' standpoint, these aberrations of belief were a minor achievement of the Devil's. They were 'in vogue among the common people', notes Thiers, which is equivalent to acknowledging how remote the latter might be from the 'true' practice of religion: and all the more so because these aberrations had long been accepted or tolerated, thereby acquiring not only the patina of prestige that was possessed in those days by everything that had a long history behind it, but also an appearance of truth which it was hard to challenge. As matrices of widespread errors, these deviations called for the greatest vigilance on the part of pastors: 'Some see these things and think nothing of them, and some are guilty of them without realizing it.'

This long-term campaign was not pursued at the same pace in all parts of the Catholic world. In Italy and in Spain it was less lively than in France, where the influence of the Oratorian and Jansenist logicians was felt very early on in this domain (it was no accident that the second large treatise on superstitions to be written in French was the work of an Oratorian, Pierre le Brun, at the beginning of the eighteenth century). Where, as in Italy and Spain, this pressure was much less felt (it was even negligible in Spain), the purificatory movement proceeded slowly. In South Germany, however, Catholic but penetrated by Protestant influences, the same transformation took place as in France, being expressed, on the plane of decoration and building, in the ornamental motifs adopted by a distinctive ecclesiatical baroque, aimed at bringing believers back to the essential themes – the Trinity, the Passion, certain intercessor saints – but greater freedom and diversity in religious practice was retained there, at the price of a struggle by the laity against the efforts of the clergy. The little-known contentions of Godeau and Thomassin in their diocese of Vence, and the conflicts between the laity and the bishop at Autun in Roquette's time, give us a confused impression of what such debates were like; a clearer one comes across from the diary of the parish priest of Sennely, in Sologne, Christophe Sauvageon, which has been remarkably interpreted by Gérard Bouchard in his monograph on this village in the seventeenth and eighteenth centuries. Even more significant perhaps is the testimony of those preachers in the second half of the seventeenth century who mention the despair of believers who had been gradually deprived of an important part of their religious outlook: Catherine de Francheville and Father Huby, in Brittany, and, especially, somewhat later, the extraordinary Grignion de Montfort, tireless missionary, founder of an order, and great composer of hymns to be sung by the people. Through the evidence of documents which are not always explicit we can make out a process of putting matters to rights, an authoritative redefinition of beliefs and practices on the part of the Church – a break with the past which was felt as an injury by a man like Grignion but, on the contrary, accepted and wished-for as a boon by the 'post-Tridentine' clergy.

On a different level, which was at once religious and political, 'popular' voices were raised, in at least one country, England, giving harsh expression to feelings of impatience and ambition which were a cause of trembling in some quarters. The Levellers and Diggers, who played so big a role in London in 1647–52, before they were crushed by Cromwell, represent in the movement of ideas in seventeenth-century Europe a factor that was of vital importance in its time and place. To be sure, political writing had formed a large proportion of printed publications long before the pamphlets of the Lilburnes and the Winstanleys. The debates provoked by the Wars of Religion, and later the writing of learned treatises devoted to asserting royal authority, had occasioned an enormous number of publications in France, in most cases bearing the names of magistrates who enjoyed the reputation of Nestors in their own circles, such as Cardin le Bret and Jérome Bignon, in the middle of the seventeenth century. In Germany, too, treatises a hundred or two pages long, affirming the rights of the princes, describing the ways in which secularization of Church property should be carried out, and discussing relations with the Emperor, had appeared in great numbers since printing was introduced, and still today occupy the shelves of old libraries, in the section entitled *Politica* – not to mention the genealogical publications, the *Leichpredigten*, and evocations of princely ceremonies of a more cheerful kind. But, basically, all of this abundant political writing was produced by magistrates, chancellors and, in general, representatives of sovereigns, and, even in the case of polemics regarding the more or less absolute monarchy, its purpose was primarily to improve and strengthen the established order.

The Levellers and Diggers of London gave forth a different message, which soon made itself heard, to the great terror of the 'Establishment'. When, after the ephemeral Parliamentary victory of the Presbyterians, the sects supported Cromwell in 1648–9 and overwhelmed the Calvinist legalists, the magnitude of their popular success was soon perceived. In October 1649 Lilburne, brought to trial, was acquitted under the pressure of angry street crowds, after a brief three-day hearing. Reducing these people to silence and inaction was no easy task for Cromwell, despite the divisions that existed among them. (It was completed after the Restoration, under Clarendon.) The power they wielded was due both to the exceptional political context of the 1640s in England, when thousands of pamphlets were written, read and discussed, at least in London, during the long crisis lasting nearly twenty years, and to the exceptional talent of the writers and orators involved, who were in many cases ministers of religion left without employment by a Church that found them hard to put up with, who had joined Cromwell's army and fought ardently to defend the people's cause.

Richard Overton, who edited for over a year (July 1648 to September 1649) the journal *The Moderate*, in which their views on questions of the day were set forth each week; John Lilburne, a puritan pamphleteer who became an officer in Cromwell's army; and William Walwyn, more of a preacher than a political orator, formed the leading group of the Levellers (though the movement was in no sense an organization, a party in the modern meaning of the word). On his own stood Milton, the poet who defended freedom of the press, the vigorous denouncer of established hypocrisies, of the sanctimonious silences maintained by parish clergy warm and comfortable in their slippers, and of the muddy ponds of conformity – Milton who asserted his fidelity to Christianity in his rejection of any and every ecclesiastical institution. Rediscovering the original inspiration of Luther, these men based their political demands upon the Scriptures. Their great manifesto, the *Agreement of the People*, of which there were two versions (1647 and 1649), called for sovereignty of the people, or, more precisely, of the 'free people', excluding domestic servants, beggars and even the propertyless in general. In opposition to the dominant political doctrine, they declared that all power was derived from the people and must be exercised for the people's good. Representation of the people was to be realized by a Parliament elected annually, which would pass a budget based on a single direct tax. Whoever governed against the people was a tyrant, whose execution would certainly be no crime. Against the dogmatisms of the established Churches, Anglican and Presbyterian alike, they proclaimed freedom of religion, to be extended to all the sects (but not, of course, to Papists) and they recognized the legitimacy of any individual form of worship.

However, the Levellers, who succeeded for several months, with their speeches, pamphlets and petitions, in stirring up the lower orders of London – craftsmen, shopkeepers, soldiers – had no social programme (though their name of 'Levellers' refers, perhaps, to the opponents of 'enclosures', who wanted to level hedges). Overton published in 1645 a *Discourse on Tithes*, condemning these levies as being contrary to New Testament teaching. When they failed, however, in 1647 at Putney, in their attempt to secure decisive influence in the Cromwellian army and its staff, the Levellers thereafter gradually lost all the political clout they had acquired. But the ebbing of their power was due also to their internal divisions, their lack of organization, and the presence beside them of more 'radical' elements, the True Levellers, or Diggers, who looked beyond political democracy.

Less numerous than the Levellers, the Diggers were both inspired spirituals, 'true seekers', like the elusive Fifth Monarchy Men, and also revolutionaries who wanted to abolish the landlord regime and introduce a kind of rural communism: their master-preacher, Gerard Winstanley, an author of hymns and sermons, was, according to Christopher Hill, 'the most radical figure in seventeenth century England'. His point of departure was the same as that of the Levellers: a free and inspired commentary on the Old and New Testaments. But his point of arrival was quite different. Winstanley and his associates denounced, from 1649 to 1652 (when the Leveller writers were in prison) the beasts who were sucking the blood of society – landlords, clergy, lawyers. Their mystical invocation of Jesus, leader and exemplar of True Levellers, led them to demand the pure community life of the lost Golden Age, which was to be recovered by abolishing private ownership of land. The first stage of their programme was the confiscation of lands left uncultivated by the Crown and the Church, and their distribution among penniless beggars, while the second implied the peaceful establishment of communities in which owners and vagrants would join together freely to cultivate the soil in common. The Levellers vehemently denounced the laws of the Conqueror, the 'Norman Yoke', though without showing any nostalgia for the laws of the Saxons. They wanted to create a nation of free producers who would elect their Parliamentary representatives, their officials and their pastors. At the same time, in 1649–50, some of Winstanley's followers attempted a brief experiment in rural communism according to their lights, by occupying some waste land in Surrey. The new foundation did not last long, though long enough for Winstanley to celebrate the joy felt by the Diggers. But this programme of agrarian revolution evoked an echo in the countryside, and, here and there, landlords newly established on their estates were attacked, fences pulled up, hedges knocked down. Winstanley's 'community with freedom' disappeared along with its prophet in the repression of 1653–4.

No greater success in drawing the masses after them or winning an exceptionally wide audience was achieved by the prophets of the Fifth Monarchy, who announced that the Millennium would arrive in 1666. Enthusiasts like John

Rogers (who eventually fled to America) and other servants of God who proclaimed the coming of the new kingdom wrote, sermonized, published, and held their ground in the streets of London in 1653, announcing a new world where there would be no tithes or customs-dues or taxes, and where the people would be led by men who had received enlightenment from God. Persecuted after 1660, they quietly left the scene.

Nevertheless it is possible to sketch the extent of the impression made by these movements upon English opinion: by the copiousness of their contribution to the immense 'pamphlet war' which was a feature of the twenty years of civil strife, and by the place that Clarendon, writing under the Restoration the history of these years, accords to these 'fanatics' who challenged the very foundations of English society. It was indeed a different language that such upholders of the traditional order heard spoken in those times, and they were not to forget it. Those clerics, straight out of England's universities, had advocated a new political organization, lending their voices and their pens to the cause of the people who had always been subject to authority. Denunciation of the 'Norman Yoke' and of the lush benefices of the established Church was indeed nothing new in English political polemic: Hartlib, a scholar more concerned with astronomy and pedagogy than with politics, had written of the Norman yoke as a sinister reality in England's history. But the novelty of what was said in these little groups which addressed themselves to the people in the streets, to the communities of town and country, and carried on agitation in the New Model Army as well as in public places, was that they set forth in a coherent fashion a political or social programme in which the lower orders recognized their own interests, and which established 'good society' could not contemplate. The 'fierce and untamable beast' feared by the freethinking horse-breakers and the theoreticians of absolutism found in the England

of those days a systematic expression of its will: a programme which, in a sense, began to be put into effect with the
execution of Charles I, which, denounced by Saumaise as a
barbarous act, all the less admissible because the King was a
Protestant, was justified by Milton, who said that 'there
appears much more of God in the people when they depose
an unjust prince than in a king that oppresseth an innocent
people'.

The *Agreement of the People*, in its version of 1 May 1649,
represented the outcropping of a popular political consciousness forged in the feverish atmosphere of London in the civil
war years by the agency of sectarian prophets who carried
certain Gospel precepts to their ultimate conclusions, with
more effect than had previously been obtained by the disciples of Jan Hus or Thomas Münzer. The thirty articles of
the *Agreement of the People*, signed by John Lilburne, William
Walwyn, Thomas Prince and Richard Overton, prisoners in
the Tower of London, and published with the complicity of
a censor well-disposed towards the Levellers, was indeed, as
has been shown by Olivier Lutaud, editor of a full translation
of the document into French, a real social contract: the last
great manifesto of the Levellers, applauded by a whole section of London's people, it certainly caused fear, and not for
only a short time, either.

But this phenomenon was strictly English, and produced
little echo on the Continent, either in Mediterranean Europe,
still living under the domination of a picaresque and theocratic
Spain that was remote from any comparable concerns, or in
Central Europe, bled white by thirty years of war and devas-
tation and aspiring only to rest and calm, as we learn from
many letters of the time, written by princes and bourgeois.
The political and religious debate carried on at the princely
level, before and after the Peace of Westphalia, dealt not at
all with the rights of peoples, but only with how the principle
cujus regio, ejus religio should be applied, and with the balance

to be achieved between the powers of the independent sovereigns and the ambitions of the Emperor: these were matters for costly delegations which resided for months at Münster and Osnabrück, carrying on perilous negotiations in which Sweden and the United Provinces played a big part. But there was nothing said there to recall the inflammatory proclamations of the Levellers and Diggers. The only ones who might have been able to give ear to them, the last of the enthusiasts, the heirs of Franck and Paracelsus, and the Hussites of the Czech tradition, were in no position to take up such slogans.

There remains France, which between 1648 and 1653 experienced five years of troubles which were less tragic than the corresponding period in England, and saw a considerable amount of pamphleteering – less extensive, however, than what went on across the Channel. In contrast to the 22,000 pamphlets included in the 'Thomason Tracts' collection, the inventory (which was no easy matter) of the Mazarinades listed only a few thousand titles; and these were less vitriolic than the English ones, since the great majority of the French writings discussed such questions as the rights of the Parlement, the duties of the nobility, the limits of monarchical power and the abuses of the royal taxation system, or else wandered off into smutty personal attacks on the cardinal-minister and the Queen Regent. There was no proclamation of, or demand for, popular sovereignty – with the sole exception of the movement of the Ormeé in Bordeaux, in the last years of the Fronde (which was particularly lively in the capital of Guyenne, where the Parlement came out against the Governor, d'Epernon, and where, a little later, the princes sought refuge). One of the Leveller leaders, Sexby, came to Bordeaux in 1651, it seems, and a popular party there, led by advocates, merchants and craftsmen, kept up the fight against Mazarin after the princes had made peace. This party publicized the *Agreement of the People*, of which the leaders of the

Ormée produced an adaptation calling for guarantees of individual and religious liberty and a representative legislature, and by which they were more vaguely inspired in their 'Articles of the Union of the Ormée', which was a programme of municipal government with participation by the citizens and protection of urban liberties, and affirmed their loyalty to the monarchy. But the popular movement of the Ormée was not master of the city for long, and its ephemeral success was not adequate to make its political and social aspirations known beyond the bounds of Guyenne (where a memory of them was still present at the time of the revolt of 1675).

All these agitations explain, to a large extent, the repressive measures taken in England and France. In the former country, where Cromwell had for some years allied himself with the sects, supporting the most 'Independent' of them so long as they favoured his authority, the choice to be made became quite clear with the Restoration in 1660. The regime of Charles II found, without difficulty, a theoretician to justify it (though in an embarrassing way) in the person of Hobbes, who had been the new King's tutor during his stay in France: a convinced absolutist who preached the primacy of the monarchical civil power over the Church and advocated firm government in order to cause the troubled years of civil war to fade from public memory. During the first years of Charles II's reign Clarendon hunted down Independents, regicides and others who had supported the previous regime. Legislation was less important than strictly police measures. The Licensing Act of 1662, which introduced a censorship of all printed works dealing with the King and the court, was not applied very rigorously and was even suspended in 1679, and the English Government did not trouble itself to interfere in a niggling way in the activities of London's printers. But Clarendon put in prison a large number of pamphleteers and orators who had become well known among the extremist groups during the civil war period. The Baptist John Bunyan, who had served in Cromwell's army, remained in prison for twelve years, 1660–72, and Fox, the founder of the Quakers, was held from 1664 to 1666. The restoration of Anglicanism was also accompanied by the eviction of the Presbyterian clergy who had installed themselves in the parishes during the Cromwellian period: in 1662 more than 1,700 of these were expelled from their livings and compelled to live by whatever means they could find or else to go into exile in the United Provinces or in the American colonies.

In face of the persecution which was thus exerted against them for fifteen years, the harshly treated 'Puritans', Presbyterians or sectaries reacted in various ways. Rare among them were men like Dryden who, after writing, in 1659, a poem in memory of Cromwell, turned his coat and accepted the new regime, becoming the King's official historiographer. Dryden was an exception: more commonly, they gave up political and religious polemic and lived by petty writing jobs, occasionally producing pamphlets critical of the new high society of the Restoration. Marvell, a friend of Milton's, is a good example, since this former panegyrist of Cromwell published critiques of the peculation and immorality of the court, of the corrupt practices of the King's officials, and, in particular, of the court's foreign policy. But the two attitudes most frequently taken up were more significant. On the one hand, many of the victims of Anglican fury preferred to go abroad and await better times, which soon came. The universities of the United Provinces welcomed them, and certain Scots, such as John Livingstone and Robert Fleming, became ministers of the Scottish Church in Rotterdam. The Quaker George Fox went to America in 1670–73 to visit the colonies and the West Indian islands and prepare the way for the transplanting of the 'Friends' to the American continent, with the foundation of Pennsylvania in 1681. On the other hand, many of the Independents, deprived for years of all pastoral activity, worked at describing their religious conceptions, relating their experiences (like Fox) or evoking their utopian vision of a changed mankind, depending on their inclinations. John Bunyan, during his long years of imprisonment, wrote his *Pilgrim's Progress*, finished in 1678, an allegorical description of the path to the Eternal City, which, though Baptist in inspiration, enjoyed immense success. Milton, who had tried in vain to get religious freedom accepted in 1659–60, so as to avoid the re-establishment of a State Church, withdrew discreetly, wrote the poems that made his literary reputation, and then returned to religious and institutional polemic once the storm had passed, publishing in 1673 an essay on heresy, schism and toleration in which he again called for freedom for the sects. Thus, the Stuart Restoration was, on the whole, with alternations of greater and less severity, marked by a policy of repression: we see this again in the flight into exile in the United Provinces, after Shaftesbury's defeat, of John Locke and many others, not to return until after the Glorious Revolution of 1688–9.

In France, where, during the first years of the personal rule of Louis XIV, the King's Government had to cope with a many-headed agitation (popular revolts caused by famine, religious conflicts around the 'formulary' and Port-Royal, anxieties among the lawyers during the prosecution of Nicolas Fouquet), the main effort was directed, on Colbert's instigation, at the printing and selling of books. Despite the amplitude of the legislation governing the work of the presses and the establishment of a department of state specially concerned with this surveillance and responsible to the Chancellor, the inadequacy of the system was plain to see. The pamphleteering fever of the period of the Mazarinades had not subsided completely; the order for the *Provinciales* to be burnt had appeared too obviously absurd in view of the success obtained by these eighteen letters; and the difficulties met with in forming a stable of writers charged with singing the praises of the monarch had shown at the same time that a policy of active surveillance and firm repression was needed as a complementary measure. The newspapers, both handwritten and printed, were especially aimed at by Colbert, who observed in 1666 that 'it was one of the most important matters in a state to prevent this sort of publication, and though in Italy no notice was taken of them, further north they were considered to be telling the truth, however impertinent they might be'. The minister wished also to regulate all the activities of the book trade, keeping an eye on the printers, checking on the despatch of books (especially from abroad), and preventing pirate editions, which reproduced with impunity books for which copyright had been granted. All these measures converged to ensure that the Government exercised firm control over intellectual life.

After carrying out an inquiry, consulting the printers normally employed by the King for producing official documents, and visiting the corporation of printers, the Council of Police set up by Colbert followed the minister's line of reducing the numbers involved, so as to make surveillance easier, while favouring those printers who were regarded as reliable. 'The first idea that the Council had where the printers were concerned', Colbert explains, 'was to reduce their number and to exclude from their ranks those who were not respectable or capable; to this end it was decided to examine the ordinances and regulations that had been promulgated regarding the printing trade, to read the list of master-printers and look into each individual case, and to visit all the printing-houses, so that, using the information obtained in all these ways, a good regulation might be drawn up.' Actually, investigations and regulations were not so badly needed. An inventory of the eighty or ninety printing workshops operating in Paris at that time was made and revised without difficulty, and there was no lack of regulations, in the form of earlier royal ordinances governing the grant of copyright, its duration, and the requirement that books be deposited in the Royal Library and in the Chancellor's 'office of the book-trade'. Since what was wanted was to ensure effective control, the measure called for was a reduction in the number of print-ers allowed to operate in Paris, and this was brought down to thirty by an ordinance of March 1667. These thirty privileged printers were to share the largest book market in France. A few months later, in October, a decision by the Council of Police sought to deal with the problem of the pirate editions which were so often produced by provincial presses, by re-minding all printers that they were forbidden to print 'any books without a privilege, sealed with the Great Seal, nor any books or flysheets without the express permission of the prin-cipal magistrate of the place'. At the same time the *baillis* and *sénéchaux* were instructed to carry out a general inventory of the printing establishments in the area under their authority and to remind all concerned of the ban on admission of new master-printers anywhere in France.

In order to apply this rigorous control the King's Govern-ment gave plenary powers, so far as the capital was concerned, to the Lieutenant of Police in Paris, the celebrated La Reynie. All printing workshops were to be visited and checked on (this task was soon carried out by Superintendent Delamare, a specialist in such matters, in the Quartier Saint-Jacques and in the neighbourhood of the Palais de Justice). Hawkers and itinerant traders were to be licensed and supervised, and their numbers reduced. The Lieutenant of Police succeeded in applying effectively the decisions taken by the Council, but only with a certain delay which reflected the resistance put up by the printers who were to be made redundant and the (discreet) backing they received from the Paris municipal authorities. In 1679 Paris still had sixty-three printing-houses, or more than twice the number laid down in 1667. Similarly, although the agents of the Lieutenant of Police did indeed check on packets of books imported from abroad – especially from Holland, a particularly suspect source – nevertheless the penetration, even into the capital, of foreign publications (whether pernicious, in the minister's view, or otherwise) was not really stopped. Extension of this generalized surveillance to the kingdom as a whole was difficult, and proved inadequate. To be sure, the provincial printers were soon complaining that, being distant from the 'office for the book-trade', never being granted privileges, and being unable to produce pirate editions, they were driven to the brink of ruin. The truth of the matter, however, seems to have been less tragic. The *baillis* did not have a sufficiently large number of policemen at their disposal, and the printers were often helped by the local authorities, when these wished to safeguard the instruments of intellectual life in their province, even if this meant disobeying the ordinances issued from Paris.

All the same, this police surveillance of publishing deserves attention. Even if it did not fully attain Colbert's ambitious aims it did constitute a handicap for literary and scientific activity in the kingdom, of which the complaints of the publishers of Lyon at the end of the century give us some idea. They said that they were managing with difficulty to survive 'in a state of necessity to pirate books published in Paris and break the law in the ways they are blamed for, but without which they would die of hunger'. Police constraints went along with consolidation of the monarchical order. Furthermore, Colbert and Louis XIV expected much from the encouragement they gave to right-thinking writers through their 'Academy' policy, while they had the teaching of Cartesianism forbidden in the universities. Here the theological debates coincided with the 'disciplining' of science that was attempted during the first twenty years of the King's personal rule: Port-Royal and the Oratory were supporters of Descartes and Galileo. The Government of Louis XIV took its stand on Aristotle and Ptolemy, even while the savants in the observatory argued and worked on the basis of Copernicus's hypotheses, and the new science progressed steadily, as Boileau and Antoine Arnauld pointed out in sarcastic terms during the 1670s.

3. SAVANTS AND PHILOSOPHERS AFTER DESCARTES

In this atmosphere of controversy in which the weight of the machinery of government was increasing in most states, the savants who were carrying on their researches under conditions thus rendered more delicate found, in several countries, a means of providing themselves with better information and making their work more effective. This was the institutionalizing as academies of the meetings which took place between scientists, together with the creation of regular publications to analyse learned papers and new books: developments which constituted an important step forward in the transformation of the conditions under which research was carried on and that philosophical discussion conducted that was inseparable from scientific demonstration. Twenty years after the death of Descartes, at the very moment when the Jesuits were having his philosophy condemned and his works put on the Index, and when, nevertheless, schools of Cartesianism were springing up everywhere, the life of the world of learning was being profoundly changed.

This change formed a stage in a continuous process which it is not difficult to recognize. Since the great success of the gatherings of learned men in Paris, as since the expansion of Gresham College in London (which was opened in Henry Gellibrand's time to the undertaking of calculations of tonnage and the measurements concerning the magnetic compass which were asked for by shipbuilders and merchants), the requirement remained the same. Every learned man felt the need to attend regularly a gathering of the learned. If none was available, he made do with his neighbours, as Guy Patin explained to Falconet in 1658: 'I spend my evenings, after supper, quietly in the company of my two distinguished neighbours, M. Miron, *président des enquêtes*, and M. Charpentier, *conseiller aux requêtes*... If we talk about religion or the state, we do so only from a historical standpoint, without thought of reform or sedition. Our principal subject of conversation is literature, and what is new, worth attention and of value therein ...' In the heart of Germany, then emerging with difficulty from the throes of war, old Duke August of Brunswick-Wolfenbüttel continued till his death to keep up a lively correspondence with his agents in Nuremberg, Augsburg and Paris, in order that he might be well-informed regarding political developments, new publications, and all recently made discoveries. In April 1666 (the duke died in December, at the age of eighty-seven) the Paris correspondent was busying himself to find what had been ordered: 'I will seek carefully for the books of Sorel's *Science universelle* which Your Highness lacks ... I will also look for the continuation of the academic and oratorical addresses of the Sieur de Richesource, of which Your Highness informs me he possesses the first part, printed as a quarto in 1661.' The same continuity is found in the travels that form a normal feature of the activity of the learned world. Sorbière, for instance, visited England in 1663, 'to visit my friends and the learned men in that nation, and to be further instructed in matters of literature and the sciences, as well as to see the country.' He did not fail to meet the most famous writers, Hobbes especially, and also another great French traveller, De Monconys, from Lyon, whose travel diary was renowned even before it was printed: 'I found him in his element, full of the conversation of physicians and talking of nothing but machines and new experiments.' Assemblies, correspondence and travel were still the three main channels for the circulation of knowledge within the world of learning. But conditions had been greatly changed, in circumstances of a more or less dramatic character.

Some English savants had been meeting since 1644, first in a tavern near Gresham College and then in the College itself, with aims exactly the same as those of their Paris colleagues. In 1660 they began, with like-minded colleagues, moves to found a 'college for the promoting of physico-mathematical learning' but without much in the way of material resources to do this with. In Paris the break-up of the Académie Putéane at the death of the Du Puy brothers caused much concern among scholars, despite the existence of several other groups of the same sort, open to all and ready to carry on the tradition. That illustrious assembly, declared its habitués, who were surprised by the bequeathing to the King of the Du Puys' library, could not be allowed to disappear, so vital was it for the savants of Paris. When the danger became apparent, Abraham de Wicquefort, who had lived for many years in Paris and spent much time at the Du Puy brothers' house, wrote from the Hague, where he was living in 1656, to Ismaël Boulliau, expressing his feelings, which were the same as those of many others, and adding an offer of service: 'I find it hard to get over the astonishment into which I have been cast since I heard this distressing news. But we must not let our fine assembly be dispersed. The late M. Du Puy regarded you as the only person capable of enabling it to continue, and I hope that *Monsieur le Cardinal* will on this occasion render you the justice you deserve from him, and let you succeed to the position and to some of the revenues of the deceased. If I were there, I would do all in my power to contribute to this end, and I offer to do all you may ask of me, and to present myself wherever you may wish to establish the assembly ...' This scheme came to nothing, and those who had frequented the Du Puys' library were soon meeting at the house of M. de Montmor. At the same time, in Italy the *Accademia del Cimento*, 'the academy of experiment', was being founded in Florence, to carry on for a dozen years the torch dropped by the *Accademia dei Lincei* when it died with its founder in 1630. A very active body, it published *Saggi di naturale esperienze fatte nel' Accademia del Cimento.* In Germany a college of persons interested in curiosities of nature, the *Collegium naturae curiosorum*, established in Rostock in 1652, had only an ephemeral existence. What was distinctive about the academic bodies set up in England and France in the 1660s was certainly their longevity: both of them succeeded in lasting and thereby in modifying the conditions of scientific life not only in their own countries but in Europe as a whole.

The more important of the two, and the earlier in date, was the Royal Society, created in 1662 by a royal decision giving formal recognition to the group of savants, partly based in Oxford, which had been led for the previous fifteen years by John Wilkins, now joined by sympathizers from London. The new institution aimed at carrying on work for the advancement of the natural sciences, and presented some original features which are important for understanding its success. Once royal patronage had been obtained, to secure its foundation, the society wished to be independent, and called on its members (about a hundred in the first year, twice that number in 1670) to pay an annual subscription, for the particular purpose of defraying the cost of publications. The objectives outlined by Robert Hooke defined a programme focused upon experiments and practical applications. First and foremost it was explicitly stated that the university disciplines subject to discussion and political controversy (metaphysics, divinity, morals), together with the strictly literary ones (grammar, rhetoric, logic) would not enter into the society's work, which should be directed to improving the useful arts, manufacture, machines and inventions, and also to reviving ancient skills the secrets of which had been lost and the virtues of which would be tested by experiment. Furthermore, the society was to be open not only to men of science but also to merchants, navigators and specialists in the mechanical arts. The first historian and panegyrist of the society, Thomas Sprat, writing in praise of this foundation to which he had belonged since 1665, stressed the importance of participation by technicians.

Organized in commissions which were open to all of its members, the society worked on the basis of papers which were presented and freely discussed. The most frequented commission was the one dealing with questions of mechanics, while the least frequented (during the early years) was the one on astronomy. The plenary sessions were devoted to great debates which fulfilled the aspiration proclaimed at the outset to examine both systems and theories and attain to a better overall knowledge of the natural world: as Hooke put it, 'in order to the compiling of a complete system of solid philosophy for explicating all phenomena produced by nature or art, and recording a rational account of the causes of things'. These sessions of the Royal Society soon acquired a great reputation for scientific soundness. Foreign savants visiting London attended them – Sorbière, for instance, who in 1663 wrote this account of a meeting: 'There is a relation given in a few words of what is thought proper to be said concerning the experiments proposed by the Secretary. There is nobody here eager to speak, that makes a long harangue, or intent upon saying all he knows. He is never interrupted, that speaks, and differences of opinion cause no manner of resentment, nor as much as a disobliging way of speech. There is nothing seemed to me to be more civil, respectful and better managed than this meeting . . .' This passage, which clearly has to be read bearing in mind that Sorbière is making a contrast with the practices of the French learned assemblies he has attended, provides evidence of the prestige that was quickly acquired by the Royal Society.

This was all the more understandable in that the society had from the beginning attracted to membership all the active savants in England. Among the founders the first place was held by chemists, physicians and astronomers. Locke, a physician, joined the society in 1668. The mathematicians and astronomers

Robert Hooke and Edmund Halley were accompanied, from
1671, by Newton, who soon came to occupy an important
position in the society. The most unusual figure was certainly
Christopher Wren, who was another mathematician and
astronomer, but also an architect, who spent a large part of
his life rebuilding London after the fire of 1666, while participating actively in the work, observations and calculations
which led Newton to frame his theory of gravity. The man
who rebuilt St Paul's, some forty other churches and a number
of secular buildings was also a remarkable mathematician
who contributed considerably to the progression of calculations and deductions which led to Newtonian mechanics.
The Royal Society secured recognition without much difficulty. In England itself, when attacked by ill-wishers who
accused it of including too many 'Puritans', the society took
little notice, and the attack came to nothing. Elsewhere in
Europe its influence was so great that continental savants
thronged at its doors, offering communications and submitting their works for discussion by their English colleagues.
Huyghens, who had a protracted dispute with Newton, and
Van Leeuwenhoek, the Dutch inventor of the microscope,
remained throughout their careers in contact with the society
and took part in its work. Here too we have the precious
evidence of a modest person who had no remarkable experiments to his credit and did not conceal his pleasure at being
accepted by the society. Sorbière wrote in 1663 in his travel
diary: 'I shall think the society he [King Charles II] has
founded very happy if they continue, pursuant to their orders,
to go on in perfecting the arts and useful sciences they have
begun to cultivate; and I take it to be an inestimable honour
to me to be admitted a member of it, and that my weak
productions have been so favourably looked on by such
clear-sighted gentlemen as they are.'

The society's international reputation was ensured by its
publications, the *Philosophical Transactions*, which contained

the papers read at meetings and the discussions of these papers, together with notes on works by members and by foreign correspondents. The make-up of the *Philosophical Transactions* reflected, of course, the predominant concerns of the new society. In the first few years, when businessmen and 'men of action' exercised a certain influence, articles devoted to the applied sciences accounted for more than a tenth of the issues. This was the time when Robert Boyle was studying the chemical processes used in the crafts, especially dyeing, while others were studying the techniques of navigation. After 1670, when the society's proceedings were dominated by the great discussions between Newton and his opponents and rivals in astronomy and optics, the share taken by mathematical problems became preponderant, while that of technical descriptions and studies fell by half. The European scientific world now possessed a new means of circulating information, greatly superior to the traditional 'correspondence', even when that had been read out in learned assemblies. The *Philosophical Transactions* served for a long time as a model, being widely imitated as scientific academies became more numerous.

The foundation of the Academy of Sciences in Paris in 1666 took place in a rather different, though comparable, context. On the one hand, the prolonged gestation was similar, since French intellectual life had become concentrated long since in a constellation of informal assemblies where men of learning assiduously met together, like their colleagues of Gresham College and other gatherings. In the 1650s after the break-up of the Académie Putéane and of Mersenne's group (the Minim died in 1648), it was the assembly at M. de Montmor's house that constituted the main meeting place of savants in Paris. There one could find the learned men of the new generation, men like Clerselier and Rohault, who were philosophers rather than savants, and Du Prat, De Monconys and Bernier, all active experimenters, along with such survivors of the older generation as Sorbière, Guy Patin and Claude Quillet. Gassendi, too, attended this group fairly regularly towards the end of his life. Guy Patin, who valued the discussions more highly than the dinners to be had there, wrote to Spon in January 1654: 'I dined today with M. Gassendi at the house of M. H. de Montmor, *maître des requêtes*. He showed me his books, which are fine and numerous. He made me promise to come and see him once a week, but I did not promise to come to dinner: too much time is wasted in such ceremonies.' This weekly gathering, which was more scientific in character than the meetings in the study of the Du Puy brothers had been, thus perpetuated the tradition. On the other hand, the King's Government, headed at this time by Colbert, thought it might add to the royal glory by supporting scientific activities, while also looking for a way to supervise and guide the movement. The interest here shown in the sciences was of the same sort as the protection accorded to letters by Richelieu when the *Académie Française* was founded. That institution, established during the previous reign, had been assigned precise tasks aimed at defining the language, but had carried out these tasks with such merely intermittent zeal that Colbert thought it good to intervene, here too, by stimulating assiduity and productivity through the introduction of payment for proved attendance at meetings. In its first decades the *Académie Française* was an envied reward for zealous writers, an assembly of hack grammarians and dictionary-makers and an editorial office at the service of the sovereign. The minister further decided that it would be best to restrict the *Académie* to its linguistic function and to establish alongside it, in 1663, a '*petite Académie*' (later to become the *Académie des Inscriptions et Belles Lettres*), entrusted with studying the best means of exalting the King's glory.

The creation of the Academy of Sciences in 1666 belonged to this lineage, while it was obviously inspired by the aims of England's Royal Society. The new creation, which copied the form of the weekly meetings held at the house of M. Habert de Montmor, brought together about twenty savants, including Roberval and Mariotte, and soon had foreign associate members, such as Huyghens (for a few years). Pensioned by the King, the members of the Academy were given directives by Colbert which guided their work into sectors where it would be useful. Under the tutelage of the minister, down to 1683 the Academicians worked at listing the machines and inventions useful for commerce and industry, devoted some of their meetings to the measurement of longitude at sea, and prepared to construct a map of France (this project Louvois caused to be dropped later, and it was not resumed until the eighteenth century). Thus, the Academy of Sciences established in France in 1666 did not possess the freedom of research, either individual or collective, enjoyed by the corresponding body in London. Nor did it have, like the Royal Society, a periodical bulletin in which to make known the results of work undertaken by its members. The *Journal des Savants*, which was founded not long before the Academy of Sciences, in January 1665, on the initiative of a Parisian lawyer, was independent of the Academy. Nevertheless, this journal (which at once got into trouble for publishing a favourable review of a Gallican work, so that its founder, Denis de Sallo, had to suspend publication in March 1665) enjoyed a long career after 1666 under the editorship of learned abbés (Gallois, then De la Roque). But the *Journal des Savants* offered itself as a general chronicle of scientific life, and did not record the proceedings of the Academy of Sciences, as the *Philosophical Transactions* did those of the Royal Society. Its issues were mostly made up of critical notes, which were precise and measured, on recently published books, and these certainly were of great service, to judge by the journal's prolonged success and wide circulation all over Europe. Of course, ill-disposed persons were able to carp, in the eighteenth century, saying that such journals 'were invented for the relief of persons who are either too busy or too lazy to read whole books': the same critics nevertheless admitted that, 'though they pamper a lot of people in this way ... a journal of such a kind has seemed to be very advantageous and useful, and it has been imitated under various titles'.

Accordingly the Paris Academy of Sciences did not perform exactly the same functions as its elder sister in London. Governmental tutelage and the bans imposed in the same period upon Cartesian physics and philosophy kept away from it many men of learning who continued to carry on their work and their discussions outside this official and constraining framework. The foreign savants invited by Colbert did not always respond, although these invitations were accompanied by offers of generous pensions: Cassini and Huyghens were among those who did, but the latter soon went back home. When Leibniz spent some years in Paris after 1672 he would accept nothing from Colbert. The Academy of Sciences was not a magnet for savants such as the Royal Society was. The institutionalizing of the groups of learned men was carried forward in the provinces of France in a way that compromised between the two principles. While Colbert's protégés were being installed in Paris, academies were being founded in the provinces, at Caen, Arles and Soissons, and the movement gained momentum as the century drew to its close. The royal administration sanctioned these foundations by issuing letters patent, which were granted after examination of the statutes and the endowments of the new institutions. But the latter benefited by their remoteness from the capital: distance sheltered them from the directives and imperative intrusions which the Paris Academy could not avoid. The provincial academies thus perpetuated, to a greater degree than Paris, the pattern of free controversy around work undertaken out of personal interest which had been in former times that of the Du Puys' study and of the assembly in the Place Royale.

The general conditions governing scientific life were thus transformed in the second half of the seventeenth century. The establishment of these new institutions (which were to be initiated during the subsequent century all over Europe) and the creation of journals for the information of savants generally (and these journals multiplied at the same pace as the academies) provided a firmer framework for intellectual activity. These innovations certainly did not put an end to the personal exchanges, reciprocal sending of books and direct correspondence which remained an essential means of communication; but they ensured for experiments and innovating work an audience that was both wider and more definite, in so far as the published reviews and commentaries could reach far more readers than could be reached by the private correspondence which had previously prevailed, and, since they could be kept for a long time, they made possible comparisons and references which had been difficult to establish previously. These transformations helped to stimulate all the scientific activities of the time, as can be seen from the success achieved by the new publications, the ardour of the polemics developed within the setting of a society so open as that of London's 'academy' (between Hooke, Newton and Wren, for instance), and the great increase in works produced and in travel by savants about Europe.

During this period the increase in the numbers of savants active in all fields was such that only descriptions sector by sector can convey an impression of the movement as a whole. In optics there was convergent work by Huyghens and the Dane Roemer, both of them Parisians by adoption, by the Dane Erasmus Bartholin, by the Scot James Gregory, and by Newton himself. After the death of the Paracelsian iatrochemist Van Helmont who had been a keen correspondent of Mersenne's, medical chemistry was in the hands of a veritable 'English School', consisting of Robert Boyle, Robert Hooke and John Mayow, who published in 1674 his *Tractatus quinque medico-physici*, which put chemists on the trail of respiratory combustion – a big advance on the disputes about antimony of which Guy Patin quoted so many examples. Medical research on the circulation of the blood, subsequent to Harvey's discovery, was performed by the first investigators to use the microscope: Robert Boyle, Marcello Malpighi, and, later, but especially, Van Leeuwenhoek. There were convergences and rivalries, as normally in the life of researchers. Just as in the previous period the work of Torricelli and of Pascal on the weight of air had given rise to disputes over priority in discovery, so the scientific life of this period was marked by conflicts in which pride, if not vainglory, played a part: between Hooke and Newton regarding the inverse square in the mathematical expression of gravity, and between Leibniz and Newton regarding the discovery of the infinitesimal calculus. The major achievements of the time were the joint outcome of constant exchanges, in an atmosphere which could not be serene all the time.

Nevertheless, from among this numerous band, in which everyone has his place, a few great names emerge, in connexion with the problems posed by Cartesian physics and general method, alongside the many exegetes of Descartes who published their writings even while that philosopher's works were being condemned by the Catholic Church – writings of interest, such as the *Traité de l'esprit de l'homme* produced by the physician De la Forge in Paris in 1666, and shortly afterwards in Amsterdam, and the *Commentaires sur la méthode de M. Descartes* which the Oratorian Nicolas-Joseph Poisson brought out in 1671. These works did not win the acclaim given to Malebranche's *Recherche de la vérité* (he had some difficulty in getting permission to publish this book in 1674, and then it was not renewed until 1695), but they help us to form an impression of the great debates. The latter were dominated, on the one hand, by men who were more concerned with general philosophy, such as Spinoza, in his lonely position in Holland, and, on the other, by men who were founding a new physics – Newton and his comrades in the Royal Society. Closely linked with both sides of this movement was Leibniz, a man of universal knowledge who, working as a librarian in Hanover, took part in all the debates, and was quick to bring-clarity into them, from 1675 to 1680. Amsterdam, London, Hanover: in the period of the Sun King's greatest political glory, the vital work in which the sciences were being given more precise definition was not taking place in Paris, either in the King's Garden (the later Jardin des Plantes) or in the observatory in the Faubourg St-Jacques. The Oratorian Malebranche, though a physicist and logician of renown and a good Cartesian, did not cause heaven and earth to stir as did the writings of the Dutchman.

For, in the first place, there was the debate about rationalism, with the amazing personality and work of Baruch Spinoza. Heir to a good Sephardic family in Amsterdam; expelled from the Jewish community for having kept company with certain 'enthusiasts' and for having adopted consistently the philosophy of Descartes; withdrawn for most of his life from the mercantile bustle of his country and earning his living by polishing lenses; yet nevertheless a man of influence, friendly with Jan de Witt and the Grand Pensionary's collaborators – Spinoza did not train up many disciples, apart from Burgh, to whom he confided one day his certainty regarding his approach ('I do not claim to have found the best of philosophies, but I know that I am aware of the true one'), and though he corresponded with other scholars in Europe, he did not travel much, in the way that they did. Nevertheless, towards the end of his life he published, with many precautions, two works which caused an upheaval that went on for a long time in the rationalist world-outlook as it existed in the late seventeenth century. The only book he put his name to, published in 1663, was an exposition of Cartesian philosophy, *Principia Renati Descartes*, in which he showed himself a critical and consistent disciple who proposed to extend to the domains which Descartes had railed off – morals and metaphysics – the practice of methodical doubt set out in the *Discourse*. Less than ten years after the *Principia*, the Dutch sage issued anonymously, taking many precautions, which soon proved futile, two further treatises in which he gave a masterly explanation of where he stood: the *Ethics* and the *Tractatus theologico-politicus*.

In these works Spinoza showed, without any equivocation, that he was a philosopher who rejected all and every philosophy, revelation or religion that could not be grounded in reason. Neither morality nor the institutions that defined it, nor the Scriptures which were supposed to be accepted without question, nor the Churches which held men back from individual study, were spared by Spinoza. He abandoned Descartes's reservations about obeying the laws of one's country and respecting religion, to lay down an approach to wisdom which owes its principles – loving one's neighbour and perfecting one's intelligence – exclusively to a persevering exercise of reason. There was no need for a Church to provide grounds for the 'sacredness of life', which was not the privilege of believers. There was no need for any imposed *credo*, since life must be devoted to meditation and action in order to understand the ordering of this world and to find one's place in it, in a coherent whole of which man is only a part. Spinoza does not deny the existence of God, whom he finds everywhere in Nature, but he leaves it to Man, in the full exercise of his reason, to build his life in accordance with the principles which he has laid down: working to advance the mechanical arts, medicine and education means attaining that wisdom which gives life all its meaning. A hard task indeed, and easier to perform insofar as one's country's institutions facilitate it. A Dutch patriot, Spinoza realized very well that no other country in the world would allow him the tranquillity he needed. Despite dreadful aberrations such as the murder of the De Witt brothers in 1672, or the vexation he had himself suffered at the hands of the Synagogue, Spinoza remained deeply attached to his country, right down to his death in 1677, recognizing that Holland was, with all its faults, the land of freedom of thought and expression in an age that suffered from orthodoxy and absolutism.

Spinoza's two great treatises made a powerful impression throughout the European world of learning. The theologians perceived straight away the ruinous effect of this Cartesianism re-established in its full logic upon Church institutions, and even upon religion itself – an extrapolation easy to make and long since customary with them. Antoine Arnauld, the Doctor of Port-Royal, was as severe on this matter as his traditional opponents in the Society of Jesus. More significant still was the attitude of Leibniz, who visited the sage of Amsterdam, corresponded with him for several years, and was constantly concerned with his rationalism. Leibniz was at once moved to admiration by the rigour of thought shown in Spinoza's work and alarmed by his radical repudiation of any form of religion based upon revelation. When he addressed Spinoza he lavished upon him expressions of his admiration and esteem, which he maintained until the end of his life; but when he addressed others he referred to the dangerousness of Spinoza's ideas in terms no less severe than those used by the theologians: Spinoza's was a 'frightening work', he wrote to Antoine Arnauld, and to the great jurist Thomasius he spoke of the 'monstrous opinions of this Jew expelled from the Synagogue'. In Spinoza Cartesian rationalism found its most coherent expression, and this was for a long time to inspire the thinking of the new 'philosophical' generations. In the same period, Cartesian physics, called in question by the most recent work of mathematicians, astronomers and physicists, was replaced by Newton's mechanics: Leibniz found himself confronted by the most powerful of the English researchers, Isaac Newton, author of *Philosophiae naturalis principia mathematica.*

The new science which took shape in the final decades of the seventeenth century was an experimental mechanics constructed through the joint effort of all these savants who were calculating and observing, discussing and re-examining published work: the law of gravity was first defined by Newton and Hooke by means of calculations the approach to which had been divined by Galileo in his work on the falling of heavy bodies. Applied to the attraction exerted by the earth upon the moon, these calculations were brought to completion as soon as the length of the earth's radius had been established by the Paris Observatory. Additional verification was provided when Huyghens and Roemer succeeded in measuring the speed of light by studying the revolutions of the astral satellites that were easiest to observe. Newton, however, who had begun by making optical studies on the solar spectrum, work that was resumed later on, gave the principle of gravitation its full significance by a series of statements supported by calculations and observations which contributed to confirm the proof established. After showing that the force of the earth's gravity corresponded exactly to the centripetal force needed if the moon was to remain in its orbit round the earth, he renewed the observations made by Kepler regarding the movement of the planets round the sun. He also showed the flattening of the planets (and of the earth) at the poles, and their swelling round the equator, to be a function of their rotation upon themselves, explained the connexion between the tides and the attraction exerted by the moon and the sun, and at last put forward the principle of the reciprocal attraction of all bodies, in the infinitely small context just as in the infinitely large.

Leibniz, a regular correspondent of the Royal Society, in which the English physicist was undisputedly the leading figure of the time, was more than a mere witness to the reconstruction of the universe on mechanistic lines of which Newton set forth the essentials in his *Principia*, published in 1687. Working at algebraic calculations parallel with Newton's, and bringing the infinitesimal calculus to perfection at the same time as Newton did (or even earlier, according to the polemic between them), Leibniz provided, in a sense, through his notation of differential quantities, the mathematical instrument needed for the calculations accomplished subsequently, the validity of which he had himself shown by accumulating solutions to problems that could not be solved by any other method of calculation. Furthermore, being a philosopher as well as a mathematician, Leibniz revealed sooner and more easily what these discoveries meant. For example, he stated that the 'principle of continuity' in physics is a necessary component of natural operations, and this justifies the use by physicists of 'that part of general mathematics which deals with infinity'. The law of gravity, in its simplest terms, obviously demolished the Cartesian physics of vortices, and many savants, loyal to Descartes's work, refused for a long time to follow Newton, and multiplied objections to his theory, related to astronomical observations and methods of calculation which neglected very small quantities. The dispute between Newtonians and Cartesians went on far into the eighteenth century. This dispute expressed the fecundity of the experimental method which was practised by all these savants, who employed mathematics to explain natural phenomena. Leibniz and Newton were far, indeed, from sharing Spinoza's viewpoint, in that they always referred back the order which they discovered in the universe to an 'Author', and venerated Divine Providence as the creator of this harmony. Whereas Spinoza's philosophy seemed to Leibniz to present a clear danger to European thought, the achievements of experimental science seemed to him to fortify the faith of the savant who discovered the order established by the Creator throughout the solar system. In Europe's world of learning, Newtonian mechanics and the many discoveries now being made, year by year, constituted a step forward: the first step in a progress that was to be continued by leaps and bounds in the succeeding decades.

However, Leibniz, who, with Newton, continued to dominate European scientific exchanges until the beginning of the eighteenth century, gave a new dimension to intellectual life and to the savant's image in the world. To a greater degree than Newton, who was discreet about his Unitarian beliefs and had no difficulty in supporting the regime established in England in 1689, Leibniz did not separate his scientific activity from his political concerns. He lived the life of his time very passionately: his legal studies had equipped him to carry out historical research, and he spent years studying the formation of the German states and their relations down to the seventeenth century. As a German patriot he advocated the unity of Germany, but few of his fellow-Germans aspired to *that* in those days: nevertheless, he did not hesitate to appeal to a German national consciousness, especially during the wars with France. He addressed Louis XIV directly, urging him to undertake a crusade; he protested against France's acts of force in 1681–5, and even more strongly against the campaign of arson waged in the Palatinate; he made it his business to reply to the juridical arguments used by French writers with counter-arguments drawn from the archives he had studied, and, later, wrote and published a treatise establishing the right of the Austrian Archduke Charles to the throne of Spain. Still later, this librarian to the court of Hanover cultivated great dreams of unity, which he extended in all directions: unity of all Christians, overcoming their antagonisms, among Protestants first, and then between Protestants and Catholics; unity of savants, who already possessed common institutions, but should create still more of these (he himself founded the Academy of Berlin, and he negotiated with Prince Eugene and Peter the Great with a view to founding others, in Vienna and St Petersburg); political unity of Europe, and even of all mankind, about which he wrote particularly to Peter the Great, because the Russian Empire formed a bridge between East and West. These projects of his, which were usually just sketched out rather than fully elaborated, came up against the inertia and scepticism of sovereigns who were more concerned with maintaining their power than anxious to innovate. Neither Louis XIV nor Peter the Great paid much attention to him. The Elector of Hanover, who employed him for so long as his librarian, does not seem to have understood him any better, and did not even take him with him to England in 1714. Nevertheless, this man of universal mind who cultivated with equal success all the sciences that existed in his time gave a vital new dimension to the image of the intellectual: participating in the struggles of the age, he prefigures to some extent the philosophers of the Enlightenment; but, above all, he offers the example of a savant whose investigations themselves lead him to become a man of action.

CONCLUSIONS

UNDER the influence of a book of great prestige, recently reissued*, the concluding decades of the seventeenth century have been categorized as those which experienced a 'crisis of European consciousness', just as the changes occurring in the previous century have been arbitrarily labelled (with reference to a somewhat mythical 'Middle Ages') 'the great turning-point of Western civilization'. In both cases this means putting the emphasis upon the 'disruption' aspect, to a greater extent than is called for. The men of the Renaissance were no less closely linked with preceding generations than were, at the end of the seventeenth century, the contemporaries of Louis XIV and of William III. The crisis of European consciousness was, to say the least, a protracted affair, which persisted all through those two centuries, in which intellectual life was ceaselessly refreshed, as generation followed generation, and as new problems were raised by scientific development and the conflicts between clerics. Thematic and statistical studies, such as the one carried out by H.-J. Martin on the book-stocks held by the Bibliothèque Nationale in Paris, show clearly the gradual progress in the production of printed books in the French cultural area; upon a stable foundation in which certain main sectors are well defined – lives of the saints, narratives of travel, moral works, and books about the occult – a series of fashions, transient 'explosions', are seen to be superimposed, such as the burlesque poetry of the mid-seventeenth century,

* i.e. Paul Hazard's *La Crise de la conscience européenne*, first published in 1935 and reissued in 1961: translated, 1953, as *The European Mind, 1680–1715*.

or the Jansenist writings of the 1640s. Also apparent is the
decline of printing in Latin, which reflects the rise of cultural
nationalism: though still more than 30 per cent of total production at the beginning of the seventeenth century, it falls to
less than 10 per cent in the last decades. Are the same tendencies to be observed in other parts of Europe – in England,
Italy and Germany? This remains to be demonstrated with the
same precision as has been achieved in France. Random
samplings in comparable large libraries, that of the British
Museum and the Bibliotheca Augusta at Wolfenbüttel (which
at the end of the seventeenth century was considered the best
library in Europe) have given approximate results pointing in
the same direction.

Let us return, at the close of this difficult voyage of exploration, to the more illuminating distinctions which were
proposed at the outset, and, in the first place, to the contrast
between 'old' and 'new' intellectuals. On the one hand there
were the changes affecting the traditional ideological framework, provided by the Church: the disruption of Catholic
cultural hegemony did not only give rise to new orthodoxies,
which established themselves with a zeal no less fervent than
that of the old one, and soon ran into the same problems as the
Catholic Church, as we have seen; though these were certainly limited in their geographical extent by the limited
territorial structures established, around Wittenberg, Geneva
and Canterbury, and also limited doctrinally owing to the
way they had originated. The Catholic world was, on this
plane, of greater significance, for the disruption caused long-
lasting disturbance and uncertainty in that world, divided
within itself on the question of the road to be followed for
reconquering lost ground, and even on points of doctrine. The
rivalry between Jansenists and Jesuits spread all over the
Catholic world very quickly after the ending of the ephemeral
'Peace of the Church', and the Southern Netherlands, the
great Arnauld's refuge when the dispute with the Jesuits broke

out afresh, became the place where the second phase of Jansenism developed, as a stormy resurgence at the end of the century, led by new 'doctors', like Father Quesnel. The laymen who played an increasingly important part in this debate incited the clerics to carry their doctrinal antagonisms to extremes. At the same time, disputes broke out in every direction on the slightest provocation. There was Madame Guyon, a mere laywoman who led the Archbishop of Cambrai, Fénelon, further than he had expected to go in the definition of quietism. More elusive are Antoinette Bourignon, the mystic who fled to the United Provinces, or the complex figure of the prophet Labadie, who moved from Calvinism to Jansenism: 'Christians without a Church', at the frontiers of Catholicism and yet not wanting to leave it, these are reliable witnesses to the difficulties encountered by the post-Tridentine Church in keeping the élite of its membership within its own fold.

However, these cases do not constitute the most important evidence: the tensions of greatest significance are those that appeared in relations between the religious orders whose functions caused them to play a role in the intellectual life of the Catholic countries. The rivalry in the educational field between Jesuits and Oratorians was not, especially in France, just a matter of competition between two theories of education, but also a conflict between defenders of the most strictly orthodox tradition in doctrinal questions and those who had decided in favour of an 'opening' towards scientific work. Charged with Cartesianism, the Oratorians, even after their submission, remained in conflict with the order which had taken its stand for over a century as the stern and well-equipped guardian of true doctrine. Historians, knowing what was to happen later, have concluded too readily, perhaps, that religion itself bore the cost of these polemical ardours within the Catholic Church: it would be better to confine oneself to saying that they reflect an undeniable and substantial decline in discipline, that is, a weakening of the system which, established long before, had been safeguarded by organs that were firmly rooted and still active. There was no question of lack of vigilance by the Curia in this matter, as the compiling of the *Index librorum prohibitorum* shows well enough. What did *not* function so well as in the distant past, when the circulation of books was slight and all intellectuals were members of the Church, was the submissiveness of the laity, who were now involved in the development of science, and were also drawn into controversy by the attitude taken up by their rulers: Galileo's truth, on the one hand, and, on the other, the Gallican and Spanish challenges to Rome.

It was certainly not accidental that the Jansenist sect should have received, when it got its second wind at the end of the seventeenth century, support from the firmest defenders of Gallicanism – all those, members of the Parlement and others, in administrative circles and among prosperous bourgeois, who were fiercely opposed to Ultramontane influences and sought protection against them behind royal (which now meant national) sovereignty. It is quite obvious, moreover, that, on the scale of Europe as a whole, political authority had been strengthened, even in the intellectual sphere, at the expense of religious authority: in Paris the role of the Sorbonne, which had been a vital one in the first half of the sixteenth century, when Francis I submitted to it every book dealing with religion, had declined in face of the control exercised by the Parlement and, especially, by the King's *ad hoc* department serving this purpose. France was perhaps ahead of the rest of the Continent in this respect, but the same tendency was observable in the small Lutheran states of Northern Germany and in the England of William and Mary. When a prince published his ecclesiastical regulations concerning ceremonies and practices within his territory, laying down the law about the teaching of the catechism, the induction of a new pastor, the hours of prayer and the formulas of excommunication, he showed himself more of a master of his Church than Colbert advising a reduction in the number of religious holidays or imposing episcopal control over pilgrimages.

In both France and England, however, this extension of political authority was based, to a greater extent than elsewhere, upon an upsurge of national artistic and literary activity: the quarrel of the Ancients and the Moderns and the rise (even if only ephemeral) of a court art at Versailles, in which Boileau, Molière and, especially, Lulli were the leading figures, enter into this setting, along with England's post-Shakespeare theatrical tradition (and the Golden Age of painting in the United Provinces). This upward movement in literature and art, which no 'Bigots' Caucus' could manage to control, intensified the general tendency to draw apart from the Churches – to a smaller extent, no doubt, than with scientific work, the results of which directly called into question certain dogmas that were regarded as untouchable, but considerably, nevertheless, and all the more so because this form of communication was accessible to a larger number of people.

It is not a paradox to say, indeed, that the élites in some ways presented the Church, challenged in its ideological role, with more problems than were presented by the masses who had for so long been neglected and badly served. More precisely, the gap between the Church and the masses was of a different kind and could, in a sense, be bridged more easily. As seminaries were established in the dioceses and the training of priests (now in the hands of experienced theologians) improved, and as the teaching of the catechism to children became widespread, and missionary activity inside the country, with retreats and instruction for adults, was carried on by better methods, the bringing into line of the masses in town and country could progress slowly, and in a way which is not immediately apparent to us today – whereas the disputes between divines and casuists are there for anyone to see, filling shelves in bookshops and private libraries. The amount of work that needed to be done in this field was, however, as we have seen, very great indeed, and the process of reconquest, about which we know little, had to overcome the widest cultural gap that existed in the societies of the Ancien Régime.

On the other hand there was the rise of the 'new' intellectuals – mathematicians, physicists, chemists, jurists who defined at length the role of the state in the modern world, philosophers who meditated upon the logic of the sciences and the world's harmony. Undoubtedly, a new stage was entered at the end of the seventeenth century, when knowledge became systematically organized around the general hypotheses put forward by Newton: the laws of mechanics by which Western science was to live for the next two centuries had been defined with sufficient certainty for progress now to be maintained. The dialogue between Leibniz and Newton, which went on until 1716, is an illustration of the continuity, and of the fruitfulness, of a mathematical and experimental method which produced wonderful results in all sectors, and particularly in optics and physics. Works on astronomy (observations of the satellites of Jupiter and of comets, expositions of the system of the universe) were certainly still the most frequently produced and most frequently reissued, but works on physics, mathematics, algebra and geometry were also numerous in the last years of the century. In Paris there appeared, shortly before 1700, the first volume of the *Mémoires de mathématiques et de physique tirés des registres de l'Académie des Sciences*, an enterprise which echoed, thirty years after, the regular publications of England's Royal Society.

Meanwhile, new scientific academies were being set up all over Europe: all so many convergent signs showing still more clearly the influence exerted by the world of learning, while creating better conditions for the work of that world to be carried on. Contemporaries, and notably the greatest among them, did not always realize the magnitude of this movement.

In 1698 Leibniz deplored, in a communication to the *Philosophical Transactions*, a slackening off in philosophical speculation about the sciences: he lacked partners in discussion whose thought was developing on the same level as his own. Yet, for many years already, not only had the public interested in scientific questions been increasing, so that there were now many members of high society who possessed telescopes through which to observe eclipses and the satellites of Jupiter, but savants had also been taking the trouble to make recent discoveries known to this public and to explain their philosophical significance: Fontenelle, for instance, the future Perpetual Secretary of the Paris Academy of Sciences, with his *Entretiens sur la pluralité des mondes*.

Meanwhile, in the sphere of the humane sciences, progress in the latter part of the seventeenth century was almost as striking as in the sphere of mathematics applied to the cognition of Nature. Two names dominate these final decades: the Huguenot Pierre Bayle, a refugee in Holland, and the English philosopher John Locke. (There would have been three, with the addition of the Oratorian Richard Simon, if, after the appearance of his *Histoire critique du Vieux Testament*, in 1678, the works of this founder of philological and historical criticism of the Scriptures had not been destroyed at the demand of Bossuet, and their author obliged to hide away and carry on his work in a clandestinity which certainly restricted its influence.) Bayle, who had taken up residence in Holland shortly before the Revocation of the Edict of Nantes, first became known through a critical work on the comets, which lacks the clarity of Fontenelle's demonstrations. He spent many years writing for newspapers published in the United Provinces, reporting events, both big and small, in the world of letters. His major work, which was read in numerous editions all over Europe, was a *Dictionnaire historique et critique*, first published in 1696. Though presented by its author as merely a compilation – with a quotation from Scaliger:

'Such men serve scholars in the capacity of porters, gathering everything together, and that is of great help to us' – this big dictionary was a great deal more than a collection of quotations. The author did indeed follow the traditional method of referring to what had previously been written on a subject, duly quoting all this and even translating it. What he wanted to say was conveyed gradually, cautiously, article upon article, without any striking conclusion being drawn – for this conclusion had to be deduced by the reader himself, not hammered home by any one article. From this unusual dictionary, in which marginal notes and references occupy more space than the articles written by Bayle, scholars found much to learn even later, in the eighteenth century. More important than the scepticism which is usually denounced in it, there was shown in the *Dictionnaire* a marked predilection, even in the choice of subjects for articles, for heretics and deviants of all kinds, who were presented with a sympathy that urged the reader towards favouring peaceful toleration. It was a method for attacking accepted ideas, and also established dogmas, protected by stern institutions, which was used by the philosophers of the next century: the oblique attack, allusive rather than deductive. The *Dictionnaire historique et critique*, while renewing the velvet-gloved audacities of the learned freethinkers, took a step forward in aggressive boldness, thus carrying criticism of institutions and dogmas forward along a new path.

John Locke's contribution was of a different order. This philosopher-physician, a member of the Royal Society, who had fled from England at the height of the Stuart reaction and lived for several years in the United Provinces among the Calvinist pastors and 'sectarian' preachers of the cities of Holland, went back home in the train of William of Orange, and, on the morrow of the Glorious Revolution and of the negotiations between the Stadtholder and the English Parliament, he published, one after the other, in 1690, two works setting forth his philosophy and expounding, so to speak, the political theory of the event which had just occurred in England: the *Essay concerning Human Understanding* and the *Two Treatises on Government*. Here were developed in a most convincing way, based upon what had just been experienced, the theory of the social contract on which all human society is founded. The protracted dialogue in 1689 between the candidate for the kingship and the nation's representatives provided a good illustration of the positive and reciprocal undertaking which defines the agreement made between society and the person to whom power to govern is delegated. It is not greatly important that Locke does not trouble about ensuring representation of the entire nation but considers as citizens only 'free men', well-to-do property-owners. What mattered most, and what caused his work to have such influence, was the theory of contract and of the separation between executive and legislative powers which he constructed, a necessary corollary of the twofold definition given: the representatives of the nation exercising the essential power, namely, that of law-making, while the delegated executive authority agreed to by the people is secondary and subject to revocation, even by means of revolt in the event of oppression. In face of an almost completely monarchical Europe, and of Bossuet drawing 'from the very words of Scripture' justification for an absolutism of which the monarchy of Louis XIV provided the model, John Locke proclaimed the principles of the new law which had now been twice asserted *de facto*: in the United Provinces during the long struggle from the end of the sixteenth century until 1609 and 1648, and in England during the struggles of the Civil War (the 'literature' of which Locke had read) and during the Glorious Revolution. In this way the movement of men and ideas hastened onward: beyond the quarter-century 1660–85, into a complex process of the decline of political and theocratic absolutism. At the end of the seventeenth century, as the number of academies and the size of the readership of scientific and literary works increased, the new intellectuals who were not churchmen, and who thought of themselves as members of a republic of letters and sciences, were steadily enlarging their influence.

This is another way in which the balance-sheet of the sixteenth and seventeenth centuries can be drawn: a major mutation had taken place in Europe's intellectual life, as a result of which the historian is able to define differently the social function assumed by these new clerics, who had escaped from the traditional institution and sought for a long time to discover where they stood in a society in which their position was not predetermined. The savants and writers who spoke to their contemporaries no longer from a pulpit and in full certainty of knowledge, but as the progress of their work and their inspiration prompted, formed a social group that had taken a long time to become integrated. When to form a learned society working regularly for the advancement of science and the honour of literature became a point of prestige for a city or a state, the new intellectuals began to occupy an enviable situation and they could now hope to secure more effective recognition of their role. But this change took place gradually: the resistance of the established institutions accounted for this slowness, just as the efforts made by the political and administrative leaders who wanted to counterbalance the ideological weight of those institutions showed the effective support which was available to these societies, academies and assemblies, which were now factors in the ordinary 'game' of social relations, and even of worldly vanities.

What was still most lacking at the end of the seventeenth century was the support of a public that would guarantee economically the place of these new 'clerks' in society. Their books were produced in editions limited in most cases to a few hundred copies, and the bookseller-publishers paid, irregularly and without great generosity, royalties which had not yet become generally established practice. Church livings, pensions from princes, administrative jobs – all these expedients to which intellectuals usually had recourse show how dependent they were in the economic sense, and thereby also the limits imposed on their freedom of expression. Indeed, the political authorities soon realized how they could use these learned pen-men to strengthen their power, by employing them in the governmental machine as diplomats, secretaries, commissioners, and so on, to use the modern terms. They encouraged the intellectuals to write in order to inform public opinion and defend the policies of the rulers, as Richelieu did with Théophraste Renaudot's *Gazette*. They organized them, hoping to find within the honorific setting of their academies those who would burn incense to their sovereignty. Historians were paid to hymn the glory of their prince, and Colbert did not forgive Mézeray for having drawn a good pension while describing the excessive burden of taxation and the poverty of the lower orders.

The complexity and the precariousness of the situation in which these new intellectuals found themselves, no longer able to become integrated in society in the traditional way, are revealed by this interplay of contrasts: the changes in the world in these two hundred years had consummated the break-up of the Church framework but had not, in themselves, brought into being a new framework that was as clearly delimited as the old one. The old and the new coexisted in a condition of anarchy in which every sovereign state sought and defined its own formula for accommodating the intellectuals, outside of the old-established method – except, of course, in the theocratic Papal State itself. Censorship of new books, which was maintained, and seemed to be a permanent necessity, was carried out in accordance with different principles in Spain, France and the Holy Roman Empire. In reply to these meddlesome efforts at regulating their trade, the booksellers busily produced pirate editions and smuggled

them out, thereby considerably whittling down the effectiveness of these various attempts at policing literature. At the end
of the seventeenth century, despite the rise of the academic
societies which formed the only firm framework within
which scholarly and philosophical activity could be concentrated, the place of the lay intellectuals (using 'lay' in its
original sense, in contrast to 'clerical') was not yet clearly
decided, in any European country. Their lot, in the everyday
sense of the word, and their social function were still un-
certain, not only in the eyes of the Churches and the state,
obsessed by the idea of taming them to its own advantage, but
also in those of public opinion and of the intellectuals themselves, for whom the republic of literature and science remained an entity without well-defined social borders: even,
as Leibniz put it, a republic that was much more invisible
than visible.

These uncertainties were due to a large extent to the scale of
the shake-up suffered by the old order since the beginning of
the sixteenth century. The movement that began then had not
stopped, of course, but had rather gone forward in every
direction, in consequence of that fundamental *questioning*
which the first generation of the sixteenth century had experienced so intensely. When the humanists, comfortably
installed in their libraries, began to discuss, in even, quiet and
calm voices, some statement by St Paul or some flight of
oratory in Cicero's speeches against Catiline, they brought
in, together with all their learning, a ferment of criticism,
advanced more or less systematically, which was thereafter
always regarded as necessary for the liberation of men's
thinking. When the monk Luther, reflecting on the future of
the world in his sometimes abrupt way, defined the wretchedness of every society in the phrase, so often quoted since:
Lege lata, fraus nascitur,★ he at once pointed to the precariousness of institutions and the necessity for challenge that is

★ 'Once law is made, crime begins.'

implied when a law is established. The fact that, subsequently, this same Luther founded a Church in his turn, laying down rules and laws, and thereby provoked a revolt that was inspired by his own initial attitude, with a proliferation of 'sectaries' demanding freedom for the individual Christian, was in full accordance with a dialectic the validity of which has by now been fully proved.

There is no need to retrace the stages of this endless movement: in a sense, they are summed up in the right to choose they implicitly assume. *Oportet haereses esse:** this phrase is merely the corollary of the one previously quoted. Heretics are men who have chosen to stand outside the consensus of the majority, rejecting the rule laid down and the considerations that justify it. To those who bring against them the established law and orthodox principles they counterpose a different vision of things and beings. These disputes seem to be hopeless when the upholders of tradition possess the means to reduce to silence those who deviate and stray. In this sense, *oportet haereses esse* might well be rewritten as *oportet haereses fieri:*† outlawed heretics help those who defend conformism by their presence and the repression they attract. Yet the game becomes more complicated, from that very moment. The way that the unequal dialogue winds this way and that shows this to be so. The advocates of a different approach, all those who are not content to reassert, or to demonstrate afresh, the validity of the good old principles inherited from a consecrated tradition, identify themselves with a different conception of the truth. Like Jan Hus before his judges at the Council of Constance, all who call for reforms and place themselves above, or outside, the law, can proclaim: 'Truth will prevail.' That is certainly a noble expression of idealism when one faces the stake or imprisonment. But what is most important, in a sense, is to see how, through a hundred dead-

---

* 'It is necessary that heresies should exist.'
† 'It is necessary that heresies should be created.'

ends and a thousand ambushes, this concern to seek a truth that cannot be imposed by decree has made its way in the world: savants obsessed with the secrets of Nature and the system of the universe, moralists or humanists anxious to discover the norms and limits of their knowledge, all reject a truth established once for all time, and insist on their right to call it in question and to undertake a fresh exploration. Well-known is the fine phrase of Descartes's biographer, Baillet, writing of the philosopher's death in Stockholm and 'the truth that he had sought for all his life long'. The paths thus opened cross and re-cross unceasingly. Some there were who thought that the quest for truth in the sciences could coexist with a tranquil discretion in the domain of theology, while others perceived the extent to which the two domains, physics and metaphysics, are inseparable. Some studied at length the skills of the navigator or the peasant's labours, in order to find their method, while others looked for it in the observation of infinite space. All had this in common: they were engaged in a passionate quest that could never come to an end and must accept no limits.

And yet this view of things should not give rise to the illusion of a linear progression. To be sure, the conflicts that punctuated the development of European thought during those two centuries reveal very clearly the opposing camps: the vigilant defenders of orthodoxies under attack, on the one hand, and, on the other, the forces of innovation. But each new situation, each new clash reveals the complexity of the facts. Catholic orthodoxy was defended, first and foremost, by an order freshly created for the purpose, an order which worked out new forms of struggle, applying itself to the task of taking over a large part of what the humanists had established, in order to make of this a preparation for religious devotion. A century after its foundation, this order (whose growth had been hindered by scabrous misadventures, expulsions and bans inspired by the success of its theory of tyrannicide), found itself being indicted within the Catholic Church itself, reproached with indulging in worldly cultural activities and fostering a deterioration in Christian morality which endangered the foundations of Catholicism. A substantial proportion of the order's 'clientèle', laymen who were not to be led by the nose and wanted to think for themselves about the mysteries of their Church, therefore refused to follow those definers and upholders of orthodoxy.

In the other camp, which was full of variations, there was no single and simple definition. The new Churches soon showed themselves to be as repressive as the old one where orthodoxy was concerned, and the 'enthusiast' founders of sects, the Anabaptists and the rest, sometimes suffered persecution from several of the constituted Churches at once. These outsiders, who constantly reaffirmed the rights of the thinking individual to decide for himself, represented, of course, the extreme position over against the formal organizations which had been maintained or newly created. Their numerical weakness, the silence that surrounded them for so long, the blame they attracted, all are elements showing the limited character of their activity. The tempting polarization by which all the thinkers of the time are to be grouped around one axis or the other – defence of the established order, in accordance with a principle of necessary social regulation, on the one hand, and, on the other, attack upon this order and definition of a new order to replace it – is therefore not quite satisfactory. The creators of Utopias, the dreamers who imagined the model of a future society – Thélème, or the City of the Sun – did indeed belong to the second group, along with those more modest reformers whose ambition went no further than the recasting of one small part of society that was disagreeable to them.

When we look at the picture as a whole, however, the dialogue between the supporters of the established order and the utopian innovators turns out to be more complicated. The Catholic Church, attacked from within for a century, reaffirmed in 1563 the truth of its dogma – but at the same time undertook to reform itself, thereby unquestionably admitting the well-foundedness of certain criticisms made earlier. This Counter-Reformation, which went on for a century and a half at least, defined the camp of orthodoxy upheld, no less than the anathemas solemnly pronounced at the close of the Council of Trent. Similarly, the political and social Utopias of the Levellers and Diggers in England were suppressed and persecuted with hatred and violence for twenty years: and yet, when Locke set forth his theory of government in 1690 he implicitly acknowledged some of the essential features of the political Utopia of the Levellers, and he, the theoretician of the Parliamentary regime, discreetly ratified these features, so to speak.

To this to-ing and fro-ing in the institutional sphere must, of course, be added, as regards the sphere of the sciences then in full development, the exchanges of information, borrowings and recoveries, verifications, and controversies which made up the daily round, and which underlie the difficulties so often met with in identifying which discoverer deserves the honour and glory of a new theory, or the explanation of an astral anomaly, and so forth. But the new sciences thereby became an example to intellectual life as a whole, since they presupposed joint work and a kind of peaceful coexistence which was not yet the rule, by any means: to such an extent indeed that another complicating factor introduced into this changing world of learning was the hesitations and recantations of some of its members, when, in debates wherein what was at issue was both that eternal salvation which nearly all of them were concerned about and, in this life, their future security, more than one shrank from following the better path. And not just from publicly stating what he considered the better path (as we have seen, many hid behind the mask of an admitted prudence): there were hesitations regarding the path itself. To reject a quiet life and

honours and subject oneself to a perpetually nomadic existence was no agreeable prospect. It happened to many prominent 'converts' that they grew tired of the struggle, tired
of proclaiming and summoning a new world, and returned to
the fold. Germany was particularly rich in princes who went
over, from the Lutheranism they had inherited from the sixteenth century, to Calvinism or Catholicism. In England and
the United Provinces, amid the confusion of proselytizing
sects which coexisted and competed with each other, in
Amsterdam and in London, conversions were common. In
France there were not so many, apparently, to judge from the
emotion aroused in the middle of the seventeeth century by
the conversion of Sorbière, who became a Roman Catholic
'at the entreaty of the Bishop of Vaison', as Patin wrote,
adding, bitterly: 'such are the miracles that happen in our
time, which, however, are political and economic rather than
metaphysical in character.'

Furthermore, there were the contradictions that might
exist within many individuals and which it was not so easy to
resolve. Here is one example, which has the merit of concerning a famous man. Colbert, who fought against the producers of newspapers and set up controls over printing and
the sale of books, appears in this connexion as an enemy
(acting in the name of the defence of royal dignity) of the
freedom of expression which was needed by savants. Yet,
at the same time, he worked to promote the organization and
proper functioning of the academies, distributed pensions to
men of letters and scientists, and intervened in 1672 to put an
end to witch-trials in Béarn, Guyenne and Normandy. Remorse and revulsion, pressure and persuasion, protracted
wandering and uncertainty – so many processes which tested
character rather than conviction, and which make more complicated the task of defining the situation and function of
intellectuals in modern European societies.

They all contributed, from different angles, to lay down the coordinates of a new society and a new world that were coming to birth. Some were filled with nostalgia for a mythical past which they projected into a future that would repeat this past. Others took their stand as defenders of the established truths which had provided, *ad aeternum*, the foundation of order on earth and in heaven alike. Yet others dreamt of a changed mankind, and even of a changed world of Nature, revealed by experiment and calculation. These were all the more persuasive and better listened-to because they spoke and wrote the language of their contemporaries, and no longer that universal Latin (now already residual) which was the language of the 'clerks' who remained within the Tradition. They won the attention of these contemporaries the more effectively because they fulfilled long-expressed desires for a better knowledge of Nature which would enable men to dominate it more fully, and for a better understanding of men themselves, which would mean a different social order, with different relations between individuals and groups. These great debates in which all the groups and classes of the societies of the Ancien Régime took part, though unequally, with the main role being played by the rising classes, the bourgeoisie and the new nobility, were to come to a climax as the eighteenth century progressed.

FURTHER READING

THE purpose of these bibliographical notes is merely to list the most thought-provoking works that have been used in writing the present book, and which may help the reader to advance his understanding of the evolution outlined in it. Most of the works mentioned include elaborate bibliographies giving references to sources, both printed and otherwise, and to monographs.

GENERAL IDEAS AND METHODOLOGY

General histories embracing the development of states and nations, and the transformations undergone by movements such as Protestantism, always furnish a useful frame of reference.

CHAUNU, P., *La Civilisation de l'Europe classique* (in the series 'Les Grandes Civilisations'), Paris, 1966.

DELUMEAU, J., *La Civilisation de la Renaissance* (in the same series), Paris, 1967.

FLICHE, A., and MARTIN, V., *Histoire de l'Eglise*, Vols. XVII and XVIII, Paris, 1952.

LÉONARD, E. G., *A History of Protestantism*, 2 vols., London, 1965 and 1967.

MOUSNIER, R., *Les XVIe et XVIIe Siècles* (in the series 'Histoire générale des civilisations'), Paris, 1957.

TATON, RENÉ, *A General History of the Sciences*, Vol. II, London, 1964.

New Cambridge Modern History, Vols. III and IV, Cambridge, 1968.

Certain works need to be mentioned here for having made a particularly important contribution to the way the present book was conceived.

FEBVRE, L., *Le Problème de l'incroyance au XVIe siècle: la religion de Rabelais*, Paris, 1947.

FEBVRE, L., *Au cœur religieux du XVIe siècle* (articles previously published in periodicals), Paris, 1957.

FRANCASTEL, P., *Peinture et société: naissance et destruction d'un espace plastique, de la Renaissance au Cubisme*, Lyon, 1951.

GOLDMANN, L., *Recherches dialectiques*, Paris, 1959.

GRAMSCI, A., *Gli intellettuali e l'organizzazione della cultura*, Turin, 1949 (translated, in part, in Hoare, Q., and Nowell Smith, G., eds., *Selections from the Prison Notebooks of Antonio Gramsci*, London, 1971).

MINDER, R., *Allemagne et Allemands*, Paris, 1947.

I. NEW WORLDS AND NEW INTELLECTUALS

FEBVRE, L., and MARTIN, H.-J., *The Coming of the Book: The Impact of Printing, 1450–1800*, London, 1976.

HUIZINGA, J., *Erasmus of Rotterdam*, London, 1952.

KOYRÉ, A., *Mystiques, spirituels, alchimistes du XVIe siècle allemand*, Paris, 1971.

KOYRÉ, A., *From the Closed World to the Infinite Universe*, Baltimore, 1968.

RENAUDET, A., *Préréforme et humanisme à Paris pendant les premières guerres d'Italie*, 2nd edn, Paris, 1953.

RENAUDET, A., *Etudes érasmiennes, 1521–1529*, Paris, 1939.

2. FROM CHURCH TO CHURCHES

BATAILLON, M., *Erasme et l'Espagne*, Paris, 1937.

BLOCH, E., *Thomas Muenzer als Theologe der Revolution*, Munich, 1921.

CANTIMORI, D., *Prospettive di storia ereticale italiana del Cinquecento*, Bari, 1960.

FEBVRE, L., *Martin Luther: A Destiny*, London, 1930.

FEBVRE, L., *Origène et des Périers, ou l'Enigme du Cymbalum mundi*, Paris, 1942.

GODIN, A., *Spiritualité franciscaine en Flandre au XVIe siècle: l'homéliaire de Jean Vitrier*, Geneva, 1971.

SKALWEIT, S., *Reich und Reformation*, Berlin, 1967.

STROHL, H., *Luther jusqu'en 1520*, 2nd edn, Paris, 1962.

WENDEL, F., *Calvin: The Origins and Development of His Religious Thought*, London, 1963.

3. REGROUPINGS AND CONFRONTATIONS

DAINVILLE, F. DE, *La Naissance de l'humanisme moderne: les Jésuites et l'éducation de la société française*, Paris, 1940.

GEISENDORF, P., *Théodore de Bèze*, Geneva, 1949.

HOOYKAAS, R., *Humanisme, science et réforme: Pierre de la Ramée*, Leyden, 1958.

MESNARD, P., *L'Essor de la philosophie politique au XVIe siècle*, 2nd edn, Paris, 1951.

RABB, T., and SEIGEL, J., eds., *Essays in Memory of E. H. Harbison: Action and Conviction in Early Modern Europe*, Princeton, 1969.

TOUCHARD, J., et al., *Histoire des idées politiques*, 2 vols., Paris, 1963 and 1965.

4. MYSTICS AND FREETHINKERS

BLEKASTAD, M., *Comenius: Versuch eines Umrisses von Leben, Werk und Schicksal des Jan Amos Komensky*, Oslo and Prague, 1969.

BRÉMOND, H., *Histoire littéraire du sentiment religieux en France depuis la fin des guerres de religion*, 11 vols., Paris, 1916–36.

HILL, C., *The Century of Revolution, 1603–1714*, London, 1961.

KOYRÉ, A., *Etudes galiléennes*, Paris, 1966.

LENOBLE, R., *Mersenne, ou la naissance du mécanisme*, Paris, 1943.

LENOBLE, R., *Esquisse d'une histoire de l'idée de nature*, Paris, 1968.

MACFARLANE, A., *Witchcraft in Tudor and Stuart England*, London, 1970.

PINTARD, R., *Le Libertinage érudit pendant la première moitié du XVIIe siècle*, Paris, 1943.

ROUSSET, J., *La Littérature de l'âge baroque en France*, Paris, 1953.

5. THE SCIENTIFIC SPIRIT

BORKENAU, F., *Der Uebergang vom feudalen zum buergerlichen Weltbild*, Paris, 1934.

BOUCHARD, G., *Le Village immobile: Sennely-en-Sologne au XVIIIe siècle*, Paris, 1971.

GOLDMANN, L., *The Hidden God*, London, 1964.

LABROUSSE, E., *Pierre Bayle*, The Hague, 1963 and 1964.

LUTAUD, O., *Les Niveleurs, Cromwell et la République*, Paris, 1967.

MANDROU, R., *Magistrats et sorciers en France au XVIIe siècle*, Paris, 1968.

MARTIN, H.-J., *Livre, pouvoirs et société à Paris au XVIIe siècle*, Geneva, 1969.

ORCIBAL, J., *Jean Duvergier de Hauranne, Abbé de St. Cyran, et son temps*, Louvain and Paris, 1947.

THOMAS, K., *Religion and the Decline of Magic*, London, 1971.

VEIT, L. A. and LENHART, L., *Kirche und Volksfrömmigkeit im Zeitalter des Barock*, Freiburg, 1956.

CONCLUSIONS

HAZARD, P., *The European Mind, 1680–1715*, London, 1953: reissued, Harmondsworth, 1964.

KOLAKOWSKI, L., *Chrétiens sans Eglise: la conscience religieuse et le lien confessionel au XVIIe siècle*, Paris, 1969.

MAPS

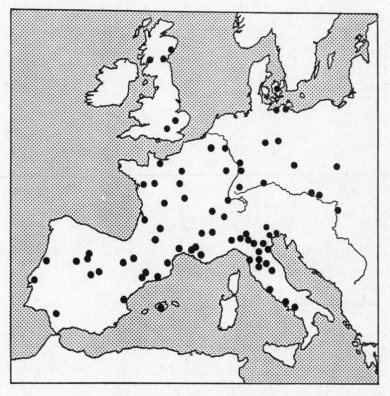

The universities of Europe in the first years of the sixteenth century.

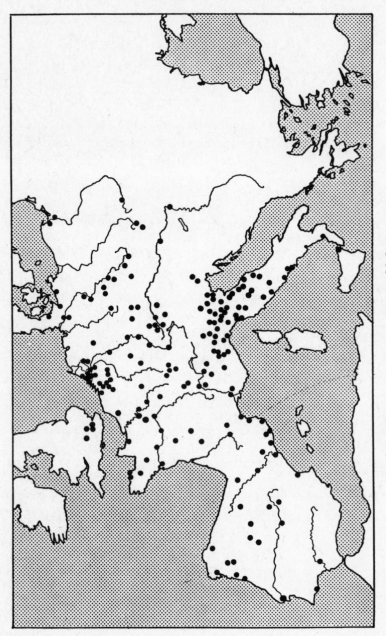

Towns with one or more printing establishments *circa* 1500.

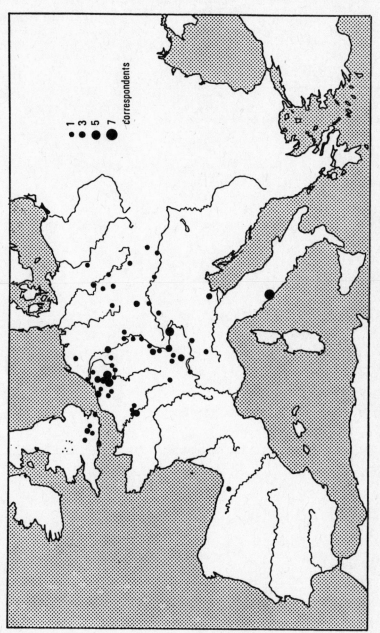

Erasmus's correspondents, 1517–24 (geographical breakdown).

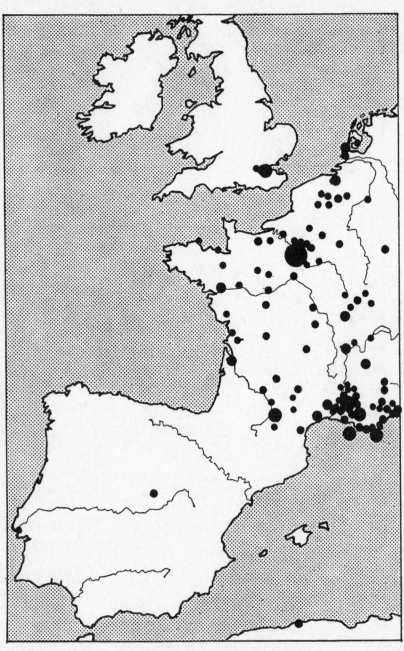

The correspondents of Nicolas Peiresc, according

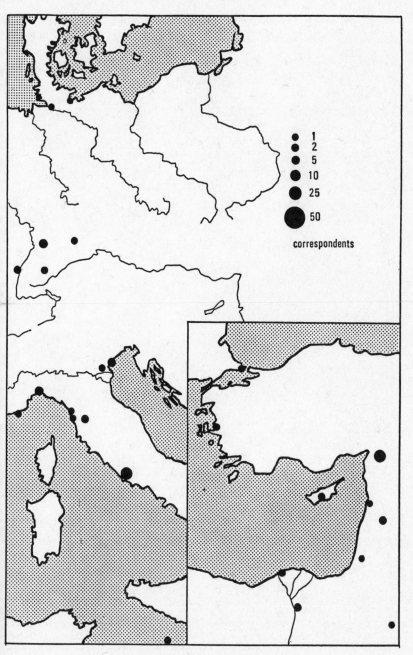

to the Carpentras lists (geographical breakdown).

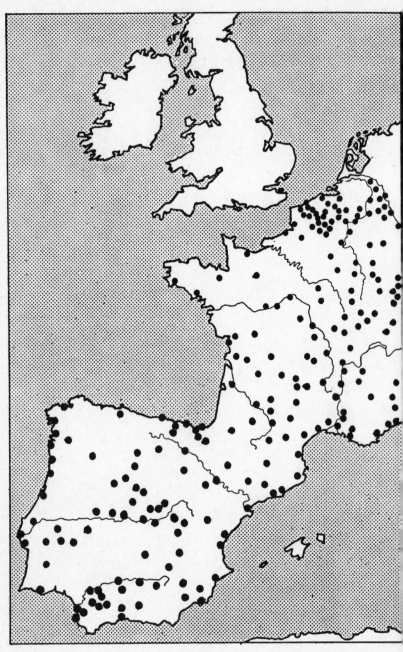

The Jesuit Colleges in Europe in the

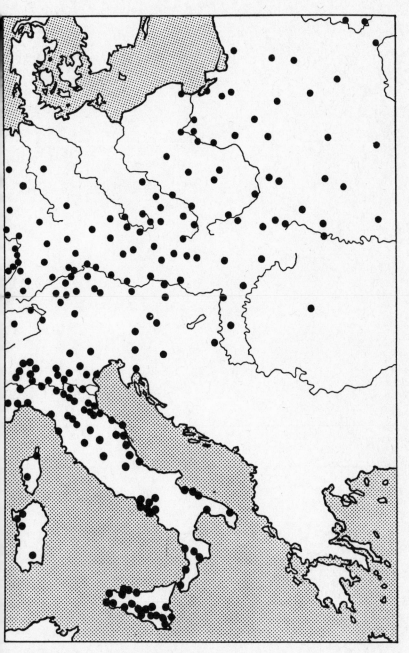

middle of the seventeenth century.

INDEX